AMC River Guide

MAINE

Fourth Edition

WELCOME TO THE AMC

Welcome to the Appalachian Mountain Club! Founded in 1876, we are America's oldest conservation and recreation organization. We promote the protection, enjoyment, and wise use of the mountains, rivers, and trails of the Appalachian region. The AMC has twelve chapters from Maine to Washington, D.C., comprised of tens of thousands of outdoor enthusiasts like you.

By purchasing this book you have contributed to our efforts to protect the Appalachian region. Proceeds from the sales of AMC Books and Maps support our regional land conservation efforts; trail building and maintenance; air- and water-quality research; search and rescue; and environmental education programs for school-age children, at-risk youth, and outdoor enthusiasts.

The AMC encourages everyone to enjoy and appreciate the natural world because we believe that successful conservation depends on such experiences. So join us in the outdoors! We offer hiking, paddling, biking, skiing, and mountaineering activities throughout the Appalachian region for outdoor adventurers of every age and ability. Our lodging destinations, such as our state-of-the-art Highland Center, are Model Environmental Education Facilities, demonstrating our stewardship ethic and providing a place for you to relax off-trail and learn more about local ecosystems and habitats, regional environmental issues, and mountain history and culture.

For more information about AMC membership, destinations, and conservation and education programs, turn to the back of this book or visit the AMC Web site at www.outdoors.org.

AMC River Guide

MAINE

Fourth Edition

Edited by John Fiske

Appalachian Mountain Club Books
Boston, Massachusetts

The Staff of AMC Books

Heather Stephenson, Publisher   Dan Eisner, Editor

Bryan Davidson, Production Manager

The AMC is a non-profit organization and sales of AMC books fund our mission of protecting the Northeast outdoors. If you appreciate our efforts and would like make a donation to AMC Books, contact us at Appalachian Mountain Club Books, 5 Joy Street, Boston, MA 02108.

http://www.outdoors.org/publications/books/.

Cartography by AMC Books
Cover Design by Eric Edstam
Front-Cover Photographs © iStockphoto
Back-Cover Photographs © iStockphoto

Library of Congress Cataloging-in-Publication Data

AMC river guide. Maine / edited by John Fiske. -- 4th ed.
   p. cm.
  Rev. ed. of: Appalachian Mountain Club river guide. Maine. 3rd ed. c2002.
  Includes index.
  ISBN 978-1-934028-15-5
  1. Canoes and canoeing--Maine--Guidebooks. 2. Maine--Guidebooks. I. Fiske, John. II. Appalachian Mountain Club. III. Appalachian Mountain Club river guide. Maine. IV. Title: Maine. V. Title: Appalachian Mountain Club river guide. Maine.
  GV776.M2A46 2008
  797.1'2209741--dc22   2008003434

The paper used in this publication meets the minimum requirements of the American National Standard for Information Sciences—Permanence of Paper for Printed Library Materials, ANSI Z39.48-1984. ∞

Due to changes in conditions, use of the information in this book is at the sole risk of the user.

Printed in the United States of America.
Printed on recycled paper.

 10 9 8 7 6 5 4 3 2 1

Contents

Preface

This, the 4th edition of the *AMC River Guide: Maine*, is the most complete and thorough iteration to date. With use of the Internet, we have been able to reach stakeholders throughout Maine and here present the best information available. To be sure, there have been changes in Maine's rivers since the 3rd edition in 2002. We have documented changes in access, land ownership, and man-made "features," such as dams and bridges. More often than not, though, our volunteers in the field reported "no changes" when scouting a river for us.

Knowledge of Maine's rivers lies with real people, the volunteers who willingly provided the accurate information here. Thanks to these folks throughout Maine who have contributed; special thanks to Sue Szwed, of Wytopitlock, Maine, for her extensive rewrite of the section on St. John River.

We have endeavored to provide up-to-date phone numbers and Internet addresses. While this information is subject to change, rivers, on the other hand, change at a much slower rate. Because of this, we are confident that you'll be able to refer to this guide for some time to come. That said, as soon as this edition of the *River Guide: Maine* was published, something, somewhere, did change. Please forward anything noteworthy you observe to AMC Books at amcbookupdates@outdoors .org.

John Fiske
Revision Editor

Protecting Rivers

As river users we all share the responsibility to make sure the rivers are properly protected. If boaters just rely on other boaters to protect their interests, the public voice for river protection will be weak. You can do a number of things to help. First, join a river protection organization like the Appalachian Mountain Club (www.outdoors.org). The AMC, through the large and collective voice of its chapter members as well as its policy and research staff, has been and continues to be a major river steward in the Northeast.

The AMC and the Relicensing of Hydroelectric Dams

The AMC has been both a regional and national leader in the relicensing of hydroelectric dams. The waters of our rivers are publicly owned. Hydroelectric dams might be granted a license to dam and divert water to generate power for 30 to 50 years. In effect, the dam owner is a tenant, and the public is the landlord. Thanks, in part, to efforts by the AMC, a federal law passed in 1986 requires that during the licensing process the Federal Energy Regulatory Commission (FERC) must now consider a river's environmental and recreational value on an equal basis with its value as a power source when it issues the terms of a new hydro-dam license.

Dams frequently reduce water quality, block fish movement, flood out boating opportunities, and at times turn flows on and off like a faucet spigot. When hydro dams were licensed more than a half-century ago, they had to meet few standards. Many of these original licenses are or will soon come due for renewal for new 30- to 50-year licenses. The AMC works hard to achieve updated license conditions during these renewals. This includes mitigation for the impacts of dams on rivers' recreational opportunities and ecosystems and a better balance of priorities.

Since the 1990s AMC has been a leader in nine major hydroelectric dam relicensing settlements in New England, which has culminated in the protection of more than 42,000 acres of waterfront lands, has guaranteed more than 500 scheduled river releases for whitewater boating along with access and egress, has enhanced the flows in several hundred miles of river to protect aquatic resources, and has created almost $20 million in river enhancement funds. The AMC collaboratively works on these settlements with its partner organizations.

The AMC-led Deerfield River Settlement in Massachusetts/Vermont was one of the first and biggest of its type in the nation—and is now a national model. In Maine, the AMC's hydro-relicensing efforts resulted in protected watershed lands on the West Branch of the Penobscot; on the Kennebec River including the Moosehead Lake's East Outlet; on Indian Pond; on parts of the Kennebec River to the Wyman Dam and river reaches in Madison; and on the Androscoggin River additions to Rangeley State Park, the Rapid River, at Upper Dam on Mooselookmeguntic Lake, and further downstream in the Jay area. Guaranteed whitewater releases as well as access and egress were achieved in the Kennebec drainage at the East Outlet and the Kennebec Gorge, and in Madison and on the Dead River; in the Androscoggin drainage on the Magalloway and Rapid Rivers; and below the Canada Falls, Seeboomook, and the Ripogenous Dams on the West Branch of the Penobscot.

To be a good river steward you need to understand how the region's rivers are currently managed. Few undammed or unregulated rivers exist today. Most are dammed with some form of storage that captures the natural high flows during spring snowmelt or major storms and releases the water during the low flow periods of late summer to early fall (a very unnatural situation for the aquatic biota). This is called regulated flow, and the impoundments providing these services usually have major fluctuations in water level. Some impoundments collect and release large quantities of water in short periods over 24 hours to match hydroelectric generation with the variable demand for electricity on the grid over a day. These are called peaking flows. Other dams might just store water during floods and release it as quickly as possible for the sole purpose of flood control—true of many U.S. Army Corps of Engineers dams. If a dam merely capitalizes on the head it creates and instantly passes all the water entering its reservoir, it is called run-of-river. A large river basin likely has a mix of all of the scenarios mentioned.

Managing to meet hydroelectric demand, provide flood control, protect aquatic resources like fish, and keep paddlers in sufficient water can be very complex. Ensuring the best use of these competing demands requires an understanding of the issue's many facets.

Of course, the ideal situation is to have an entirely unregulated, undammed river, but hundreds of years of dam building in the Northeast has made that more of an ideal than an achievable reality in the near future. However, that trend is reversing as some dams that have low economic value and high negative ecological impact are actually being removed to restore river reaches, increase boating opportunities, and allow fish access to more habitat. The removal of the Edwards Dam on the Kennebec River in Augusta has been a national example.

Protecting Flows and Public Access

In addition to working on hydroelectric dam licensing, the AMC works to secure public access on the state's rivers and to make those sites better known. The AMC seeks the appropriate balance among ecological protection, motorized craft, and human-powered boaters (paddlers) when seeking public access. The AMC has recently published informative map guides to the Saco and Androscoggin Rivers, Acadia region, and Southern Piscataquis County and sells the Northern Canoe Trail maps for Maine (http://www.outdoors.org/publications/index. cfm). In 2007 Maine passed state regulations to protect instream flows from excessive water withdrawals, a process that the AMC participated in.

What Can You Do for Your Rivers?

- First, make sure you have the basic knowledge about your watershed. A good starting point is the U.S. Environmental Protection Agency's "surf your watershed" website (http://www.epa.gov/surf/).
- If a dam near you is coming up for relicensing, go to the Hydro Reform Coalition (the AMC is a founding member and major participant) for a toolkit to learn how to be an effective participant and to obtain a toolkit (http://www.hydroreform.org/hydroguide/ citizen-toolkit-for-effective-participation).
- To learn about dam removal on your favorite river, visit American Rivers at www.americanrivers.org and look up the dam removal toolkit.

- Join a river cleanup day.
- Support your local land trust to protect river waterfront property and create river greenways.
- Nominate your river for protection under state or federal river designations, like the Wild and Scenic Program.
- Support free flows, but do not be a freeloader on the river protection efforts of others.

Your river will say thanks.

Ken Kimball
Research Director
Appalachian Mountain Club
November 2007

Introduction

During the last ice age, which ended approximately 15,000 years ago, Maine was covered by glaciers up to one mile thick. These glaciers removed much of the existing topsoil and gouged out the bedrock. When the glaciers retreated, the state we now call Maine was dotted with numerous valleys, rivers, and lakes.

Canoeing and kayaking are excellent ways to enjoy the scenery created by the glaciers. The purpose of this book is to describe Maine's rivers and a few of its lakes. This book should enable the reader to locate put-ins and take-outs for specific river trips and offer a very good idea of what to expect on the river between the two points. The rivers described range in difficulty from flat water to Class IV whitewater.

Safety

Although this book was prepared carefully, no guidebook should be used on blind faith. It is a helpful companion, along with a map, to have when you run a river, but it will not prevent every problem.

If you are a new boater, or would like to improve your skills, take advantage of the many outfitters, private schools, and national and local organizations (including the AMC and the Maine Chapter of the AMC) that offer canoe and kayak instruction. Join a local group that runs rivers together; boating with a responsible, safety-conscious group will help improve your skills. You can also find many books to read on the subject. Ultimately, though, it is your responsibility to know the limits of your skills and to paddle within them. The Safety Code of American Whitewater is included in Appendix A; it contains many good suggestions for safe boating.

Be aware, too, that canoeing and kayaking have changed considerably in recent years. Today, high-tech boats are being built to deal with the more difficult rapids. More and more, former portages have turned into standard runs for experts. The problem of rating rivers, already made difficult by variations in water levels, is further compounded by the type of boat used. A rapid that is an "easy Class III" to an expert in a specially designed boat with a full set of airbags might still be a portage to many people. In this book, rivers marked "runnable" in high water that have Class III and above rapids are rated for whitewater boats. If you are paddling a flatwater canoe, you should increase the rating at least one class.

If you are attempting rapids that are rated Class III or above, you should consider yourself a whitewater boater and outfit your boat and yourself accordingly.

- Always wear an approved life jacket.
- Use a full set of airbags in your boat.
- Use thigh straps to help keep you stable in the canoe while going through large drops or turbulent water.
- Wear a helmet.
- Learn to self-rescue; then learn an Eskimo roll.
- Check your equipment carefully before leaving home.
- Carry an extra paddle, a throwbag, and a first-aid kit when you paddle.

As a sport, boating involves certain risks that can be minimized with the proper training, forethought, caution, and equipment.

Be Considerate of Landowners

Many put-ins, take-outs, and portages are open for public use. Others require that you cross private property. Note that many landowners whose property borders popular paddling rivers have posted their property against trespass. You can prevent additional closings by being thoughtful. Always ask for and obtain permission from landowners; don't damage vegetation; don't park cars where they block roads; pick up litter. Make your portage expeditiously and leave; don't picnic or make a disturbance. Don't expect local residents to be responsible for rescuing you and your canoe or kayak. Dumping boats and getting them pinned on whitewater rivers happen to the best of us. You should prepare before launching by having suitable equipment, clothing, and a large enough group. Access to put-ins and take-outs is the right of a private landowner and the privilege of the user. Access is becoming limited on some rivers, so it is increasingly important to maintain good relations with property owners.

River Stewardship

You can get active in efforts to ensure that boat access will be available in the future. Part of doing so involves accepting the responsibility of thinking of rivers as complex ecosystems serving the needs of many. Nothing guarantees that put-ins and take-outs that exist today will be around tomorrow. You should be aware of the issues that surround rivers. Water quality, wildlife habitat, drinking water, dams, recreation, and land ownership all affect rivers and the paddling experience.

Fortunately, many resources are available to paddlers who are interested in having a role in river stewardship. Local watershed councils and river groups; local conservation commissions; nonprofit recreation groups such as the AMC (www.outdoors.org), the American Canoe Association (www.americancanoe.org), and American Whitewater (www.americanwhitewater.org); and national river conservation groups such as American Rivers (www.americanrivers.org) are excellent resources for information on rivers and how to become a steward. By knowing all the facts about river issues, you can be a better advocate in protecting the rivers you love.

Using the River Guide

Organization

Each chapter begins with a map that identifies the rivers described in the text. The principal river is described first and then the tributaries in descending (downstream) order. In the coastal watersheds, the rivers are arranged from west to east.

Format for River Descriptions

Each description starts with general information about the river as a whole. Longer rivers are then broken into sections that are of reasonable length for a canoe or kayak trip and omit unrunnable sections of rivers. These sections are introduced by a boldfaced heading and, in most cases, a table that summarizes significant information about that segment.

Map numbers from the DeLorme *Maine Atlas and Gazetteer* are a new addition to the description. We recommend that you investigate drops and other obstacles on all rivers.

The tables present significant information about that section of river. In the descriptive text that follows the tables, cumulative distances from the section's starting point are placed within parentheses.

TABLE FORMAT

STARTING POINT ➤ ENDING POINT   **TOTAL MILES**

Description:	(Difficulty of the river in this segment)
Navigable:	(Recommended water levels and seasons)
Scenery:	(What you will see from the boat)
Maps:	(U.S. Geological Survey quadrangles, the DeLorme *Maine Atlas and Gazetteer* map numbers, and other maps)
Portages:	(Where to, when to, and how far to carry)

Terminology: Difficulty of River

The following terms appear opposite the "Description" heading in the summary table and describe the difficulty of the water to be paddled:

Lake. The segment being described flows through a lake, or it is necessary to paddle across a lake to reach the beginning of a river.

Flatwater. Little or no current exists, and the river's surface is smooth and unbroken. Paddling upstream is easy.

Quickwater. The river moves fast. Its surface is nearly smooth at high water levels but is likely to be choppy at medium water levels and shallow at low water levels.

Marsh/swamp. Vegetation often obstructs the river. Paddling might be slower than the distance alone would indicate.

Class. Difficulty of rapids in a segment is rated according to American Whitewater classifications: Class I, II, III, or IV. See Appendix A for a description of these classifications.

When two or more terms appear together opposite the "Description" heading in the summary table, expect to encounter all of the conditions in that segment of the river.

Judging the difficulty of rapids is subjective. It depends on the type of boat, on how well you read the river, and on how skillfully you maneuver your boat. The difficulty of rapids changes with the water level. A given stretch of rapids might become easier or harder when more water is in the river. Water level affects different parts of the same river differently. As a general rule, more water washes out a river with low gradient and small rocks, but it generates larger waves and more turbulence in a river that drops steeply through large rocks.

As water level rises, current picks up. Be aware of this. If the river is high and the air and water are cold, increase the rating by at least one class, and possibly two classes.

On small rivers, fallen trees present a greater hazard to you than do rapids, especially because their location cannot be documented in advance. Barbed-wire fences frequently cross rivers in rural areas and are hard to spot. Be alert and have your boat under control.

Terminology: Water Levels

The following terms appear opposite the "Navigable" heading in the summary tables. They describe the water level recommended for paddling a particular segment. The dates and conditions most likely to produce the recommended water level follow.

Low water. A clearly defined shoreline exists below the bank. Small rocky rivers will not be passable, but flatter stretches and rapids in large rivers will be navigable.

Medium water. The river extends to the bank, and soft vegetation along the shore might be underwater. Marshy areas might be wet. Larger whitewater rivers, depending on the type of rapids, will be navigable at this water level, and dodging rocks will be the major entertainment.

High water. The river is near the top of its defined bank, and alder along the shore might be underwater. This is an acceptable water level for small whitewater rivers.

Very high water. Large trees or clumps of smaller ones have their roots in the water. Reaching shore might be difficult or impossible. This water level is recommended only for experts who are familiar with the particular river and its features.

Flood. The river overflows its banks and makes pillows on large trees. This stage is dangerous for everyone.

Levels lower than those recommended do not necessarily mean that the river is not runnable; a river for which high water is recommended might be traveled in medium water, but it is likely to be scratchy, and you might have to wade down some sections.

Terminology: Scenery

The following terms are used in the tables to describe the territory that borders the river.

Wild. This describes long sections of semiwilderness, with no more than a few isolated camps and occasional road access. Dirt roads might parallel the river within sight or sound but only for short distances; they do not noticeably alter the semiwilderness atmosphere of the trip. These roads might be closed to the public or altogether impassable.

Forested. Banks on both sides of the river look densely wooded, but good dirt and asphalt roads follow along the river or are not far from it. These roads might approach or cross the river frequently. Farms and houses might be nearby, but not many of them are visible from the water.

Rural. Farms are visible from the river, and some fields might extend down to the water.

Towns. Small and isolated towns border the river. Aside from their effects on water quality, these towns have little impact on the trip.

Settled. Many houses or small buildings are within sight or sound of the river.

Urban. Multistoried buildings are visible. The shorelines are frequently unattractive.

Maps

Each map includes pertinent topographical maps in 7.5-minute series unless followed by "15" to indicate that they are in the 15-minute series. Topographical maps can be ordered from map dealers or from the U. S. Geological Survey (USGS) itself at its website (www.usgs.gov); by mail from Map Distribution, USGS Map Sales, Box 25286, Federal Center, Bldg. 810, Boulder, CO 80225; or by phone at 888-ASK-USGS (275-8747).

The DL indication in the tables stands for *The Maine Atlas and Gazetteer*, which is published by DeLorme and is widely available at bookstores and outfitters. The same company also publishes Maine's official highway map. The publisher's address, phone, and website are as follows: DeLorme, Two DeLorme Drive, Box 298, Yarmouth, ME 04096 (800-511-2459), www.delorme.com.

For information on Canadian maps, write to the following: Canada Map Office, Policy and Product Promotions Office, Centre for Topographic Information, Natural Resources Canada, 615 Booth Street, Room 180, Ottawa, Ontario, Canada KIA 0E9, http://maps.nrcan.gc.ca/.

For information on tidal sections of the big coastal rivers, National Ocean Survey charts provide excellent information. Contact is as follows: FAA Distribution Division, AVN-530, National Aeronautical Charting Office, Glenn Dale, MD 20769 (800-638-8972), http://chartmaker.ncd. noaa.gov/nsd.

Portages

The portages listed include all unavoidable carries (such as dams and waterfalls) and difficult sections where you usually find insufficient water to make them runnable. In addition, some rapids are listed if their difficulty significantly exceeds the rating of that portion of the river. For example:

Portages: 2.5 mi R dam 50 yd
                    5.0 mi e ledge
                    (11.75 mi L dam 500 yd)

The first dam is 2.5 miles from the start and should be portaged on the right for 50 yards. The ledge at 5.0 miles from the start can be portaged on either side. The distance varies with the height of the water and the skill of the paddler. In some cases, it might possibly be run, but it is well above the level of difficulty given in the chart above. The parentheses around the dam at 11.75 miles indicate it need not be portaged by those ending their trip there.

Unlisted portages can occur where you encounter fallen trees, low snowmobile bridges, or where you carry around rapids you do not wish to run.

Campsites

Information on campsites is listed as follows:

Campsites: (6) mi L 5th St. John Pond (near canal) permit
                    1.5 mi R Red Pine Grove (poor) NMW $ car

- Parentheses around the distance indicate that the campsite is located off the route normally followed and opposite or in line with a point 6.0 miles along that route.
- "L" indicates the left-hand side of 5th St. John Pond.

- The name or location of the campsite is followed by special directions (near canal) or a comment (poor).
- A fire permit is needed for those sites that are followed by the word "permit." They can be obtained at a Maine Forest Service Ranger Station, including those indicated on the chapter maps.
- Administering organizations are also noted: Allagash Wilderness Waterway (AWW), Maine Forest Service (MFS), and North Maine Woods (NMW).
- Fees are charged where the symbol "$" appears, and when a campsite is also accessible by road, the word "car" is written.

Abbreviations

The following abbreviations are used in the summary tables:

AWW	Allagash Wilderness Waterway
BPL	Bureau of Parks & Lands
cfs	flow of water in cubic feet per second
CMP	Central Maine Power
CNTS	Canadian National Topographical Survey
DL	*The Maine Atlas and Gazetteer*
e	either
FoPR	Friends of the Presumpscot River
ft	foot, feet
L	left
MFS	Maine Forest Service
mi	mile, miles
NMW	North Maine Woods
R	right
yd	yard, yards

Example: How to Read a Summary Table

SMITHVILLE ➤ BROWNVILLE   3.75 MI

Description:	Class I, II
Navigable:	High water: April to early May
Scenery:	Forested
Map(s):	Greenwood, DL 15
Portages:	1.5 mi L dam 15 yd
	2.0 mi L two ledges 100 yd

Smithville ➤ Brownville The starting point for this imaginary segment is Smithville. The end point is Brownville.

3.75 mi The total distance to be covered is 3.75 miles.

Description: Class I, II You will encounter Class I and II whitewater on this segment. Most of the segment is Class II.

Navigable: High water: April to early May The river is runnable at high water levels, which are most likely to occur during April and the first part of May.

Scenery: Forested You will pass between wooded banks, but access roads might exist in the woods, close to the river.

Maps: Greenwood; DL 15 The topographical map for this segment is the USGS Greenwood 7.5-minute quadrangle; the *Maine Atlas and Gazetteer* map number is 15.

Portages: 1.5 mi L dam 15 yd
              2.0 mi L two ledges 100 yd

You will have to carry your boats for about 15 yards around a dam about 1.5 miles from Smithville. The best route for the portage is on the left as you face downstream. You have another portage in 0.5 mile, 2.0 miles from the starting point at Smithville. The best route is also on the left, and you have to carry your boat about 100 yards to avoid two ledges. The last portage is not the take-out point for the end of this section, however. If it were, it would appear in parentheses to indicate that only those paddlers wanting to continue downriver need to complete that portage.

Security

Crime is common. At put-ins for some popular rivers, the burglary rate of the parked cars is high. To discourage this, do not leave money, cameras, or other valuables in cars. The first place thieves look is in your bag of dry clothes; leave your wallet at home. Take only the cash and cards you need, and carry them in a waterproof folder in your pocket. If this is not possible (for example, on an extended trip), pay to park your car at a gas station or at a house.

Time

It's impossible to estimate time realistically for a river trip. Too many factors influence the length of time. For example, the water height affects the speed of the current. The boater might pursue paddling as an athletic endeavor or might prefer to float silently with the current, observing surroundings. A small, well-qualified party might scout nothing, whereas an instruction trip might scout everything. You might spend time bailing out canoes, taking pictures, or negotiating blowdowns.

On a large river with the current and wind favorably behind, the miles whiz by. A paddler, on the other hand, might take hours to travel a single mile on a small stream blocked with alder thickets and fallen trees. The same mile requires far less time when it is free of obstructions. It is good practice to select alternate end points for a trip, especially on an unfamiliar river.

River Levels in Maine

The water-level information given in the summary tables for individual rivers includes approximate dates, which are subject to wide variation from year to year. Some of the factors that influence water levels are discussed here.

Snow depth, temperature, rainfall, and transpiration are four seasonal factors that affect river levels. Runoff is generally greater and swifter when the ground is frozen. As the snow cover disappears, temperature becomes less important. After the leaves are out, surface runoff decreases substantially because plants use a great deal of water during transpiration. Conversely, the fall foliage season invariably signals a rise in water levels following rain.

Terrain also must be considered. A river flowing from steep-sided hills and mountains quickly collects the runoff from rainfall and melting snow. On the other hand, lakes, swamps, and gently rolling hills buffer the spring runoff; the result is an extended paddling season despite the weather. Knowledge of Maine's topography and familiarity with its weather will be helpful to you.

You must also take into account the nature of the river itself. If a river is flat, weather affects navigability only slightly. If the river is steep and full of rapids, then heavy snow, warm temperatures, and moderate rainfall all might be necessary to keep it runnable. Farther north, access to the water in early spring is hindered, first by snow and later by mud. Also, ice shelves along the banks are hazardous in rapids and an inconvenience elsewhere.

If you wish to run rapids in mid-March, coastal Maine is the place to go. By the end of March, the season moves to central Maine. By May, the rivers of northern Maine, which are fed by melting snow, are usually at optimal levels. Sometimes they are passable through Memorial Day, but in some years the season is over in late April.

River levels can vary tremendously from season to season, and unusually heavy rainfall can make any river passable at any time. If you do enough canoeing and kayaking, you will probably eventually meet someone who will defend winter boating and will claim that the canoeing season includes any sunny day when the temperature is above freezing.

Over several years, a person who runs a lot of rivers develops a sense of river levels. Those who fish the ocean acquire an instinct for the tides, those who live off the land can almost smell the weather, and so it is with river people. After a while they get to know when a river runs and when it does not.

Water Releases

With many of Maine's rivers passable for only a few weeks in the spring or after an unusually heavy rainfall, releases of water from dams can extend the paddling season in some localities. Three types of releases occur. The first type of release comes from dams used to generate power. The West Branch of the Penobscot, the Kennebec, the Androscoggin, and the Magalloway are all runnable throughout the summer because they are used as a source of power.

The second type of release is one scheduled solely for the benefit of paddlers. These are arranged by whitewater clubs. They take place on scheduled weekends during the spring, summer, and fall. The Dead River in the Kennebec watershed is a good example of this type of release.

The third type of release is the annual drawdown of lakes that are used primarily for summer recreation. These releases generally take place in the fall. A drawdown often takes several weeks to complete. Rivers that are drawn down in the fall include the Dead River and the Kennebec River.

Administering Organizations

Maine Department of Conservation
Bureau of Parks and Lands
Northern Parks Region
106 Hogan Road
Bangor, ME 04401
207 941-4041
www.maine.gov/doc/parks

> If you are planning a trip on the Allagash Wilderness Waterway, write to the preceding address. You will receive an excellent map of the waterway and a copy of all rules and regulations pertaining to the Allagash.

Maine Forest Service
Department of Conservation
22 State House Station
Augusta, ME 04333
207-287-2791
1-800-367-0022 (within Maine only)
www.maine.gov/doc/mfs

> In many sections of Maine, the Maine Forest Service has established authorized campsites where fire permits are not needed. However, at many campsites located along the rivers, you need a permit in order to build a fire. Information regarding many such sites is given in the individual river descriptions. Fire permits can be obtained at the locations shown on the chapter maps. If you have further questions, contact the Maine Forest Service at the preceding address.

North Maine Woods, Inc.
P.O. Box 425
Ashland, ME 04732
207-435-6213
www.northmainewoods.org

> North Maine Woods is an organization that was set up to regulate the access to most of the timberlands north of Baxter State Park and west of Route 11. On behalf of the many landowners of that region,

North Maine Woods coordinates the uses of the area by companies engaged in logging operations and by the general public seeking recreation. It maintains checkpoints on the roads that give access to the region and at campsites within.

A camping fee is collected at the checkpoints on arrival. Several flying services are authorized to issue permits, and anyone arriving by plane should inquire about this ahead of time. Season registrations are also available.

Because rules and fees are subject to change, write for current information.

Rentals

You can rent boats in many places in Maine. Outfitters and retailers all rent canoes and kayaks. You can also run an Internet search or use the Yellow Pages.

Fire Safety

Always properly extinguish campfires. If you should need to report a fire to the Maine Forest Service, call 888-900-3473.

USGS Gauges in Maine

The U.S. Geological Survey maintains gauges in many locations throughout the region. Many of these transmit data that is posted on the Web at http://waterdata.usgs.gov/me/nwis/. The list below is provided for information only.

On many rivers you find hand-painted gauges, on bridge abutments, for example. These gauges are meaningless except if you know and are familiar with the river in many water levels or you were the one who painted the gauge in the first place. Never substitute a gauge reading, particularly when you might not be familiar with the river, for your own commonsense, river-reading judgment.

It is the belief of the editors, therefore, that gauges are of secondary value to river runners, and this river guide only inconsistently mentions them.

St. John River Basin
St. John River at Ninemile Bridge
Big Black River near Depot Mountain
St. John River at Dickey
Allagash River near Allagash
Saint Francis River near Connors
Fish River near Fort Kent
St. John River at Fort Kent
Aroostook River near Masardis
Aroostook River at Washburn
Williams Brook at Phair

Saint Croix River Basin
Saint Croix River at Vanceboro
Grand Lake Stream at the city of Grand Lake Stream
Saint Croix River at Baring

Machias River Basin
Pleasant River near Epping
Old Stream near Wesley
Narraguagus River Basin
East Bear Brook near Beddington
West Bear Brook near Beddington
Narraguagus River at Cherryfield
Cadillac Brook near Bar Harbor
Hadlock Brook near Northeast Harbor

Penobscot River Basin
Seboeis River near Shin Pond
East Branch of the Penobscot at Grindstone
Mattawamkeag River near Mattawam
Piscataquis River at Blanchard
Kingsbury Stream at Abbot
Piscataquis River near Dover
Piscataquis River at Medford
Penobscot River at West Enfield
Penobscot River at Eddington

Ducktrap River Basin
Ducktrap River near Lincolnville

Sheepscot River Basin
Sheepscot River at North Whitefield

Kennebec River Basin
Kennebec River at The Forks
Spencer Stream at its mouth
Kennebec River at Bingham
Carrabassett River near North Anson
Sandy River near Mercer
Sebasticook River near Pittsfield
Kennebec River at North Sidney
Kennebec River at Augusta
Cobbosseecontee Stream at Gardiner
Kennebec River at Gardiner

Androscoggin River Basin
Diamond River near Wentworth
Androscoggin River at Errol
Androscoggin River near Gorham
Wild River at Gilead
Androscoggin River at Rumford
Swift River near Roxbury
The Basin outlet at North Auburn
Townsend Brook near Auburn
Bobbin Mill Brook near Auburn
Little Androscoggin River near South Paris
Androscoggin River near Auburn

Royal River Basin
Royal River at Yarmouth

Presumpscot River Basin
Presumpscot River at Westbrook

Saco River Basin
Saco River near Conway
Saco River at Cornish

Suggested Rivers

SUGGESTED CANOE CAMPING TRIPS

Chapter	River
5	**Allagash** (Telos Landing ➤ Churchill Dam)
5	**Allagash** (Churchill Dam ➤ St. John River)
6	**Aroostook** (Munsungan Lake ➤ Masardis)
6	**Big Black** (Depot Stream ➤ Allagash)
3	**Bow Trip**
6	**Fish River** (Portage Lake ➤ St. John River)
8	**Machias** (Fifth Machias Lake ➤ Machias)
8	**East Machias River** (Pocomoonshine Lake ➤ East Machias)
4	**Mattawamkeag, West Branch** (Island Falls ➤ Haynesville)
4	**Penobscot, East Branch** (Grand Lake Dam ➤ Medway)
4	**Penobscot, West Branch** (Roll Dam Campsite ➤ Ripogenus Dam)
1	**Saco** (Center Conway ➤ Hiram)
8	**St. Croix** (Vanceboro ➤ Kellyland)
6	**St. Francis** (Estcourt ➤ St. John River)
4	**Sebois** (Grand Lake Road ➤ Lunksoos Deadwater)
8	**Union, East Branch** (Steep Landing ➤ ME 179)
4	**Webster Stream** (Telos Landing ➤ Grand Lake Dam)

Symbols:
+ Trip can be easily lengthened
- Trip an be easily shortened
x Predominant features
• Occasional features

Miles	Portages	Lake	Quickwater	Class I	Class II	Class III	Passable in summer
33.75	1	x					x
53.0	1–2	•	x	x	•		x
47+/-	0–1		x	•			•
53+			x	x	•	•	
34.0	1–2	•	x	•	•		
44.5+/-	1–2	x			•		x
76.5-	2–8	x	•	•	•	x	
45-	1						
24.5+	0–1	x	x	x	•		•
47.5-	4–6		x	•	•	•	x
43.5+		x	x	x			x
43.25+/-	1		x	•	•		x
33+/-	1	•	x	•	x		x
56-		•	x	x	•	•	x
19.75+	1		x	•			
14.25	0–2	•	•	•	•	•	•
24.0-	2–6	x	x		•	x	x

SUGGESTED WHITEWATER RUNS OF CLASS II DIFFICULTY

Chapter	River	Miles	Class III Rapids	Passible in summer
6	**B Stream** (Hammond ➤ Houlton)	4.25		x
2	**Bear River** (North Newry ➤ Newry)	6.75		
3	**Carrabassett** (Kingfield ➤ New Portland)	6.5		
3	**Dead, North Branch** (Chain of Lakes Dam ➤ Eustis)	19.0	2	
8	**Dennys** (Meddybmps ➤ Dennysville)	20.75	1	
8	**Grand Lake Stream** (West Grand Lake ➤ Big Lake)	3.0		x
3	**Kennebec River** (The Forks ➤ Caratunk)	9.0		x
4	**Kenduskeag** (Kenduskeag ➤ Bangor)	16.0	1	
1	**Little Ossipee River** (Davis Brook ➤ ME 5)	11.25		
4	**Nesowadnehunk Stream** (Nesowadnehunk Lake ➤ Campgound 5)	5.0	1	x
4	**Piscataquis River** (Dover Foxcroft ➤ Derby)	18.5		x
3	**Sandy River** (Phillips ➤ Fairbanks Bridge)	17.25	2	x
7	**Sheepscot River** (Whitefield ➤ Head Tide)	6.0		

SUGGESTED WHITEWATER RUNS OF CLASS III DIFFICULTY

Chapter	River	Miles	Class IV Rapids	Passible in summer
8	**Blue Hills Falls**			x
3	**Carrabassett River** (Kingfield ➤ New Portland)	10.0		
3	**Dead River** (under 2,500 cfs) (Spencer Stream ➤ The Forks)	16.0		x
6	**Machias Stream** (Big Machias Lake ➤ Aroostook River)	32.0		
4	**Pleasant River, West Branch** (K. I. Words ➤ Brownville Jct.)	9.75		
3	**Roach River** (Kokad-jo ➤ Moosehead Lake)	6.5		
1	**Saco River** (Limington Rips)	0.5		
4	**Souadabscook Stream** (Vatiades Landing ➤ Hampden)	9.0	1	
2	**Swift River** (Byron ➤ Mexico)	13.0	1	
8	**Union River, West Branch** (Great Pond ➤ Amherst)	11.0	2	
2	**Webb River** (Lake Webb ➤ Carthage)	4.5	1	
2	**Wild River** (Campground ➤ Gilead)	8.0	1	

SUGGESTED WHITEWATER RUNS OF CLASS IV DIFFICULTY

Chapter	River	Miles	Big Water Rapids	Ledge Drops	Passible in summer
6	**Aroostook River** (Fort Fairefield ➤ St. John River)	11.0	x	x	x
3	**Dead River** (2,500+ cfs) (Spencer Stream ➤ The Forks)	16.0	x	x	x
3	**Kennebec River** (East Outlet ➤ Indian Pond)	3.5	x		x
4	**Mattawamkeag River** (Kingman ➤ Mattawamkeag)	12.5	x	x	
2	**Rapid River** (Middle Dam ➤ Lake Umbagog)	6.0			x
3	**Sandy River** (Smalls Falls ➤ South Branch)	5.5		x	

Chapter 1
Lower Saco Watershed

Saco River

The Saco is one of New England's most popular paddling rivers. Melting snow and spring rains provide whitewater boating for the novice to the expert near the headwaters in spring and early summer, while below the Maine–New Hampshire border the river is mostly flat and passable at all water levels. The river begins at Saco Lake just north of Crawford Notch. It drains the southern slopes of the Presidential Range and, in New Hampshire, flows through the Mount Washington Valley. From Conway, New Hampshire, it winds generally southeast to the Atlantic Ocean south of Portland, Maine.

Although settlement along the Saco began early in the seventeenth century, few towns were located next to the river. To this day, it remains a pastoral stream passing through only a few small settlements until it gets almost to the sea. The Saco River Corridor Commission, which cooperates with local communities in matters relating to zoning and land-use planning, offers state-supported protection of the Maine portion of the Saco.

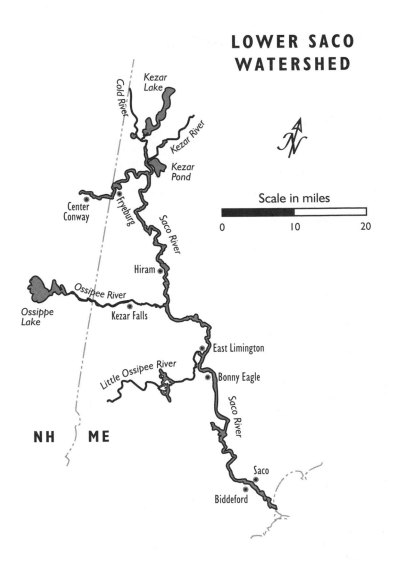

LOWER SACO WATERSHED

Kezar Lake

Cold River

Kezar River

Kezar Pond

Center Conway

Fryeburg

Saco River

Hiram

Ossipee River

Ossippe Lake

Kezar Falls

East Limington

Little Ossipee River

Bonny Eagle

Saco River

NH ME

Saco

Biddeford

Scale in miles

0   10   20

This book does not include the Saco River or its tributaries in New Hampshire, which are primarily whitewater trips. It also does not include the New Hampshire tributaries of the Ossipee River, which flow into Ossipee Lake and are primarily quick water. Descriptions of these rivers are available in the *AMC River Guide: New Hampshire/Vermont.*

The Little Ossipee is a good choice for an overnight trip in the spring. The Saco between Conway and Cornish is very popular for camping trips throughout the paddling season.

Spring whitewater is available on the Ossipee and Little Ossipee, while the Saco at Limington Rips can be used all summer. The Saco has a good current and can be run at all water levels. Flat water is available on lakes and in pools behind dams.

The Saco River: A History and Canoeing Guide by Viola Sheehan (Saco River Corridor Association, 1976) discusses the Saco River in Maine. Available from the Saco River Corridor Association (207-625-8123, www.srcc-maine.org) for $6.50, it provides an excellent history of the Saco River and several drawings of the Little Ossipee, Ossipee, and Saco Rivers as a paddling guide.

CENTER CONWAY, NH ➤ HIRAM, ME   44.25 MI

Description:	Flatwater, quickwater, Class II
Navigable:	Spring, summer, fall
Scenery:	Forested, rural
Maps:	North Conway 15, Ossipee Lake 15, Fryeburg, Brownfield, Hiram, DL 4
Portage:	10.0 mi R Swan's Falls 300 yd
Campsites:	10.0 mi R Swan's Falls AMC $ car
	14.0 mi R Canal Bridge (ME 5) commercial $ car
	23.5 mi L Walker's Falls AMC $
	29.5 mi R Woodland Acres commercial $ car
	29.5 mi L River Run commercial $ car
	35.5 mi R Burnt Meadows commercial $ by reservation only

From Center Conway, New Hampshire, to Hiram, Maine, is the "sandy" Saco, where low water during the summer months exposes many miles of beaches. A quickwater river in a wide valley of farms and forests, it flows alternately along the edges of fields and through stands of pine and swamp maple. A few small towns are nearby, but none infringe upon the river.

The setting is so peaceful and the water so clean that the Saco attracts people (thousands of them on a nice summer weekend). Because of the large crowds and the impact that high-density use can have on a river, river-use regulations are in place. In addition to the river-use regulations, the AMC encourages all paddlers to adopt the Leave No Trace principles outlined at the end of this book. All trash must be carried out (not buried). Nothing is to be washed in the river; all washing should be done in buckets and the waste water poured on the soil away from the river. Human waste should be buried at least 6 inches deep in topsoil and at least 200 feet from the river's high water mark. Fire permits are required. Only cooking fires on sand bars are allowed; no bonfires are permitted. All fires should be extinguished with water (not covered with sand). The land along the Saco is privately owned. Paddlers need to get permission before wandering. Other than at campgrounds, camping is permitted on unposted sand bars from the Maine state line to Hiram. Never dive head first into the river! The river generally is shallow, even where it looks deep—deaths and serious injuries have occurred far too often on the river.

For further information and maps on the river, contact the AMC campgrounds at Swan's Falls (207-935-3395) and Walker's Falls, the Saco Bound, 2561 E. Main St., P.O. Box 302, Center Conway, NH 03813 (603-447-2177), or any of the canoe liveries. Fire permits are available in Fryeburg from the town fire warden. Check on this with the liveries.

At least nine other parking sites exist along the river; some charge fees and others are free. Many offer only unsupervised parking. You can find parking at Canal Bridge on ME 5, at Walker's Bridge on US 302, at the Brownfield Bridge on ME 160, at Weston's Bridge off ME 113 west of Fryeburg, and at the Lovewell Pond access that is reached by a road that leaves ME 5/113 southeast of Fryeburg and north of a railroad crossing. The AMC *Saco River Trip Leaders' Guide,* $2.00, lists all available parking (as well as complete information and helpful hints for a successful Saco River trip) and is available at the AMC Saco River Campgrounds as well as from the AMC campground registrars. Please be considerate of landowners and park only at designated areas.

Now you are ready for your Saco River trip. The river is clearest in the 17.5 miles from Center Conway, New Hampshire, to the confluence with the Old Saco. In this section of the river, the current is stronger, the river generally shallower, the banks more open, and the sand bars more numerous. As you approach and pass the Old Saco entering from the north, you will notice that the banks are more heavily forested and the water darker.

Just below the US 302 bridge near Center Conway, New Hampshire, soon after the river flows between the abutments of the old covered bridge, you encounter some Class II rips that are bony in low water. The remaining 9.0 miles to Swan's Falls are mostly quick water. The main highway approaches the river across from McSherry's Nursery (3.25 miles). The next landmark is Weston's Bridge (6.75 miles). Weston's Bridge and Beach is the Fryeburg town beach. Organized swimming lessons and activities are held in the river every day, so you are advised to stay far river right on the outside of the curve. In another 3.25 miles is Swan's Falls (10 miles), where you find a dam that should be approached cautiously in high water. Portage on the right.

About 1.0 mile past Canal Bridge (14.0 miles), the river swings to the north, and a channel enters on the right. The stream can be followed upstream 200 yards or so to Bog Pond, a small and secluded body of water. The next landmark is the Old Saco (17.50 miles), which enters on the left.

The Old Course of the Saco, as the name implies, was once the channel of the river. The Saco today follows a canal dug in 1817 for flood control. The western end of the Old Saco is silted in, but the eastern portion of it still drains Kezar Lake.

From the Old Saco (17.5 miles) quick water continues for 6.0 miles past Walker's Bridge, US 302 (21.0 miles), and the outlet to Pleasant Pond (23.25 miles) to Walker's Falls (23.5 miles) where the short, easy rapids become flooded out at high water. Pleasant Pond is very close to the river and provides good views of the mountains.

Below Walker's Falls 2.0 miles the outlet from Lovewell Pond enters on the right. Then the Saco meanders, passing to the west of the Brownfield Bog Wildlife Management area, which is a nesting area for ducks, great blue herons, bald eagles, and other colorful and rare birds. The Department of Inland Fisheries and Wildlife has set up rookeries here in an attempt to encourage nesting. Below the ME 160 bridge (29.5 miles) the river continues to meander for the next 13.75 miles to Hiram (43.25 miles).

HIRAM ➤ BONNY EAGLE DAM (ME 35)   25.25 MI

Description:	Flatwater, quickwater, Class I, II
Navigable:	Spring, summer, fall
Scenery:	Forested, rural, towns
Maps:	Hiram, Cornish, Sebago Lake 15, Buxton, DL 4
Portages:	2.75 mi R Great Falls Dam 0.25 mi
	14.75 mi L Steep Falls 50 yd
	25.25 mi R Bonny Eagle Dam 70 yd
Campsite:	19.25 mi Limington Rips (island at top)

The Saco is a fairly large river rising in Crawford Notch. The rapids are much more difficult in high water, especially Limington Rips, which generate big waves. This portion of the river is used much less than the section preceding it. The water is not as clear as it is near Fryeburg, but the scenery is comparable. The occasional rapids are a feature not found on the section from Center Conway, New Hampshire, to Hiram.

In the late spring when water levels are generally medium, you can make a nice 20.75-mile run by starting at Kezar Falls, running the Ossipee River to the Saco near Cornish, and then continuing down the Saco to the ME 25 bridge in East Limington.

From Hiram you encounter flat water for 2.75 miles to Great Falls Dam. **Caution!** In high water, go left of an island after a sweeping left turn. You should land on the right above the dam and portage along the trail there. Two-thirds of a mile below Great Falls Dam you find a Class I rapid at a short left turn. Quick water continues past the mouth of the Ossipee River (5.75 miles) to the ME 5/117 bridge in Cornish (6.25 miles).

Just past the Cornish bridge are riffles. After 2.75 miles, you reach Old Bald Rapid, a short Class II pitch with large waves in high water. You find more riffles in the remaining 5.5 miles to Steep Falls.

Steep Falls (14.75 miles) is a dangerous 7-foot drop that must be portaged. You are apt to come upon it suddenly, especially in the fast-moving current of high water. Be alert for the sound of falling water, a glimpse of a house on the left bank, or the sighting of a green girder bridge below the falls. When you notice any of these, get quickly to the left bank where you find a short portage. After the falls, you have 0.25 mile of rapids, Class II in low water, but rougher in high water. The rapids continue under the bridge and past the remains of a dam.

Below Steep Falls, riffles continue intermittently for 1.0 mile, followed by almost 3.0 miles of quick water to Parkers Rips, a short Class II rapid near a house on the right where the river swings left. In 0.75 mile, you reach Limington Rips, a 0.5-mile set of Class II rapids in low water, but Class III with heavy waves in medium water.

The left-hand side of the island requires more maneuvering and is usually used in low water. The drop is steeper on the right, but scouting is easier and the shore closer in case of mishap. The take-out above the rapid is also on the right, to a road immediately adjacent. Although the hardest section of this rapid is near the end, below the ME 25 bridge (19.75 miles), most mishaps occur before the bridge.

Just past Limington Rips, the Little Ossipee River enters on the right (20.0 miles). Deadwater continues for the remaining 5.25 miles to Bonny Eagle Dam (25.25 miles) just below the ME 35 bridge. Take out on the right bank near the powerhouse. If you are continuing down the river, portage beyond the building about 50 yards to a gravel path to the river.

BONNY EAGLE DAM (ME 35) ➤ BIDDEFORD   19.0 MI

Description:	Lake, flatwater
Navigable:	Spring, summer, fall
Scenery:	Forested, rural, towns
Maps:	Buxton 15, Kennebunk 15, Biddeford 15, Portland 15, DL 2, 3
Portages:	1.5 mi L dam at West Buxton
	6.75 mi R dam at Bar Mills
	10.0 mi R Skelton Dam
	(20.0 mi dams)

More than half of this section consists of deadwaters behind a succession of dams. Near the ME 4A/117 bridge (8.0 miles) at Salmon Falls (flooded out), you enter the third deadwater. As the river opens into the wide lake behind Skelton Dam at Union Falls (10.0 miles), head southeast after a short portage around the dam.

A couple of miles after the ME 5 bridge (14.5 miles), the flat water is broken by a short rapid. Below the Maine Turnpike (18.75 miles) you find a convenient take-out on the right at Rotary Park (19.0 miles). Below dams in Biddeford and Saco the river is tidal.

Old Course

Kezar Outlet drains Kezar Lake south to the Old Course of the Saco, a bit west of the latter's northernmost point. The upper (western) portion of the Old Course is now only a series of sloughs, its entrance from the Saco unidentifiable. The lower portion is kept active by the outlets from Kezar Lake, Charles Pond, and Kezar Pond. Wildlife is abundant; almost every stump and rock is covered with turtles in season.

KEZAR OUTLET ➤ SACO RIVER   8.0 MI

Description:	Quickwater
Navigable:	Spring, summer, fall
Scenery:	Forested
Maps:	Fryeburg 15, DL 4

The current flows briskly, and vegetation covers the bottom, waving sinuously. Red School Bridge on US 5 (4.0 miles) and Hemlock Covered Bridge (6.5 miles) also allow access.

The outlet from Kezar Pond enters left just above the covered bridge. The Saco River is another 1.5 miles.

Kezar Lake Outlet

This route is popular as an access to the Saco River, making an interesting variation. Swimming is not as desirable here as on the main Saco.

KEZAR LAKE NARROWS ➤ OLD COURSE   4.5 MI

Description:	Lake, flatwater
Navigable:	Spring, summer, fall
Scenery:	Forested
Maps:	Fryeburg 15, DL 4
Portage:	4.25 mi dam 10 yd

From the landing at Kezar Narrows, paddle southwest into the lower bay and across it to the outlet (1.75 miles). The lake level is raised by a small dam on the outlet just above the confluence with the Charles River (4.5 miles). The wire grating above it must also be lifted over.

Below the dam, the river flows quickly, passing under a bridge near the confluence. It might be rocky in low water.

Charles River

The Charles River is the outlet to Charles Pond. The river flows from Charles Pond to the outlet from Kezar Lake; they meet and flow together into the Old Course of the Saco.

CHARLES POND ➤ KEZAR OUTLET   1.5 MI

Description:	Flatwater, quickwater
Navigable:	Spring, summer, fall
Scenery:	Forested
Maps:	Fryeburg, DL 10

The Charles River leaves from the east side of Charles Pond. It is rockier and wider than the Cold River and might require occasional wading to pass when the Cold River is runnable. It passes under a bridge just above the confluence with Kezar Outlet.

Cold River

The Cold River is a small stream that rises on Baldface Mountain in New Hampshire, flows to Charles Pond, and ultimately to the Saco River. Because it is a narrow stream with a good watershed, it can be run after summer thunderstorms as well as in spring.

PINE HILL ROAD ➤ CHARLES POND   10.0 MI

Description:	Quickwater
Navigable:	Medium water: late spring or after heavy rain
Scenery:	Forested
Maps:	North Conway 15, Fryeburg 15, DL 10

Put in from the road to Pine Hill. The river is very small but flows mostly over a smooth, sandy bottom with deep pools here and there. The river flows into the north side of Charles Pond, which is about 0.5 mile in diameter. The outlet, marked by a large rock, is only a few hundred feet to the left. Follow the outlet approximately 1.0 mile to the road that runs along the Old Course of the Saco.

(For an exciting, if frigid swim, find Emerald Pool, near the AMC Cold River Camp, off ME/NH 113, north of Fryeburg.)

Kezar River

This small stream drains the Five Kezar Ponds in Stoneham and flows southwest to the Old Course of the Saco just north of Kezar Pond.

NUMBER FOUR ➤ LOVELL   2.25 MI

Description:	Quickwater, flatwater
Navigable:	Summer: after a heavy rain
Scenery:	Forested
Maps:	North Conway 15, Fryeburg 15, DL 10

This stream can be run from here after a heavy summer rain. It is a canoe-width wide at the start, with overhanging bushes. After 1.5 miles, it opens up into the flowage above the dam at Lovell, with pond lilies and attractive wooded banks.

If you are continuing, you can portage right through a culvert under the highway.

LOVELL ➤ OLD CHANNEL   3.50 MI

Description:	Quickwater, flatwater
Navigable:	Summer: after a heavy rain
Scenery:	Forested
Maps:	North Conway 15, Fryeburg 15, DL 10

The bottom is sandy where it circles around Smarts Hill. The river enters Swimming Bog about 2.0 miles from Lovell and somewhat disappears into it. By keeping to the right-hand channel, you might be able to work through it down to the Old Saco. When the river is up, much of the water overflows into Kezar Pond.

Ossipee River

The Ossipee River flows east for 17.5 miles from Lake Ossipee, across the Maine border, and into the Saco River near Cornish. It has dependable flow in the spring, but by summer the water level is too low to run the lower section.

OSSIPEE LAKE ➤ KEZAR FALLS 10.75 MI

Description:	Quickwater, Class I, II
Navigable:	High and medium water: spring
	Low water: passable, some lining at rapids
Scenery:	Forested, rural, towns
Maps:	Ossipee Lake 15, Kezar Falls, DL 4
Portages:	10.5 mi first dam at Kezar Falls (across island)
	30 yd
	10.75 mi R second dam at Kezar Falls 30 yd

Quick water characterizes this section, although you find one nice rapid just above the NH 153 bridge in Effingham Falls. You encounter several more short rapids before Kezar Falls, but for most of the distance the river is smooth. Vacation cottages line the banks near the beginnings, and below East Freedom you find more cottages and houses, with a main highway close by on the left bank for much of the distance. Anyone seeking a paddle in remote surroundings will not find it here.

The dam at the outlet of Ossipee Lake is at the end of a side road 0.5 mile west of the junction of NH 25/153 in Effingham Falls. Put in below the gatehouse and run down the sluiceway to a pool of slack water. Soon, there begins 0.25 mile of rapids that are Class II or III, depending on the water level. They are the most difficult on the river, and they lead up to the NH 153 bridge (1.5 miles).

You travel 1.5 miles of quick water past the NH 25 bridge (2.0 miles) to East Freedom, where 0.25 mile of Class II rapids leads under a bridge (4.5 miles) to the Maine border. The remaining distance to Kezar Falls is mostly quick water with two short Class II rapids, one before and one after the ME 160 bridge in Porter (7.75 miles).

In Kezar Falls, go to the right of the island and take out at a small bridge (10.5 miles). If you are continuing downstream, carry across the island to the foot of the main dam and continue 0.25 mile through the town to the second dam (10.75 miles). Take out on the right, carry across the canal, and put in below the dam.

KEZAR FALLS ➤ SACO RIVER   6.75 MI

Description:	Quickwater, Class I, II
Navigable:	High and medium water: early to late spring
Scenery:	Forested, rural
Maps:	Kezar Falls, Cornish, DL 4
Portage:	4.25 mi dam 10 yd

Below the second dam in Kezar Falls, the Ossipee River takes on a different character. It is a scenic run past forests and farms almost all the way to the Saco River, with quick water or rapids for the entire distance.

When the water level is up, the run from Kezar Falls to the ME 5/117 bridge over the Saco can be made in a little over an hour. Or, it can be done at a leisurely pace with a lunch stop. But if you continue down the Saco for another 14.0 miles to the ME 25 bridge, you can make a long, scenic trip of mixed flat water and rapids. Note, however, that Limington Rips, which begin just above the bridge, are severe rapids in high water.

East of the ME 25 bridge in Kezar Falls 0.5 mile, turn north onto Garner Avenue (at the house with a red metal roof), turn left at the end (one block), and take the first right to reach the dam and power station. The gate is usually locked, so boats must be carried or wheeled down the access road. You find two steep put-ins in river right: one along the sluice, one at the pool at the end of the sluice.

Below the dam are some nice Class I and II rapids for 1.0 mile to Which Way Rips, where the river abruptly divides around an island. Quick water and Class I rapids continue to the first bridge (3.5 miles), with more quick water to the second (5.5 miles). Below the second bridge and past a few cottages, you find some easy Class I to II rapids that lead almost to the Saco River (6.75 miles). At the Saco, go right 0.5 mile to above the ME 5/117 bridge east of Cornish (7.25 miles). You find a nice take-out with granite steps on river right, just below the bridge.

Little Ossipee River

The Little Ossipee is a fairly popular trip in southwestern Maine. It flows east from Balch Pond, a small lake on the Maine–New Hampshire border, to the Saco River just downstream from the ME 25 bridge at East Limington.

In high water, it is an easy 2-day trip of 28.25 miles from Davis Brook near North Shapleigh to East Limington just above the confluence with the Saco River. The hardest rapids that are normally run are at Newfield, and they are Class II. Those at Hardscrabble Falls below ME 117 are so difficult that all but the last 100 yards are usually portaged. The section below Ledgemere Dam is usually passable through the summer.

DAVIS BROOK ➤ ME 5   11.25 MI

Description:	Flatwater, quickwater, Class I, II
Navigable:	High and medium water: early spring to late April
Scenery:	Wild, forested, towns
Maps:	Newfield 15, DL 2

The most remote part of the Little Ossipee River is the section above Newfield. Much of the area was burned in 1947, and today it is covered with scrub growth, predominately gray birch. In medium water, all the rapids are shallow, so high water is recommended.

ME 11 crosses the Little Ossipee at the Newfield-Shapleigh town line. Just south of this point, follow Mann Road east for 0.9 mile to the double culvert over Davis Brook.

Alternatively, you can start at the culvert on ME 11. Rocks inside are difficult to dodge in the darkness. The first mile to Davis Brook contains shallow rapids that might be choked with debris and might require short carries.

Davis Brook is a small stream that flows into the Little Ossipee 0.25 mile from Mann Road. Then, in the next 4.25 miles, the main river is a mixture of quick water and short, easy Class I–II rapids. The river flows through some small meadows, and you encounter at least one beaver dam.

Approaching Newfield, you find a Class II drop over some ledges. Just east of Newfield, ME 11 crosses Chellis Brook. If the depth of the water over the cement brook bed under the bridge is between

1.25 and 1.5 feet, the Little Ossipee is probably at medium level. In that case, the recommended start is at Chellis Brook, which joins the main river in 100 yards. If the water under the bridge is less than 8 inches, this section will be scratchy in many places.

Most of the remaining 6.25 miles to ME 5 at Ossipee Mills is quick water with no significant rapids. About halfway down, you pass between the two old abutments of Clark's Bridge.

ME 5 ➤ LEDGEMERE DAM   5.75 MI

Description:	Lake
Navigable:	When lake is full
Scenery:	Forested
Maps:	Newfield 15, Buxton 15, DL 2 and 4

The flashboards on Ledgemere Dam might not be in place, with the result that the level of the lake might be down a few feet. Ledgemere Flowage (renamed Lake Arrowhead by real estate developers peddling house lots) will then have some sections of shoals and extensive mud flats with exposed stumps. In some places, sandy beaches will be exposed. Portions of the lake are attractive; others are not. You see many houses; most of the shoreline is developed.

The lake poses navigation problems. The topographical map shows the normal pool elevation, but the lake usually is kept at full pool.

LEDGEMERE DAM ➤ EAST LIMINGTON   11.75 MI

Description:	Flatwater, quickwater, Class II
Navigable:	Spring, summer, fall
Scenery:	Forested
Maps:	Buxton 15, DL 2 and 4
Portages:	4.25 mi R Hardscrabble Falls 0.5 mi
	11.25 mi L falls at East Limington 300 yd
Campsite:	4.75 mi R Hardscrabble Falls (end of portage)

The Little Ossipee is much larger below Ledgemere Flowage than it is above it. The banks are heavily wooded all the way to East Limington, and near the end it flows through a small, narrow valley with steep slopes close to the riverbank. The river is mostly flat water in this section, and you find almost no easily runnable rapids. The first of the two ledge drops, Hardscrabble Falls, should be portaged, whereas the second one is just after a logical take-out point near the end of the river.

The current is fast for 1.0 mile or so to a short Class I drop. Then it is slow past the ME 117 bridge (1.75 miles) to the second bridge (4.25 miles), which is at the top of Hardscrabble Falls. **Caution!** Stop on the right above the bridge. The falls, which are 0.5 mile long, begin and end with Class II rapids, but the middle section consists of a steep drop over a series of ledges that should not tempt you. The portage follows a rutted dirt road close to the right bank and makes a sharp right turn after passing a field on the right.

From the end of Hardscrabble Falls (4.75 miles), the river is flat and winding for 6.0 miles to a short Class II drop within sight of, and 0.25 mile above, the last bridge on the Little Ossipee. **Caution!** This bridge at East Limington is located just above a dangerous pitch. Stop above this bridge (11.25 miles). You should look at the approach, particularly in high water. Take-out and/or portage is on the right above the bridge. If you are continuing the last 0.5 mile to the Saco, go across the road and take an old trail that follows the southern bank of the river. Another 0.25 mile of flat water brings you to the end of the Little Ossipee. Limington Rips is 0.25 mile to the left, and Bonny Eagle Dam is 5.25 miles down the deadwater to the right.

Access at East Limington: The bridge above the last portage on the Little Ossipee is about 1.0 mile by road from the ME 25 bridge over the Saco River. Heading west from the latter, take the first left.

Chapter 2
Androscoggin Watershed

Androscoggin River

After the glaciers in the last ice age retreated some 15,000 years ago, the present-day Androscoggin valley was made up of a chain of lakes linked by short rivers. In time the Androscoggin as we know it emerged. The beautiful valleys, or intervales, along the Androscoggin mark where the lakes once were.

The Abenaki tribe of Native Americans used the river as a means of transportation and as a source of fish. When the Europeans arrived, they used the waterway as a power source and an industrial waste and sewer system. During the first half of the last century, the Androscoggin was one of the most polluted rivers in the United States. The Federal Water Pollution Control Act of 1972, better known as the Clean Water Act, has led the way to a much cleaner river. The main force behind the legislation was Senator Edmund Muskie, who grew up along the Androscoggin in Rumford. In addition, recognizing the need for continuing improvement, the state of Maine enacted the Color,

ANDROSCOGGIN
WATERSHED

Aziscohos
Lake

Cupsuptic
River

Kennebago River

Kennebago
Lake

Wilson's
Mills

Magalloway
River

Rangeley
Lake

Rangeley

Errol

Rapid
River

Mooselookmeguntic
Lake

Umbagog
Lake

Upton

Richardson
Lake

Milan

Androscoggin River

Berlin

Byron

Webb
Lake

Gorham

Shelburne

Sunday River

Bear River

Andover

Ellis River

Swift River

Weld

Carthage

Webb River

Rumford
Point

Rumford

Mexico

Wild River

Bethel

Androscoggin River

Dixfield

Sevenmile River

Jay

West Paris

West Branch

Nezinscot River

Parker
Pond

Vienna

Norway

Buckfield

Dead River

North Wayne

Turner

Androscoggin
Lake

Little Androscoggin River

Mechanic Falls

Auburn

Sabattus
Pond

Lewiston

Sabattus

Sabattus River

Lisbon Falls

Merrymeeting
Bay

Brunswick

NH   ME

N

Scale in miles

0   0   10   15   20   25

Odor, and Foam Reduction Act in the spring of 1990 to reduce the level of those three pollutants in the rivers of Maine. As the river's water quality has continued to improve, recreational use of the river has grown dramatically. A few sections have rapids that need to be respected, and, as always, water levels affect difficulty. The river's novice-friendly nature, ease of access, and beautiful scenery make the waterway a great paddling river.

The Androscoggin River begins north of Errol, New Hampshire, at the confluence of the Magalloway River and the outlet of Umbagog Lake. This is no longer a clearly defined spot because the dam at Errol floods many miles up both branches. The lakes in the headwaters form a vast storage area of impounded water to run the mills and power stations on the Androscoggin. This makes summer paddling possible.

LAKE UMBAGOG ➤ BERLIN, NH   34.25 MI

Description:	Flatwater, quickwater, Class I, II
Navigable:	Spring, summer, fall: controlled release
Scenery:	Forested, rural
Maps:	Errol 15, Milan 15, Berlin
Portages:	3.75 mi L Errol Dam
	21.75 mi R Pontook Dam
	(34.5 mi Berlin Dam)
Campsites:	4.5 mi R Errol Bridge private $ car
	8.0 mi R Mollidgewock private $ car

This is the clean water section of the Androscoggin. Below the Errol and Pontook Dams two whitewater runs exist all through the summer. Although the runs are neither long nor difficult, they are popular in July and August, with few other whitewater alternatives in New England. The valley is attractive, though not wild because NH 16 follows the river closely almost the entire distance. For this reason, it is rarely used for overnight trips.

Below Lake Umbagog, the river is wide, with extensive marshes on both sides. In 3.0 miles, it reaches NH 16 where you find a launching ramp; 0.75 mile beyond this ramp is the Errol Dam (3.75 miles), which is portaged on the left.

The section from Errol Dam to just below the NH 26 bridge, 0.75 mile long, consists of a short rapid, a pool, and another 0.5 mile of easier Class I–II rapids. Because of the slack water below where Clear Stream enters on the right (which is immediately after the rapids) and the proximity of the road, these rapids are not as dangerous as the size and difficulty of the river normally would indicate. If you plan to run this section by itself, the best way to reach it is to park your car in the field at the put-in beside the pool on river right above Errol, run the rapids, and take out on river right either near the bridge or at the end of the rapids. Then carry or wheel your boat back to the parking lot at the bridge.

Below Clear Stream (4.75 miles), you travel 3.25 miles of flat water to Mollidgewock Brook (8.0 miles). Downstream 3.0 miles of Class I–II rapids are separated by pools, with mixed smooth water and riffles for the remaining distance to Pontook Reservoir. You can find an access point at the Dummer-Cambridge town line along NH 16. It is a section of old NH 16 and is right along the river. Just above Seven Islands is a bridge (12.75 miles), with a nice wave. Bog Brook (18.25 miles), which enters on the left, is the next landmark. Portage at Pontook Dam (21.3 miles) on the right.

Caution! At the dam you encounter a strong, consistent, and dangerous reversal. This hydraulic is more dangerous than it looks; people have drowned here. Heed the warning signs, and do not go upstream to play in the reversal! The parking lot and public boat landing is on river right and includes restrooms. Pre-arranged water releases on summer weekends provide enough water to create Class I–II rapids. Call 603-449-2903 for release information. You can find a public boat launch at the Paul O. Bofinger Conservation Area, on the right side of the river, 2.2 miles below the Pontook Dam. This area has parking, restrooms, and interpretive signs. This take-out is a nice place to swim as the water is usually warm. Paddlers often do a morning run, have lunch, and run it again. The Mollidgewock campground, New Hampshire, is nearby if you want to make it a 2-day event.

The remaining 10.5 miles have a good current but no rapids. The bridge in Milan can be used as an access point, although the bank is very steep. Park on the left side of the river. The Nansen Wayside Park is also a good access point, with an easy paddle down to Berlin, New Hampshire, from here. You come to a bridge in Milan (27.75 miles). In Berlin, you should take out at the playground (34.5 miles) located on the left below the first bridge or continue down to the new boat launch and float installed in the summer of 2000 by the Northern Forest Heritage Park. It is on river right, but close to the Berlin Dam, so paddle cautiously.

BERLIN, NH ➤ SHELBURNE DAM   11.50 MI

Description:	Flatwater, quickwater, Class I
Navigable:	Spring, summer, fall: controlled release (not recommended, dams)
Scenery:	Urban, forested
Maps:	Berlin, Shelburne
Portages:	7 dams

The river valley is attractive, with views of the Presidential Range to the southwest and lower mountains to the east. A recommended paddle would be to put in at Gorham and paddle down to the Shelburne Dam. No portages are necessary, and the views of the Presidential Range in this section are wonderful. The river has been cleaned up substantially. You can hardly discern the difference in water quality in this section from the first section. The seven dams above Gorham can each be portaged individually, or in series.

SHELBURNE DAM ➤ BETHEL   17.75 MI

Description:	Flatwater, quickwater, Class I
Navigable:	Spring, summer, fall: controlled release
Scenery:	Forested, rural
Maps:	Shelburne, Gilead, Bethel, DL 10

The water in this section is less polluted than in the past and the river valley is scenic, with views of the Presidential Range to the southwest and lower mountains to the east. The river can sometimes have an odor, but not everyone can detect it.

Put in below the dam at the bridge on which the Appalachian Trail crosses the river. Two log cribs dominate the view upstream over the dam. You have a good current with pleasant riffles for many miles, as the river continually separates around numerous islands.

At 2.75 miles, you come upon a bridge. Above the next bridge near Gilead (8.75 miles) is the most difficult rapid in this section, dropping past rocky outcroppings. You find a boat launch on river right above this bridge. Although Route 2 runs along the river, this section has a wilderness feel, and you get a good view of the White Mountains in one bend. This is a nice section to run in summer, or as a fall foliage trip. At 14.0 miles is the Newt's Landing Access site, owned and maintained by the Mahoosuc Land Trust. It is on the south bank and easily recognized by the log steps leading up from the river. Parking and river information are available here. The current continues slower to Bethel and the US 2 bridge. Arrangements can be made with Bethel Outdoor Adventure (207-824-4224) to rent canoes and/or take out at their beach on river left below the bridge. They can also provide shuttle service.

BETHEL ➤ RUMFORD   23.50 MI

Description:	Flatwater, quickwater, Class I
Navigable:	Spring, summer, fall: controlled release
Scenery:	Forested
Maps:	Bethel, Bryant Pond, East Andover, Rumford, DL 10 and 18
Portage:	(24.25 mi L Rumford car recommended)

This is a beautiful stretch of river, still in the mountains, with fine views in every direction. The river flows through meadows in an open valley, offering many opportunities to enjoy the views. You encounter many riffles, but no major rapids, and the current is good. The views toward Grafton Notch are particularly interesting, and birds are abundant. The river is large, however, so wind can cause considerable trouble.

The best access at Bethel is at the private campground next to the US 2 bridge. Ask for and obtain permission from the property owners before accessing the river. Here the river turns north; it passes a highway rest area just before the Sunday River enters on the left (4.0 miles) in North Bethel. Just beyond the riffle at the mouth of the Bear River entering left at Newry (6.5 miles), the river resumes its eastward course. A newly built boat launch (11.0 miles) in Hanover offers access to this section of the river, which is sometimes used for floatplane launches and landings. The Ellis River enters on the left (13.75 miles) shortly before the bridge at Rumford Point (14.25 miles).

The remaining 10.0 miles to Rumford have a good current and are good going all the way. Another public boat launch is at about mile 23, next to the McDonalds on US 2.

Take out at the bridge above the first dam at the pulloff on the left. Three dams and a major waterfall make it advisable to carry the whole city in one long portage, cutting across the northward loop of the river where the Swift River enters.

RUMFORD ➤ LIVERMORE FALLS   24.0 MI

Description:	Quickwater, flatwater
Navigable:	Spring, summer, fall: controlled release
Scenery:	Forested, rural, towns
Maps:	Rumford, Dixfield, Worthley Pond, Canton, East Dixfield, Wilton, Livermore Falls, DL 19 and 11
Portage:	(24.0 mi 1 dam)

In this stretch, the river is still in mountainous country, although the higher hills have been left behind. The Androscoggin can be accessed easily at the Mexico boat launch on the Swift River, with the Mead Paper Company on the opposite bank for the first mile or so. From Rumford it is 4.0 miles with a good current to the West Pen Bridge and then to Dixfield, where the Webb River enters on the left. A public boat launch on river left is in Dixfield and is the last easy access point. A bridge in Canton is passed at 15.0 miles and then a portage on river left at the Riley Dam (21.2 miles). You now encounter a series of dams owned by International Paper in this region—be attentive! The remaining 5.0 miles to Livermore Falls present no problems. At first, the river remains in a narrow valley, but then gradually the valley becomes more open and the bottom lands wider and more rural. Some 16.0 miles below Dixfield, Sevenmile Stream enters on the left. A big dam at Livermore Falls is best carried on the left.

LIVERMORE FALLS ➤ AUBURN-LEWISTON   30.0 MI

Description:	Quickwater, flatwater, Class II, III
Navigable:	Spring, summer, fall: controlled release
Scenery:	Rural, towns
Maps:	Livermore Falls, Turner Center, Lewiston 15, DL 11

Portages:	25.5 mi Gulf Island Dam
	26.5 mi Deer Rips Dam
	(29.0 mi dam and cascades)

A boat access site below the dams in Livermore Falls is on river right, about 0.5 mile south of the ME 4 bridge. You encounter two sets of rapids in this section before you come to the twin bridges of ME 219. Just below the bridge is a ledge-type rapid, which should be scouted before running. Portaging is possible through the island that the twin bridges cross. The 6.6 miles from the twin bridges to Center Bridge is wonderful calmwater paddling, with white pine lining the banks. The current is almost nonexistent because of the Gulf Island Pond Dam another 9.0 miles downstream. The Turner Bridge has a boat launch with parking, but no restroom facilities.

From here, it is all slack water for 7.0 miles down Gulf Island Pond to the Gulf Island Dam. Many paddlers take out here, but you can continue 1.3 miles more to the Deer Rips Dam, another high dam. Below that is another 2.6 miles to the first dam in Auburn-Lewiston, where you have a long carry on river right around the dam and cascades below.

Gulf Island Pond has an interesting feature a few miles down. In a state-mandated effort to increase oxygen levels in the impounded water, pure oxygen is bubbled into the water through an underwater diffuser. A line of effervescent water crosses the river from bank to bank—an unusual sight.

AUBURN-LEWISTON ➤ DURHAM   10.0 MI

Description:	Flatwater, quickwater, Class II, III
Navigable:	Spring, summer, fall: controlled release
Scenery:	Rural
Maps:	Lewiston 15, Freeport 15, Bath 15, DL 5 and 6

In this section, the river flows through the rolling country of southern Maine, with less spectacular but still pleasant rural scenery. The Little Androscoggin River joins with the Androscoggin in Auburn. You find a set of rips, Dresser's Rips, below the confluence of the two rivers that are Class II–III, depending on the water level.

DURHAM ➤ BRUNSWICK 12.50 MI

Description:	Flatwater, quickwater, Class II
Navigable:	Spring, summer, fall: controlled release
Scenery:	Urban, rural
Portages:	4.0 mi L Worumbo Falls Dam 0.5 mi
	7.5 mi R dam at Pejepscot 0.25 mi
	(12.5 mi R dam at Brunswick)

A fine public boat launch is found in Durham, on river right. This section of the river is beautiful, and you can see lots of wildlife. From Durham it is 3.0 miles to the boat launch at the confluence with the Sabattus River, which enters on the left upstream of Lisbon. You encounter some Class I–II riffles in this section. Another 1.0 mile brings you to the Worumbo Falls Dam; portage on the left. Another 0.5 mile downstream on river left is the Lisbon Falls boat ramp. Flat water for 3.0 miles brings you to the Pejepscot Dam; portage on river right along the trail. A cleverly designed boat slide helps you get back down the steep bank to the river downstream of the dam. Most of the remaining 4.0 miles are quick water. The large red I-95 bridge hums with traffic, and then the Brunswick take-out is at the Mill Street boat landing, on river right. The river is cordoned off with log booms from this point on because of fast current, rapids, and the dam below. For those willing to brave traffic, portage on river right to below the rapids at the 250th Anniversary Park. You also find a boat launch and parking in Brunswick, reachable by Water Street on the right side of the river. Check the tide charts before going on the Topsham side of the islands; you encounter mud flats at low tide. You can find a public boat launch and small park on river right at the site of the Bay Bridge, which went out in a flood in the late 1800s. You can continue on to explore Merrymeeting Bay, which is tidal. Keep an eye on the weather, as this expanse is wide and unprotected.

Magalloway River

The Magalloway River is a beautiful, wildlife-abundant, little-used river in western Maine. Beginning in Moose Bog near the Canadian Border, the river runs through Aziscohos Lake and then meanders its way into New Hampshire before joining the outlet of Umbagog Lake to form the Androscoggin River. Above Aziscohos Lake, you have no public access.

Aziscohos Lake offers many miles of paddling as well as a number of campsites. Below Aziscohos Dam, the Magalloway River offers both whitewater and flatwater trips, which can be run in combination with trips across Umbagog Lake and/or the Androscoggin River.

Camping in the area is uncrowded but limited to designated areas along the rivers and lakes. Culvert Camps on the Magalloway are administered from Mollidgewock Campground (603-482-3373), 3.0 miles south of Errol, New Hampshire.

AZISCOHOS DAM ➤ WILSONS MILLS   3.25 MI

Description:	Class II, III, IV
Navigable:	Spring, summer, fall: controlled release
Scenery:	Wild, forested
Maps:	Oquossoc 15, Errol 15, DL 28 and 27

For more information on this stretch, see the *AMC Classic Northeastern Whitewater Guide* by Bruce Lessels.

Caution! Although it might look tempting, do not put in just below the dam! Many iron rods are still embedded in the bedrock from logging days and can quickly tear any boat into pieces.

The first few hundred yards are extremely technical and can be bony at low levels. Although it is usually Class III, this stretch can be Class IV at high levels; beyond here, the rapids are less difficult but still technical. After 1.0 mile or so, on a left bend, a large ledge drop might form a large hole at high levels. A hunting camp can be seen on the right side. From this point, the river decreases in intensity as it nears the NH 16 bridge at Wilsons Mills.

WILSONS MILLS ➤ ANDROSCOGGIN RIVER   16.25 MI

Description:	Flatwater, quickwater
Navigable:	Spring, summer, fall: controlled release
Scenery:	Forested, rural
Maps:	Errol 15, DL 27

The lower part of the Magalloway offers a leisurely paddle and a chance to observe wildlife and picturesque views. The river is narrow at the start, with a 3-mph current; it meanders along with views of Aziscohos Mountain on the east, and Halfmoon Mountain and the spectacular granite cliffs on the sides of the Diamond Peaks and Mount Dustin off to the west, looping into New Hampshire for 1.0 mile.

Below the confluence with the Diamond River (6.0 miles), the Magalloway River begins to widen; in 0.75 mile it passes under the ME 16 bridge near the Magalloway schoolhouse and back into New Hampshire in another mile. From there, the river wanders, with many side channels to explore and pond lilies galore. The Sturtevant Pond outlet enters in a wide culvert from the left. Farther down, Culvert Camp is on the right. In 3.0 miles, it reaches Umbagog Lake and the Androscoggin River, when the river swings west, away from the highway.

Umbagog Lake

All of the big lakes of western Maine, Rangeley, Mooselookmeguntic, and the Richardson Lakes, drain through the Rapid River into Umbagog Lake and from there to the Androscoggin River. All of these lake levels are artificially raised, creating a dependable reservoir for power generation. They offer public launching ramps, campsites, and many miles of paddling.

Lake Umbagog is an irregularly shaped, shallow lake that is mostly wild, but accessible. Much of the New Hampshire land surrounding the lake lies within the Lake Umbagog National Wildlife Refuge. Bald eagles (one pair) have nested in a tall, nearly dead pine tree on an island near the point where the Magalloway River enters the lake.

Lake Umbagog is a popular, though expensive, place to camp. Settlement is only at the southern end, along NH 26, where reservations for campsites should be arranged.

You can find campsites at the Umbagog Lake State Park Campground at Errol, New Hampshire (603-482-3373). Reserve sites and pay a fee at the base camp located where NH 16 skirts the southern tip of the lake.

Camping at Cedar Stump Campground, at the mouth of the Rapid River, is run by Saco Bound/Northern Waters (603-447-2177) in Errol, which can also arrange shuttle service for the Rapid River.

Rapid River

The Rapid River flows from Lower Richardson Lake to Lake Umbagog and offers difficult rapids and clean water in a remote setting. The river flow is regulated at Middle Dam on Lower Richardson Lake by the Union Water Power Company for power generation and paper production on the Androscoggin. Water-release levels for the next 24 hours can be obtained from Florida Power & Light's river information line (800-557-3569).

Forest Lodge, the former home of Louise Dickinson Rich, whose book *We Took to the Woods* relates her experiences in this region, is on the tote road below Pond in the River. On the northwestern shore of Pond in the River are the remains of the steam tug Alligator, which was used to winch rafts of logs across the lake. Some of the rocks in the river have been blasted to facilitate log drives, and their sharp edges can be hazardous to boaters.

The Rapid River would be even more popular if the access were less difficult. Middle Dam can be reached by a 3- to 4-mile paddle across Lower Richardson Lake, whereas the mouth of the Rapid River can be reached by a 6- to 7-mile paddle from Errol, New Hampshire. A motorboat shuttle is often arranged by whitewater paddlers. A tote road runs from Middle Dam to Sunday Cove on Lake Umbagog, and shuttle service is available through Lakewood Camps at Middle Dam (Andover, Maine; 207-243-2959) for whitewater paddlers wishing to run the rapids or for flatwater paddlers wishing to avoid them. It is also possible to hand-carry boats up to run the last section of the rapids.

MIDDLE DAM ➤ LONG POOL   3.0 MI

Description:	Lake, Class II, III, IV
Navigable:	Spring, summer, fall: controlled release, 600–2,000 cfs runnable
Scenery:	Wild
Maps:	Oquossoc 15, DL 18

Put in at the whirlpool below the dam or 50 yards downstream at Harbec Pool. The next 0.5 mile is Cemetery Rapids, which contains Class III waves with the right side recommended for the upper half and the left side for the lower half. The next 1.5 miles are Pond in the

River. Lower Dam, at the outlet, is mostly gone, and the 2-foot-plus drop can be run if desired. Access is available via a branch road from the tote road for those wishing to start here. Then you encounter 1.0 mile of Class II–III rapids, scratchy at 600 cfs, to Long Pool, where you find a branch road. Paddlers carrying up from downstream should take the turn just after a few houses on the right.

LONG POOL ➤ LAKE UMBAGOG   3.0 MI

Description:	Class III, IV
Navigable:	Spring, summer, fall: controlled release, 600–2,000 cfs runnable
Scenery:	Wild
Maps:	Oquossoc 15, Errol 15, DL 18
Campsite:	1.5 mi Cedar Stump private $

The first 1.5 miles have difficult rapids that should be run only by expert boaters with suitable heavy-water craft. Just below Long Pool, the river curves slightly to the right and enters the First Big Pitch, which contains 4- to 6-foot waves (even at lower levels); this should be run to the right of center to avoid a large hole on the left. This is followed by several hundred yards of easier rapids to another difficult but shorter pitch, sometimes known as Elephant Rock because of the large black rock in the middle. After a short, calmer section at Cold Spring, the Third Big Pitch starts, sometimes called the Staircase because of its appearance when viewed from below, with three steps and a pool below each at the lower water levels. This rapid is longer than the first two and leads to Smooth Ledge. Here, a rock dike extends from the right bank, with a hydraulic and a pool below, which is a favored spot for lunch.

Next is an S-turn rapid called Island Rip, which is intricate at 600 cfs and contains larger waves at higher levels. Then come two hydraulics to the right of center called the Jaws of Death. The upper hydraulic is full of air and hard to get out of at 600 cfs (not quite as difficult at 1,200 cfs) and becomes a standing wave at 1,800 cfs. The lower one also should be avoided.

The Devil's Hopyard consists of heavy waves studded with boulders for the next mile. The rapids end abruptly, and just below is

Cedar Stump, a primitive campsite that can be reached by motorboat from Lake Umbagog. A carry trail up the river connects to the tote road for those wishing to hand carry. It is about 1.5 miles to Long Pool or 2.5 miles to Lower Dam.

The last 1.5 miles to Lake Umbagog are wide, and the current gradually decreases.

Cupsuptic River

The Cupsuptic River rises in a rugged mountain wilderness on the Maine-Quebec border and flows southward into Cupsuptic Lake, one of the Rangeley lakes. The last 8.0 miles below Big Falls are relatively flat and offer good paddling. Access to the start is by a private road controlled by the Seven Islands Company. Ask for and obtain permission before crossing property lines.

BIG FALLS ➤ CUPSUPTIC LAKE 8.0 MI

Description:	Flatwater, quickwater, Class I
Navigable:	High water
Scenery:	Forested
Maps:	Cupsuptic 15, DL 28
Portage:	6.0 mi R Little Falls 0.25 mi

A start can be made at Lost Brook field, just below Big Falls. The first 1.0 mile to Portage Brook has a fast current, shallow rapids, and pools. From there to Little Falls, the current moves more slowly and can be paddled either way, as the course becomes more meandering and the balsam banks give way to alder thickets. The river can be reached at the bridge on Lincoln Pond Road. You might encounter many blowdowns.

Slower current for 2.0 miles brings you to Little Falls. You can put in here to paddle upstream for about 3.0 miles until blowdowns make further progress impractical. You can find a good 0.25-mile portage trail on the right around the falls. The falls has approximately a 5-foot drop and is not recommended to run. A huge boulder sits in the middle of this 30-foot-wide stretch. Also, this is a historical fly-fishing spot. It is common to see six to eight fly fishermen on any given day. A mass of downed trees for 200 yards below the falls makes a carry imperative. You can find a portage trail on the right. Below are 2.0 more miles of slack water to ME 16 and Cupsuptic Lake.

Kennebago River

The Kennebago River rises just east of the high peaks on the Maine-Quebec border and flows south to drain the rugged mountain area north of the Rangeley lakes. In enters Mooselookmeguntic Lake close to the outlet of Rangeley River from Rangeley Lake. The dirt road that follows up the river is not open to the public, but the river can be reached indirectly from the Morton Cut-Off Road, right onto Lincoln Pond Road.

The upper and lower sections are relatively quiet, but the middle section is an expert whitewater run in the early spring.

BEAR BROOK ➤ KENNEBAGO   8.0 MI

Description:	Quickwater, Class I
Navigable:	High and medium water
Scenery:	Wild
Maps:	Cupsuptic 15, DL 28
Portage:	(8.0 mi power dams)

At high water, you can put in at the Bear Brook Bridge, which can be reached by the Canada Road. Shallow rapids lead for a distance to Little Kennebago Lake, which is a mile across to the outlet at the south end. There, you can reach a launching ramp via Lincoln Pond Road from ME 16 and Morton Cut-Off Road, or from Tim Pond Road from ME 27, north of Eustis. You can paddle upstream aways from this point. The river meanders 3.0 miles to the outlet of Kennebago Lake. It is another 1.0 mile to the first of two power dams.

KENNEBAGO ➤ BRIDGE   6.0 MI

Description:	Class III
Navigable:	Medium and high water
Scenery:	Wild
Maps:	Cupsuptic 15, Oquossoc 15, DL 28

You need to ask for and obtain permission to drive on a private road opposite the Cupsuptic MFS. Put in below the lower dam at the old settlement of Kennebago. The first 2.0 miles are Class I and II rapids and the last 4.0 miles are Class III. The rapids are continuous, and you must be able to read them as they are run.

The gauge for this run is on the ME 16 bridge that crosses the Kennebago 1.0 mile north of Oquossoc. A reading of 1.0 on the gauge is medium water, and a reading of 1.6 and over is high water. At medium water, the river is rocky and technical. At 1.6, many of the rocks are covered, and you encounter large, turbulent, boat-filling waves. You also find some sticky reversals.

BRIDGE ➤ MOOSELOOKMEGUNTIC LAKE   7.0 MI

Description:	Flatwater, quickwater, Class I, II
Navigable:	Medium water
Scenery:	Wild, forested
Maps:	Oquossoc 15, DL 28

The first 1.0 mile below here is easy rapids, which are probably scratchy in midsummer. This is followed by a good current for the next 2.0 miles to Kamankeag Brook, which can be reached by driving in 5.0 miles on Boy Scout Camp Road, off ME 16. The current slows and the river winds for the final 4.0 miles to the ME 16 bridge and Mooselookmeguntic Lake, passing the Boy Scout camp (no buildings) on the left bank partway down. This is probably the only spot on the Kennebago providing loading areas (and lots of blueberries). Moose are often seen along the river.

From the Boy Scout camp down, it is a predominantly sandy/gravel bottom and quick moving in the spring, up to Class II. In the summer you would have some dragging. Great fun for families.

A recommended put-in is at Steepbank Pool, with a take-out at ME 16. The Boy Scout camp is halfway down. Steepbank Pool is a historic fly-fishing spot, chock full of anglers. Be courteous.

Rangeley River

The Rangeley River is the connecting link between Rangeley Lake and Mooselookmeguntic Lake. It starts at the ME 16 bridge at the northwestern edge of Rangeley Lake, and it looks like a continuation of the lake.

RANGELEY LAKE ➤ MOOSELOOKMEGUNTIC LAKE   1.5 MI

Description:	Class II
Navigable:	Medium water
Scenery:	Forested, town
Maps:	Oquossoc 15, DL 28

Lift over the screens and paddle 200 yards to the dam, which should be carried left. The fish ladder has been removed, although the framework remains. Below the dam are fairly continuous Class II rapids to Mooselookmeguntic Lake. These are recommended for spring and early summer.

Wild River

The Wild River drains the Carter and the Baldface-Royce ranges in the White Mountains, flowing northeast to Hastings. There, it is joined by Evans Brook from Evans Notch and then flows north into the Androscoggin River at Gilead. Portions of the Wild River watershed received federal wilderness status in 2006.

WILD RIVER CAMPGROUND ➤ GILEAD   8.0 MI

Description:	Class II, III, IV
Navigable:	High water: mid-March to mid-April
Scenery:	Forested
Maps:	Bethel, DL 10

Take US 2 to Gilead, and then follow ME 113 for 2.75 miles to Hastings. If the snow has melted, take the gravel road that turns off to the right at Hastings; the road follows the river to Wild River Campground, which is about 5.0 miles from the start of the gravel road. To avoid a longer carry (100 yards) from the campground to the Wild, you can put in at Blue Brook, just below the campground. It flows into the Wild after a short distance. If the road is not open to the campground, you can use many alternative put-ins; in most places, the river is just a short carry through the woods. Always remember to ask for and obtain permission before crossing property lines. For information on road conditions, call the Androscoggin Ranger Station (603-466-2713).

The run is continuous with many rocks, waves, and holes. The heaviest water on the trip—Class IV—is 2.0 miles from the take-out, where the river turns away from the road (just below a large gravel turnout). It is best to scout this section on the way to the put-in. The last mile above the US 2 bridge is an easier, Class II stretch. A few inches more or less water changes the run to dangerously heavy or bony.

Sunday River

The Sunday River rises in the northern Mahoosuc Range and flows southeast into the Androscoggin River at North Bethel. It enjoys a beautiful setting in a small, peaceful valley where the Mahoosucs rise impressively in the background. The waters are perfectly clear.

ABOVE THE POOL ➤ ANDROSCOGGIN RIVER   9.25 MI

Description:	Quickwater, flatwater, Class I, II, III
Navigable:	High water: late April to early May
Scenery:	Forested, rural
Maps:	Gilead, Bethel, DL 10

Take Sunday River Road toward Ketchum from North Bethel. Shortly before you come to the bridge over Sunday River, a woods road leads to the river and a good put-in spot. The put-in here avoids the unrunnable double-ledge drop that is about 100 yards below the bridge. High water is needed, so the best time is usually around the end of April. This period often coincides with mud season, which can make the access road a Class IV experience.

The rapids are Class II for the first 1.25 miles; then Class III rapids start. There, the river splits into three branches; stop and scout. Most of the water is in the center and left; the run in the center is more difficult than the left. A small, river-wide hydraulic is formed where the branches come together.

Below the pool you come to an easy Class III rapid; then the rapids are mostly Class II for the rest of the way to the covered bridge, with a few slightly harder. Watch carefully for downed trees.

You find a new gauge on the downstream, river-right side of the concrete bridge next to the covered bridge.

Below the covered bridge is another 1.0 mile of easy rapids, and then the current gradually slows to the Androscoggin. The easiest take-out is from a side road on the right, upstream of the US 2 bridge (9.25 miles).

Bear River

The Bear River drains the south side of Grafton Notch. Most of this section is easy rapids, but you also find three widely separated Class III ledges.

NORTH NEWRY ➤ NEWRY   6.75 MI

Description:	Quickwater, Class I, II, III
Navigable:	High water: April
Scenery:	Forested, rural
Maps:	Old Speck Mountain 15, Bethel, DL 18 and 10

Put in at the Devil's Horseshoe, which is 0.25 mile north of the tiny settlement of North Newry on ME 26. The Horseshoe is a geologic feature that so much resembles a breached dam that you might question whether its origin was natural. Kayakers might be tempted to run the heavy 4-foot drop through the break.

Busy Class II water starts immediately and lasts for about 0.75 mile, to the point where Branch Brook comes in from under ME 26 on the left. Here you find a 3-foot sloping ledge with a tiny bit of a slot in it. The setup for the slot is a fast S-turn, which is Class III when the water is high.

Fast current and scattered rocks continue for 0.25 mile to a sudden, but straightforward, drop over a 2-foot ledge. The river then runs fast and fairly unobstructed for another 1.0 mile to a 2- to 3-foot ledge, which produces a strong roller and some haystacks.

The remaining 4.0 miles to US 2 are mostly fast current with occasional rocks or tight corners, none of which rates more than Class II at average mid-April flows. The Androscoggin River is 100 yards downstream of the US 2 bridge.

Ellis River

The Ellis River rises in Ellis Pond and flows westward through the hills into the Andover interval, where it meets the West Branch of the Ellis River. Above South Andover, it is too shallow to run in low water. Unlike the other rivers in this region, it is a stillwater stream that offers an easy trip in enjoyable surroundings.

ANDOVER ➤ RUMFORD POINT   17.0 MI

Description:	Flatwater, quickwater
Navigable:	Medium water
Scenery:	Rural
Maps:	Old Speck Mountain 15, Ellis Pond, East Andover, DL 18

You can put in at the crossing of ME 5 over the West Branch of the Ellis River just below the turn to South Arm. It is a small meadow brook here, winding through the intervale for 2.0 miles to the junction with the main river. It then becomes larger but continues its winding course another 2.5 miles to the bridge at South Andover. For the next 8.5 miles, the river twists through the flat valley bottoms to the bridge at the North Rumford School. The river continues, but with a somewhat less tortuous course, for 4.0 miles to the US 2 bridge, only 200 yards above the junction with the Androscoggin River.

Swift River

The Swift River rises in one of the unincorporated townships south of Rangeley and flows south through Byron, Roxbury, and Mexico to the Androscoggin River at Rumford. Its uppermost part is too steep to paddle. The river is perhaps best known as a popular place to pan for gold, although more aluminum than gold is now to be found on some rocks. It is also an excellent whitewater run, best for seasoned paddlers. The river rises and falls quickly, making it difficult to determine the best time for paddling. When low, it is impassable, and when high, it is dangerous in spots. At medium water, it can be run from above Houghton down to Byron, all delightful Class II rapids, but you must take out above Byron to avoid being swept over the falls at Coos Canyon.

Description:	Quickwater, Class I, II, III
Navigable:	Medium water: April
Scenery:	Forested, towns
Maps:	Ellis Pond 15, Roxbury 15, Rumford 15, DL 18 and 19
Portages:	(6.5 mi L Swift River Falls 100 yd)
	10.0 mi R dam and ledge 0.5 mi

Put in just below the gorge at Coos Canyon. You can reach the best put-in by turning right off ME 17 onto Tumbledown Mountain Road. After crossing the bridge over the gorge, take the next right, which is just after the bridge, and follow that for 100 yards to the Swift.

You encounter some sharp turns and drops in the first 1.0 mile or so below the gorge. Many of these turns and ledge drops offer good playing and surfing spots. The next 3.0 miles to Roxbury are Class I and II and quick water. Below Roxbury 1.0 mile (where Walker Brook enters on the left) is a Class III rapid. Here, the point at which the river begins to steepen and become more difficult, is the most interesting and challenging part of the trip. After the Walker Brook rapid, the river turns to the right and then back to the left as it passes through a steep-walled gorge. The rapids preceding the gorge can be difficult at any water level, with large waves and rocks protecting the mouth of the gorge. The gorge itself is a Class III ride with a wave train running through the center. Be alert and possibly scout after passing Walker Brook.

Below the gorge, several Class III drops occur as the river turns sharply and passes over a series of ledges. Below the gorge 1.0 mile is Swift River Falls. You can find a take-out or a portage on the left. These falls cannot be run.

After Swift River Falls, you travel quick water and Class I rapids to Hale, where there is a Class II–III ledge just above the bridge and a heavy Class III chute underneath it. Next, an impassable pitch and a dam require a long portage on the right. About 1.0 mile of Class II water brings you to Tubbs, and an S-turn drop that is harder than it looks (Class III at high water). The rapids diminish and disappear in the 2.0 miles to Mexico and the US 2 bridge 100 yards above the junction with the Androscoggin.

Webb River

The Webb River rises in Lake Webb in Weld and flows south through Carthage to form the boundary between Mexico and Dixfield, finally emptying into the Androscoggin River at Dixfield. The upper part between Lake Webb and Carthage offers a good spring run for Class III paddlers. The section below Carthage is mostly smooth water and is usable in all but a dry season.

LAKE WEBB ➤ CARTHAGE   4.5 MI

Description:	Class II, III
Navigable:	High water: late March to early April
Scenery:	Forested, rural, towns
Maps:	Weld, Dixfield, DL 19

If you are approaching Lake Webb from the south on ME 142, leave a shuttle vehicle at the take-out (a widening of the road's shoulder just more than 0.5 mile past the point where the Webb is first crossed by a small bridge on ME 142). From the take-out, drive north on ME 142 for approximately 4.5 miles to the second ME 142 bridge that crosses the Webb. Check the gauge on the downstream, center abutment of the bridge. A reading of 2 is considered minimal level; anything above 2 offers a good Class II–III run. The put-in, located 0.75 mile above this bridge, is not much more than a widening of the shoulder on the left side of the road if you are going north. The put-in is down a steep bank, and the river is narrow.

The rapids begin immediately and continue for most of the 4.75-mile run. The rapids are generally short and rocky and are often followed by pools. You also encounter a few ledge drops.

Approximately 1.25 miles from the put-in the river narrows and is lined with alder; watch for downed trees and branches that reach into the river.

Next is a small bridge that marks the beginning of a short Class III drop, usually run on the right. The next short section of the run is Class II–III rapids, which offer good surfing opportunities. Below this section are several good Class III rapids full of rocks and waves, with the last rapid being just above a bridge over the Webb at Berry Mills. This rapid is marked by a high bank on the left where the river drops sharply, turns to the right, and then straightens for a short distance before turning back hard to the left.

Below Berry Mills, the river passes through a heavily wooded section where you can choose from multiple channels. The best route is usually on the right. Watch for downed trees in the river. Below the wooded section is one more solid Class III rapid, which leads to the take-out on the right.

CARTHAGE ➤ DIXFIELD   9.0 MI

Description:	Flatwater
Navigable:	Spring, summer, fall
Scenery:	Forested, rural
Maps:	Weld, Dixfield, DL 19
Portages:	4.0 mi falls short
	8.5 mi falls

Put in at the ME 142 bridge at Carthage. You encounter 2.0 miles of meadow paddling followed by 2.0 miles more through woodlands to the falls, where a short carry should be made. Below are 4.0 miles more of marshy woodlands leading to a bridge at the beginning of a 100-yard-long rapid near the northern edge of Dixfield. In the next 1.0 mile, toward the Androscoggin River, is an impassable waterfall just before the point where the US 2 bridge is visible.

Sevenmile Stream

Sevenmile Stream rises in Carthage and flows east and then south to the Androscoggin River in Jay. Its upper stretches are too steep to run, but below East Dixfield it has a few miles of good, navigable sections. It is a relatively small stream and should be paddled early in the season when the snows are still melting on Saddleback Mountain. This is lovely, mountainous country.

EAST DIXFIELD ➤ ANDROSCOGGIN RIVER   8.0 MI

Description:	Quickwater, flatwater
Navigable:	Spring: early April
Scenery:	Rural
Maps:	East Dixfield, Wilton, DL 19

Put in at East Dixfield from a side road off ME 17. The first 2.5 miles are all rapids but not difficult. The going is almost all through open meadowland. By the time Birchland Cemetery is reached, though, the river has become much quieter, and from there to the Androscoggin River the going is all smooth water with a fair current. Take out at the ME 140 bridge, less than 100 yards above the Androscoggin River.

Dead River

The Dead River is the outlet from Androscoggin Lake to the Androscoggin River. It should not be confused with the whitewater run on the Dead River that flows into the Kennebec River at The Forks. This Dead River is a flatwater paddle and can be done at any season.

ANDROSCOGGIN LAKE ➤ ANDROSCOGGIN RIVER   7.0 MI

Description:	Flatwater (motorboats)
Navigable:	Spring, summer, fall
Scenery:	Forested
Maps:	Wayne, Turner Center, DL 12
Portage:	5.5 mi dam

The Dead River starts on the northern side of Androscroggin Lake, near the tip of the peninsula that extends almost 2.0 miles into the lake. It is nearly 2.0 miles down the river to the village of Dead River and the highway bridge. The river then winds and twists for another 3.0 miles to the next bridge, below which are 2.0 more river miles to the Androscoggin River, with an easy lift around a low dam. You can take out at a farm on the left bank just below the mouth or go on down the Androscoggin 3.0 miles to the ME 219 bridge. Remember to ask for and obtain permission before crossing property lines.

FLYING POND   2.5 MI

From the head of Flying Pond in Vienna you can paddle 18.0 miles of lakes and connecting rivers to the Dead River and another 7.0 miles of easy going down the Dead River to the Androscoggin (25.0 miles in all). All the lakes and rivers are flatwater paddling that can be done at any season.

You can put in at Vienna; from there, it is 1.0 mile to the cove on the east, where the outlet is located. A long arm of the lake is to the south of this, however. The outlet runs through a series of ponds, the last of which is 1.0 mile long and behind the dam at Mount Vernon. The dam must be carried into Minnehonk Lake.

MINNEHONK LAKE   1.25 MI

From Mount Vernon at the northern end of the lake it is only a short paddle to Hopkins Stream at the southern end.

HOPKINS STREAM   3.0 MI

Follow 200 yards of brook to Horseshoe Pond, the outlet of which takes off just to the right of the inlet. Then it is 3.0 miles down an easy stream of smooth water to the dam at West Mount Vernon, where a short carry brings you into Crotched Pond.

ALTERNATIVE START AT PARKER POND   3.75 MI

You can put in at the northern end of Parker Pond where the stream from Whittier Pond crosses under the road at the shore in Vienna. Only the northern end of the pond is in Vienna; the rest is in Fayette, although most of the shores are in Chesterfield and Mount Vernon. The outlet is at the southeastern corner where a short river takes off. After 0.5 mile, you come upon a dam. Traveling 100 yards more brings you to the millpond behind the dam at West Mount Vernon, 0.5 mile farther on. You can also reach this point from Flying Pond in Vienna and Minnehonk Lake in Mount Vernon by coming down Hopkins stream from the latter. Below this is Crotched Pond.

CROTCHED POND   3.75 MI

Crotched pond is sometimes called Echo Lake. Although the outlet is at Fayette on the western bay (where you find a small dam), you also come upon an equally long eastern bay, which also provides a pleasant outing.

LOVEJOY POND   2.5 MI

It is only 2.0 miles from Fayette to the outlet at North Wayne, but you also find a northeastern arm that invites exploration. About 0.25 mile down the outlet river, at North Wayne, you come to a dam that must be carried.

PICKEREL POND AND POCASSET LAKE   3.0 MI

Just below the dam at North Wayne, Pickerel Pond begins. It is only 1.0 mile from the inlet at the northeastern end to the outlet at the northwestern end, but a large bay to the south offers access to marshes. Pocasset Lake is 2.0 miles long and wider than some of the upper lakes. The outlet river takes off at Wayne, west of the peninsula that juts into the lake from the south. Here, you come across two dams a short distance apart.

ANDROSCOGGIN LAKE   2.5 MI

This is the largest lake in this chain. Although it is only 2.0 miles from the inlet to the outlet, you find many miles of fine flatwater paddling in the large southern and western bays.

Nezinscot River

The Nezinscot River rises in the high hills of Sumner, its East Branch forming the boundary between Sumner and Hartford. The two branches meet just below Buckfield, and the main river flows east to the Androscoggin River at Turner. The main river below Buckfield can be paddled in any but dry seasons. The river runs through pleasant valleys with open meadows and woodlands.

BUCKFIELD ➤ TURNER   8.0 MI

Description:	Flatwater, quickwater
Navigable:	Spring
Scenery:	Forested, rural
Maps:	Worthley Pond, West Sumner-Buckfield, Poland 15, Turner Center, DL 11
Portage:	8.0 mi dam at Turner

Put in at the ME 117 bridge south and east of Buckfield. The next 8.0 miles to the dam at Turner are flat river through open meadows and woodlands, with the river making several big loops a few miles above Turner.

TURNER ➤ ANDROSCOGGIN RIVER   7.5 MI

Description:	Quickwater, Class I, II
Navigable:	Spring
Scenery:	Forested, rural
Maps:	Worthley Pond, West Sumner-Buckfield, Poland 15, Turner Center, DL 11
Portages:	0 mi dam at Turner
	(7.5 mi dam at Keens Mills)

For the whitewater section, put in on river right below the dam at Turner. You encounter 0.25 mile of Class II rapids over and around low ledges. Quick water and Class I rips for 3.0 miles bring you to the first of two ME 117 bridges at Turner Center; just below this bridge is a strong Class II rapid. The second bridge is 1.0 mile below. It is then 3.0 miles more to the dam at Keens Mills, where most paddlers take out rather than go the additional 0.25 mile to the Androscoggin River.

Nezinscot River (West Branch)

The West Branch of the Nezinscot flows from West Sumner to the main river at Buckfield. The first 1.0 mile of river below the ME 219 bridge is heavily obstructed by alders and is not recommended.

Description:	Flatwater, quickwater, Class I, II
Navigable:	High water: April
Scenery:	Forested, rural
Maps:	West Summer, Buckfield, DL 11
Portage:	9.75 mi dam in Buckfield

Some of the rapids can be scouted from the bridge on the Darnit Road. The put-in is on the River Road. From Route 219 in West Sumner, at the ball field, turn left at the T, take the next left onto the River Road, which is dirt and might be passable only with four-wheel drive vehicles in the spring when the river is usually run. (This road follows the river to North Buckfield, but is too rough for most vehicles.) You come to a bridge less than 1.0 mile in with parking on both sides. Boats can be launched on the far side of the bridge.

In a short distance, the rapids begin as Class I with stretches of quick water between. You come upon a drop of 1.5 feet, which is run easily. All of the drops are runnable, with no spot more difficult than Class II. **Caution!** You might encounter blowdowns and strainers. A few small islands can be run on either side. The stream banks are picturesque, and the woods are mostly hardwood and open.

You come upon a short stretch of flat water. Then, as you approach North Buckfield, the gradient becomes steeper, and more effort and quickness are required to maneuver around the rocks. The stream is not brisk, and flow rates around 100 to 150 cfs provide the best running. Paddlers generally take out on the right at the North Buckfield bridge, on the Paris Hill Road, but parking is limited.

A few hundred feet of rapids remain; then the river flattens, flowing through meadows and woods. Approaching Buckfield, the stream becomes quite steep with numerous rocks. The dam in Buckfield spills water, and the pool above it is neither long nor still.

It is awkward to reach the river below the dam. After a short rapid, it runs into a meadow, meandering until it joins the East Branch to form the Nezinscot about 1.0 mile below Buckfield.

Nezinscot River (East Branch)

The East Branch is a shorter run and can be scouted from the bridge on Route 140. You can find a gauge under the bridge on ME 219 in East Sumner; 1 is low, but okay. The parking is a bit south of the bridge on the right. The put-in is down a steep bank to a tributary stream/eddy pool. Watch for blowdowns or strainers. The take-out is at the Jordan Road bridge on river left.

Little Androscoggin

The Little Androscoggin is one of the larger tributaries of the Androscoggin. It rises in Bryant Pond southeast of Bethel, flows southeast to West Paris, and then south through Paris to Oxford. There, it turns easterly to flow through Mechanic Falls and join the Androscoggin at Auburn. The first 4.0 miles below Bryant Pond are too steep and rapid to run. From Tubbs School in Greenwood you can paddle it all the way to the mouth, although you come upon a number of dams to be carried in some of the towns. Because of the pond at its head, all but the lower part can be run fairly late in the spring; it is apt to be too low in the summer. The scenery away from the towns is attractive but not spectacular.

THIRD BRIDGE ➤ SOUTH PARIS   12.0 MI

Description:	Flatwater, quickwater, Class I, II
Navigable:	Medium water: April and May
Scenery:	Forested, towns
Maps:	Greenwood, West Paris, DL 10 and 11
Portages:	2.0 mi e dam carry across road
	4.5 mi e Snows Falls 100 yd
	6.0 mi R Bisco Falls 20 yd
	(12.0 mi dam)

Put in at the third ME 219 bridge upstream of West Paris at a stream junction. The Little Androscoggin is small, with easy rapids halfway to West Paris and then quick water to the dam located below a bridge on a side road in the center of town. Take out upstream of the bridge, and carry across the road.

For 0.5 mile the rapids below the bridge are more difficult than those above. Then the river is smooth until it reaches Snows Falls at a highway rest area on ME 26. Rapids and small ledges extend for 0.25 mile; then quick water leads to Bisco Falls and an 8-foot dam at a natural ledge. Access here is difficult. Rapids continue below the falls, gradually diminishing.

Below you come upon a long stretch of smooth water with meanders. It is 5.0 miles to South Paris. You can take out where the river comes close to the road 2.5 miles below the falls, the ME 26 bridge, or 1.0 mile farther down at the ME 117 bridge.

SOUTH PARIS ➤ MECHANIC FALLS   20.0 MI

Description:	Flatwater
Navigable:	Spring
Scenery:	Rural, forested
Maps:	Greenwood, West Paris, Norway 15, Poland 15, Lewiston 15, DL 11
Portage:	1.0 mi dam

This section is largely flat water through meadows and woodlands, with many meanders. Put in just below the ME 117 bridge in South Paris. The stream continues for 2.0 miles in a southwesterly direction to a point below Norway, where the stream from Penneseewassee Lake joins on the right. The river winds for the next 7.0 miles through meadows and woodlands to Oxford; there, it passes under the ME 121 bridge. The stream from Thompson Lake enters on the right, just below the bridge. The river twists and has numerous oxbows for the next 2.0 miles to the dam at Welchville. The following 8.0 miles to Mechanic Falls are mostly through meadows and woodlands, with many meanders and more oxbows. Take out at the ME 11 bridge just west of town. Several mills and a large dam exist in Mechanic Falls.

MECHANIC FALLS ➤ AUBURN   13.0 MI

Description:	Flatwater
Navigable:	Spring, summer, fall
Scenery:	Forested, rural, towns
Maps:	DL 11 and 5
Portages:	4.0 mi dam
	5.0 mi dam

This section is all flat water. Put in below the dam at Mechanic Falls. From here to the next dam at Hackett Mills are 4.0 miles of river winding through meadows, some of which are overgrown with bushes and trees. From Hackett Mills to the next dam at Minot is 1.0 mile of paddling. The next 7.0 miles to Auburn are also through meadows, but the river does not wind and twist quite as much as above. You can find a gauging station at the bridge 4.0 miles downstream. Take out several miles below this bridge on a side road on the right bank, before entering Auburn. Several dams and an impassable rapid are located before the Little Androscoggin enters the Androscoggin River in the middle of Auburn.

Sabattus River

The Sabattus River drains the Sabattus Pond through Lisbon to the Androscoggin River. It is only 9.0 miles long and flows through pastures and woods for the first 8.0 miles. The Sabattus can be run at any time; water levels vary only slightly. The water is light green in color because of algae. You find little current, and the water quality is good since the mills have ceased operation. The last 1.0 mile below the dam at Lisbon Center flows through a steep ravine with a technical Class IV rapid that contains an undercut ledge. This last mile is not recommended.

SABATTUS ➤ LISBON CENTER   8.0 MI

Description:	Flatwater, quickwater below dams
Navigable:	Medium water
Scenery:	Rural, towns
Maps:	USGS Lewiston 15, DL 12 and 6
Portages:	3.5 mi L dam and ledge 50 yd
	(6.5 mi dam)
	(6.75 mi dam)
	(7.75 mi dam)

Sabattus has three dams, so you should put in at the ME 126 bridge that crosses the river below these dams. The river is a quiet, wandering stream that passes under a bridge in 1.0 mile and under the Maine Turnpike 1.0 mile farther. Below are 1.5 miles of large meanders that lead to the dam at Robinson Corner. **Caution!** This dam has been breached, but it needs to be portaged because of debris and snags in the river just below the old dam. The dam is marked by a low highway bridge; take out on the left before the bridge for the shorter portage. From here, it is 3.0 miles to the first dam in Lisbon, where most people take out. You come upon another dam 0.25 mile below the first Lisbon dam. Easy paddling for 2.0 miles brings you from this dam to the one at Lisbon Center, which marks the end of navigation.

Chapter 3
Kennebec Watershed

Kennebec River

The Kennebec River is one of the largest rivers in Maine. It flows from Moosehead Lake south to the Atlantic below Bath, having received the waters of the Androscoggin River at Merrymeeting Bay just above Bath. Because the river has largely been harnessed for power, most of it is smooth paddling. The upper part above The Forks is rapid and should be run by experienced paddlers only.

This river was the route of Benedict Arnold's abortive invasion of Canada in the fall of 1775. Arnold ascended the river to Carrying Place Stream about 25.0 miles above the present site of Anson and then crossed through the three Carry Ponds to Bog Brook on the Dead River, a spot now flooded by Flagstaff Lake. From there, he followed the North Branch of that river into Quebec. His tiny force of 1,100 men suffered severely, and many men were lost on the journey.

Moosehead Lake

Brassua Lake

Roach River

Second Roach Pond

Wood Pond

Long Pond

Moose River

First Roach Pond

Third Roach Pond

Holeb Pond

Jackman

Attean Pond

Indian Pond

Moose River

Little Spencer Stream

Dead River

Greenville

KENNEBEC

WATERSHED

North Branch

Spencer Stream

Kennebec River

The Forks

Caratunk

Austin Stream

South Branch

Carrabassett

Carrabassett River

North Anson

Bingham

North Dexter

East Branch

Great Moose Lake

Corinna

Stetson

Stetson Stream

Sandy River

New Portland

Newport

South Branch

Phillips

Strong

Madison

Skowhegan

Pittsfield

Martin Stream

Temple Stream

Farmington

Sebasticook River

Burnham

Wilson Stream

Farmington Falls

Smithfield

East Pond

Waterville

Twentyfive Mile Stream

Belgrade Stream

Messalonskee Stream

Readfield

Kennebec River

Winthrop

Cobbosseecontee Lake

Cobbosseecontee Stream

Gardiner

Merrymeeting Bay

Scale in miles

0   10   20   30

N

MOOSEHEAD LAKE ➤ HARRIS STATION

Moosehead Lake drains by two outlets into Indian Pond; the two outlets provide different types of paddling. The West Outlet, which leaves the lake 2.0 miles below Rockwood (halfway up the lake on the west shore), carries relatively little flow of water and consists almost entirely of a series of ponds. About 9.0 miles long and followed most of the way by a dirt road, it is passable with some carries. The East Outlet, which leaves the lake at the village of Moosehead one-quarter of the way up the lake on the west shore, is only 3.5 miles long, with heavy and continuous rapids, and is suitable for experts only. Its flow, which is controlled for power generation, is fairly constant and usually very heavy.

WEST OUTLET ➤ INDIAN POND   10.0 MI

Description:	Lake, quickwater, Class I
Navigable:	Check Long Pond's water level
Scenery:	Forested
Maps:	Moosehead Lake 15, Brassua Lake 15, DL 40 and 41
Portage:	5.5 mi lift-over

When this route has water, it is an easy run through rather wild country. From ME 15, 1.75 miles down, just below the small dam, a pond leads to Class I rapids between Long Pond and the next pond. If these are runnable, all of the rapids should be. From here to Churchill Stream each pond is followed by rapids. A dirt road on the right is not obtrusive.

Just beyond a railroad bridge, you can see a very low bridge that you might have to carry on the left. Just beyond Churchill Stream is a slightly harder rapid, followed by 1.0 mile of quick water and another rapid to Round Pond. The outlet is straight across the pond.

After another smooth 1.0 mile, 0.5 mile of rapids ends in the backwater of Indian Pond. Keep to the left around islands for another mile to the main body of the lake. A boat ramp is 1.0 mile directly across the lake to the south. You might also be able to drive to the lake at a campsite 0.5 mile to the north.

EAST OUTLET ➤ INDIAN POND   3.5 MI

Description:	Quickwater, Class II, III, IV
Date checked:	1990
Navigable:	Spring, summer, fall: controlled release
Scenery:	Wild
Maps:	Moosehead Lake 15, Brassua Lake 15, DL 40 and 41

The rapids on this run are separated by sections of quick water. At low flow (below 2,000 cfs), they are mostly Class II–III; at higher flows, they are Class III–IV.

The dam at the lake is followed by a railroad bridge and the ME 15 bridge. In 0.5 mile is a narrow chute with a long ramp and cliff on the right. Scout from the left. The next 2.0 miles alternate fast current and rapids, which are usually spread out, but you do face a few large boulders here. A dirt road, which follows high on the left bank, descends here to river's edge. At 3.0 miles, the flowage from Indian Pond comes into view, but just before reaching the pond you come upon a heavy drop over a ledge not easily seen from above. Land on the right and scout. The far left has an insignificant drop; the right is all Class III–IV and can be run in more than one place. Below, you find a quiet pool and a picnic site on the right.

INDIAN POND   9.0 MI

Indian Pond is a natural body of water that was enlarged by the Harris Dam. This long, narrow lake offers good wildlife-viewing opportunities in the wetland area at the north end, and a scenic forested shoreline with minimal development for much of the remainder of its length. It is 9.0 miles from either approach to a boat ramp at the southern end. Campsites are near the northern end, one on an island at the West Outlet and one at the East Outlet, both of which are inclined to be insect-infested. Two other campsites are halfway down, one on each side.

Take out at the landing and picnic areas to the left of the 155-foot-high Harris Dam, which is maintained by the Central Maine Power (CMP) company.

HARRIS STATION ➤ CARRY BROOK   3.75 MI

Description:	Class III, IV, V
Navigable:	Spring, summer, fall: controlled release minimum 140 cfs, usually run at 4,800–5,000 cfs
Scenery:	Wild
Maps:	The Forks 15, DL 40

Below Harris Station, the Kennebec flows through a wild gorge that is among the most impressive in size and beauty in New England. Because of its dependable water flow and continuous difficulty, it is the finest decked-boat whitewater run in Maine. However, the canyon walls, rising sheer from the turbulent river, that give the gorge its incomparable attraction make it difficult to navigate. Scouting is difficult, and the most severe drops are not feasible to portage, line, or evade. This run is only for boaters of proven skill. Most people prefer to enjoy the gorge from a commercial raft trip.

The flow in the Kennebec is most inconvenient for paddling this section of river. When the generators at the Harris Station are shut down, you find practically no water in the river. Then it must be run from Carry Brook Eddy by poling or lining down the shallow rapids. When the generators are started up in midmorning on weekdays, the river rises several feet in a few minutes' time. With all three generators operating, the flow is 6,500 to 8,000 cfs. Spring is the best time for high water on weekends.

To get the water release schedule from Harris Station for the day or the following day, call Central Maine Power's flow-information line (800-557-3569). Also, a sign at the put-in states the amount of flow and approximate duration of the flow for that day.

All boaters must sign a release form at the dam office that says that CMP is not responsible for what might happen to them on the river. The dam attendant also knows the flow. A road leads down to the river to the left of the power station. You must arrive before 9:30 a.m. if you wish to drive to the base of the dam to unload equipment. All vehicles must park at the top of the hill near where the rafting companies have their assembly points. If you arrive after 9:30 a.m., you have to carry all your equipment from the parking lot to the dam.

For more information, see the *AMC Classic Northeastern Whitewater Guide* by Bruce Lessels.

The river is extremely narrow and, because of the cliffs, can be a long, bad swim. The size of the waves varies with the water level, but unpredictably. Wave size also is dependent on whether the river is rising or falling. The river has been run by canoes from 140 cfs to 7,200 cfs. At 140 cfs, it is a very technical Class II–III trip. Keep in mind that you always face the possibility that the river might rise if a need exists for more power. It takes only 5 minutes to increase the level from 140 cfs to 8,000 cfs. If you run the Kennebec at minimum water, take out at Carry Brook; the river is too shallow at this water level to continue to The Forks.

Do not attempt to run the Kennebec unless you have an effective self-rescue if you are a canoeist, or a bombproof roll if you are in a decked boat. The swim is long and very unpleasant. If you lose your boat, it is very difficult to hike out.

The rapids begin just as you move out of sight of the dam. The waves build to 3 to 4 feet, and the current gets pushy. The first rapid with a name is Taster, so named because it gives you a taste of what the gorge is going to be like. The next rapid of any consequence is called Rock Garden. At 2,400 cfs or below, it looks like a rock garden. At 3,800 cfs and up, it is a large curling wave on the right side of the river that is best hit on the left side of the wave for a drier run. You encounter eddies from the start of the run all the way down, ranging in size from large to small; all take some effort to catch.

Below Rock Garden comes Big Mama, which used to be known as Three Sisters until the flood of 1984 rearranged the rocks—and thus the rapid. At 3,800 cfs, it is a pulsating wave; above 3,800 cfs, it begins to get more constant and continues to build. At 6,500 cfs, it is easily an 8- to 10-foot wave. Big Mama is on the right-hand side of the river and can be run anywhere, although the sides provide better opportunities to catch eddies. In a decked boat, the best ride is to head straight for the wave. If you hit it just right, the ride is incredibly gentle and smooth.

Below Big Mama, Upper Alley Way starts. Stay to the center as you approach the next two rapids. Goodby Hole is nasty if you run it right, and Whitewasher is nasty, too, if you get into it on the left. Below Whitewasher, you come upon some large 6- to 8-foot waves.

A good eddy on the left is just below these waves. From here down, it is a nice ride through waves to Cathedral Eddy. Eddies are on both the left and right here, although the left eddy starts to resemble a whirlpool and is difficult to exit at levels above 4,800 cfs. This is a good surfing spot.

Next comes Z-turn, which is another play spot. This bend is followed by 100 yards of Class II. Then Magic Rapid, Class V, begins in another 0.25 mile; it can be seen ahead where the river disappears from sight except for some large exploding waves that appear over the horizon line. The Kennebec drops 25 feet in 250 yards here. A trail on the left makes the mandatory scouting easy. The trail leads to a spot just a few yards from Magic. It is also entertaining to watch the rafts punch Magic, because a fair number of them flip. Prominent features here are two holes. At the beginning, on the left near the shore, is Magic (Rock) Falls. Just to the right of center and 50 yards below is an even worse hole called Maytag. The rest of the drop consists of large waves and smaller holes. After you pass Maytag, you find that the right side has fewer holes to avoid.

You have two basic ways to run Magic: the Highway or the Magic Hole itself. The Highway consists of a run that starts just right of Magic and then cuts behind Magic to the left to avoid Maytag farther down. A large diagonal wave just after Magic and above Maytag can be used to push to the left. If you stay left, you have to contend with Hellhole and Bonecruncher, two holes that you should avoid at low water; to do this, cut back right below Maytag.

You can run Magic itself at levels greater than 4,800 cfs; below this level, it becomes very sticky. Above 4,800 cfs it is more forgiving but still can flip rafts. The foam pile on the left of Magic Falls is another place to avoid.

In another 1.0 mile, Dead Stream enters on the right, dropping over a series of pretty falls. Carry Brook Rapid starts immediately and ends at Carry Brook Eddy.

CARRY BROOK ➤ THE FORKS   8.5 MI

Description:	Quickwater, Class I, II, III, IV
Navigable:	Spring, summer, fall: controlled release
Scenery:	Wild
Maps:	The Forks 15, DL 40

Although most of this section is an easy float, Black Brook Rapids are 0.5 mile long and unfeasible to line or portage, so the boater putting in here should be prepared to deal with them directly. At open boat levels under 3,000 cfs, the rapids are Class III; above 3,000 cfs, they are Class IV.

You can reach the put-in at Carry Brook by taking a road that leaves the Indian Pond Road at an old shack 0.5 mile north of the Black Brook Bridge. You find a parking area at the end of the road, and CMP has now put in steps from the river up the cliff, which makes this former Class V take-out much easier.

Black Brook Rapids start just below the confluence of Carry Brook with the Kennebec. They are continuous for 0.5 mile, with one easier spot in the middle, and cliffs on each side that prevent lining or portaging. Halfway down, and 100 yards above where the river bends to the right, a wide, dangerous hole exists at levels below 5,000 cfs. It is in the center of the river, so stay to either side.

Around the bend to the left is Stand Up Rips, which is Class III at most levels. One good surfing hole called Jacuzzi is on river right about two-thirds of the way through the rapid. It is fairly sticky at 4,800 cfs or less, so have a throw rope handy to pull out boaters after they tire. For the next 6.5 miles to The Forks, the current is good and the rapids are nearly continuous but easier (Class I and II).

Take out at the ballpark on the right above the bridge or on the left at the state picnic area.

THE FORKS ➤ CARATUNK   9.0 MI

Description:	Flatwater, quickwater, Class I
Navigable:	Spring, summer, fall: controlled release
Scenery:	Forested
Maps:	The Forks 15, Bingham 15, DL 40 and 30

Below the confluence with the Dead, the Kennebec becomes more gentle, offering a pleasant, easy paddle, which, though not remote like the rivers above, is attractive and away from the road for most of the distance.

A pull-off just at the confluence on the left makes a good launch spot. The rapids are continuous, but easy. In 3.0 miles, you pass Gilroy Island, with a good channel on either side and Class II rapids below. You can take out at the Appalachian Trail crossing.

CARATUNK ➤ WYMAN DAM   12.0 MI

Description:	Flatwater, quickwater, Class I
Navigable:	Spring, summer, fall: controlled release
Scenery:	Forested, rural, towns
Maps:	The Forks 15, Bingham 15, DL 30

The current gradually diminishes somewhere around 5.0 miles to the backwater from Wyman Dam, an attractive lake with steep, wooded hills rising above it. A public boat landing near the head of the lake offers access. Carry the 140-foot-high Wyman Dam in Moscow on the western end, near the powerhouse.

WYMAN DAM ➤ SKOWHEGAN   30.0 MI

Description:	Flatwater, quickwater, Class I
Navigable:	Spring, summer, fall: controlled release
Scenery:	Forested
Maps:	Bingham 15, Anson 15, Norridgewock 15, Skowhegan 15, DL 30, 20, and 21
Portages:	5.0 mi L Solon Dam 200 yd
	18.0 mi R 2 dams in Madison 1.0 mi
	(30.0 mi 2 dams on either side of the island in Skowhegan; one carry 0.5 mi)

At this point the river becomes considerably more settled and the banks more open. Below the Wyman Dam 1.0 mile you pass Bingham on the left; in another 5.0 miles, you reach Caratunk Falls and Solon Dam. Portage 200 yards on the east bank. Then it is 8.0 miles to the mouth of the Carrabassett River at North Anson. In another

5.0 miles, mostly through open meadowlands, you reach the twin towns of Anson and Madison. Here you find two dams 0.5 mile apart; between them the river loops to the east. The portage is on the west bank. You encounter a rapid below the lower dam for a short distance and then a short rip 0.5 mile below. It is then 2.0 miles to the confluence with the Sandy River at some open fields on the right bank. The next 4.0 miles to Norridgewock offer no obstructions. Another 5.0 miles largely through open fields bring you to Skowhegan, where the river is dammed on both sides of the island. Here, the river divides into two channels around an island: the North Channel and the South Channel. The best take-out spot is about 200 yards above the North Channel Dam on the left. Then you can carry along Elm, Russell, and Water Streets to the Great Eddy below the gorge. This avoids the difficult scramble down into the gorge below the dams.

This gorge can be run only by experts. If conditions are right, experienced paddlers can take out on the island between the dams and put in below to run the gorge, 1.0 mile (Class III–IV), to the Great Eddy.

SKOWHEGAN ➤ WATERVILLE   20.0 MI

Description:	Flatwater, quickwater
Navigable:	Spring, summer, fall: controlled release
Scenery:	Rural, urban
Maps:	Skowhegan 15, Waterville 15, DL 21
Portages:	13.5 mi R dam at Shawmut
	19.0 mi R dam at Waterville
	(20.0 mi L Ticonic Falls)

This stretch has no obstructions, and the river runs through rolling country with open banks and a fair and pleasant landscape for 13.0 miles to the dam at Shawmut in the town of Fairfield; there, the carry is on the right bank. Below the dam is a bit of quick water followed by 3.0 miles of pleasant country at least as far as Fairfield (3.0 miles above Waterville, where urbanization starts). Two dams stretch across the river in Waterville. The first is best carried on the right, or Waterville side; the second, 1.0 mile down at Ticonic Falls, is more easily portaged on the left, or Winslow side.

WATERVILLE ➤ AUGUSTA   20.0 MI

Description:	Flatwater, quickwater
Navigable:	Spring, summer, fall: tidal
Scenery:	Rural
Maps:	Vassalboro 15, Augusta 15, DL 21, 13, and 12

You face no obstructions in this section of the river. Below the dam 1.0 mile the Sebasticook River enters on the left, and 1.5 miles farther down Messalonskee Stream enters on the right.

The removal of Edwards Dam, completed in the fall of 1999, has transformed this section from a uniform impoundment to a river full of variety. Although this section has several rips, the only part requiring some concentration is at Six Mile Falls. You can spot the "falls," a series of small drops, in advance by a wire with orange markers stretching across the river about 9.0 miles below Waterville. The "falls" can be run easily on either the far right or far left. The Sidney boat launch provides an alternative put-in about 10.0 miles below Waterville.

AUGUSTA ➤ BATH   30.5 MI

Description:	Tidal
Navigable:	Spring, summer, fall: controlled release
Scenery:	Forested, rural, towns
Maps:	DL 12 and 6

This section is freshwater tidal and passes some large towns, most of which have public launching ramps. High tide at Augusta is 3 hours 54 minutes later than in Portland; tidal range is 4 to 5 feet. It is 6.0 miles to the Gardiner boat ramp and another 11.0 miles to Richmond and the head of Swan Island.

From the ramp in Richmond it is a 9.0-mile circuit of Swan Island. At low tide, mud flats extend 0.5 mile south of the island.

From Richmond it is 8.5 miles through Merrymeeting Bay, a freshwater tidal ecosystem where 6 rivers meet, to the Chops into Goose Bay. At the Chops one-third of Maine (the Androscoggin and the Kennebec) drains through a gap less than 0.25 mile wide. Currents can be tricky at certain tides. The eastern side of Lines Island has less current and more scenic interest as well as intriguing water conditions. You find a public ramp on the western side at the northern end of Bath and a public float above the bridge.

Moose River

Moose River rises in Beattie and Lowell townships just east of the Maine/Canadian border (plus or minus 22.0 miles as the crow flies) west of Jackman, Maine. It runs east into and out of Holeb Pond. (Holeb Stream has a unique propensity: it runs into Holeb Pond when more rain is to the west on the upper Moose and runs out of Holeb Pond when the water is higher in Holeb than it is in the Moose.) It picks up water as it makes up and flows through Attean, Big Wood, Long Pond, and Brassua, flowing easterly toward Moosehead Lake. Moose River is the primary water source for Moosehead Lake and thus plays a major role as headwater source of the Kennebec River, which flows southerly to the Atlantic.

The Bow Trip, a favorite for groups, makes the Moose one of Maine's better rivers for canoe or kayak camping, especially if the group wishes to put in and take out at the same spot. The Bow Trip is 34.0 miles of lakes and river; it starts and finishes at the end of the access road to Attean Pond. (The Holdens, who operate Attean Lake Camps and maintain the state landing at the north end of Attean, request that Bow Trippers park on the left at the sign-designated space and offload and upload to the left at the beach site, thus leaving a cleared space to the Holdens' dock.)

The Bow Trip is popular because it can be canoed in 3 days. The fact that whitewater is at a minimum appeals to families and new paddlers. Wild game abounds, and you find little human presence on both the river and lakes. Popularity has its price, however. The river is heavily traveled in the summer and on long weekends in the spring and fall. Weekend traffic can best be circumvented by starting your trip on a Monday. The next best way to beat weekend numbers is to start your trip one day before or one day into the weekend. Good advice to any trip leader is to speak to any paddlers along the way to coordinate with them where it is best for each group to camp for the night. Campsites are too few for all groups to head for the same destination each night.

Many paddlers choose to preclude the 1.25-mile portage between Attean and Holeb, as well as much of the lake travel. The potential for encountering winds on the lake and a long portage has to be weighed against the inconvenience of shuttling cars between a new/different put-in site and the Attean take-out site. You can shuttle between Turner Brook Beach (at road's end on the north shore of Holeb Pond), or you can shuttle between a put-in at the old Moose River bridge site (next right off the Beaudry Road, past the RR crossing). If you put in at Turner Brook beach on Holeb Pond, you subtract 7.75 miles of lake paddle and 1.25 miles of portage—thus making your Moose River trip a total of 25.0 miles. If you choose to put in at the old Moose River bridge site, your Moose River trip is all river and 27.0 miles long.

The road to Attean Pond leaves US 201 just south of the junction of US 201 and ME 6/15. Turn left off US 201 and travel to the road's end. For those shuttling to either Holeb Pond or the old Moose River bridge site, turn left off US 201, 3.25 miles north of the bridge over the Moose River in Jackman. Follow the well-traveled dirt road 10.0 miles and, just after mud pond on the left, make a sharp left-hand turn onto the small, rough dirt road that ends at Turner Brook beach at Holeb Pond. If you wish to put in at the old Moose River bridge site, continue 5.0 miles past the 10.0-mile turnoff to Holeb Pond to a right-hand turn, which ends shortly at the old Moose River bridge site.

BOW TRIP   **34.0 MI**

Description:	Lakes, flatwater, Class I
Navigable:	Spring, summer, fall
Scenery:	Wild
Maps:	USGS 1:24,000—Attean, Holeb Pond, Catheart Mountain, DL 39. Contact the Bureau of Parks & Lands for its Holeb brochure/map (207-287-3821).
Portages:	4.25 mi from Attean Pond to Holeb Pond 1.25 mi 19.25 mi L, Holeb Falls
	30.25 mi L, Attean Rips; then R, Attean Falls

(Each of these rips can be run in high water. The first set, Attean Rips, can be taken with a setting pole at low water. Both rips and falls have been blasted and harbor sharp rocks.)

Campsites:	All campsites on the Moose River require fire permits from the Maine Forest Service. If the party is guided, the guide can acquire a blanket permit for all permit sites. If not guided, call the Maine Forest Service Old Town office at 207-827-1800 to get a permit number.
Campsites:	1.25 mi 1 site—N, Attean Pond
	4.25 mi 1 site—W end of Attean at beginning of portage
	6.0 mi 2 sites—E end of Holeb Pond at end of portage; 1 site—N at rocky point
	9.0 mi 2 sites—N, Holeb; sandy beach cove, due east of Turner beach put-in
	12.0 mi 1 site—Barrett Brook outlet on S shore
	14.0 mi 1 site—N shore just before 1st Camel Rips; 1 site—N shore at 1st Camel Rips
	18.5 mi 1 site—beginning of Holeb Falls portage; 3 sites—end of portage
	19.25 mi 2 log cabins—off the portage trail, one L and one at end L; both cabins are left open for Moose River; 1 site—S shore at the bottom of the last pitch; 2 sites—Mosquito Rips, just around the bend from the Holeb Falls portage put-in, 1 N, 1 S
	22.75 mi 1 site—Spencer Rips, N shore
	30.75 mi 3 sites—Attean Falls, 2 R above falls, 1 L below falls

After off-loading vehicles and packing boats, you leave the north shore of Attean and paddle west for 4.25 miles down the long arm of Attean Lake to the portage. At least three trails lead westerly from this point. The middle trail, just to the left of the campsite, is the correct one. If you do not cross railroad tracks within 1.0 mile, you are too far south.

You have a 3.25-mile paddle the length of Holeb Pond to the outlet, Holeb Stream (9.25 miles). In 1.0 mile, Holeb Stream meets the Moose River (10.25 miles). From Holeb Stream, it is 3.75 miles to a minor ledge drop at first Camel Rips (14.0 miles). Second Camel Rips is in a 90-degree left turn about 500 yards downriver. As you approach the

Holeb Falls portage, be on the lookout for a high, rocky ledge on the right and large boulders in the river. At this point, take the smaller left branch and immediately turn right. Follow this branch past two short drops with rock ledges on both banks. Just past the still water on your left, at a point 0.5 mile from the last left turn, take another left turn into a narrow streamlet. It is imperative that you take these two left-hand turns off the main river; at each turn the river gets markedly smaller. Follow this narrow stream to the end, off-loading on river left at the beginning of Holeb Falls portage trail.

The portage trail, about 0.5 mile, has seen many years of use and is rather rough. Boats can be partially unloaded here, hoisted over the hump, passed downstream on this left tributary about 100 yards farther to a campsite on the left, and portaged from there. Other campsites are at the pool at the foot of the portage trail. On the trail to the outhouse a private cabin is available to paddlers on a first come basis with a preference for organized educational or conservation groups.

The river meanders for 11.0 miles from Holeb Falls to Attean Falls (30.25 miles). In summer low water, you find almost no current. Mosquito Rips is a sharp drop, just around the bend from the put-in from Holeb Falls portage. **Caution!** At Mosquito Rips invisible rocks hide just below the surface in the backwash on river left; you can line the boats to the right if the water is too low. Be very cautious of slippery ledges. Although parts of the ledges might look dry, wet shoes or feet can lubricate the invisible, dried slime into a dangerously slippery surface. Spencer Rips, about 3.5 miles further on, can be run at high water and poled at lower pitches. Be careful. This drop, the site of a long-gone bridge, has been dynamited, leaving sharp, jagged rocks. Portage river right to just beyond the bridge abutment, or to the open campsite about 100 yards downstream.

Attean Rips begins 7.0 miles farther, just above Attean Falls (30.25 miles). Attean Falls is a misnomer—it is a quick drop laden with sharp rocks and preceded by Attean Rips. Each of these pitches has also been dynamited in the past to facilitate long-log passage down the Moose in the late 1800s and early 1900s. The resultant sharp and jagged rocks make each pitch difficult in low water. They both can be run in high water. Attean Rips can be poled at low to medium pitch. A portage to the left above Attean Rips bypasses both the rips and

Attean Falls. If you choose to run the rips, start in the middle, moving somewhat right and then into the pool on river right, just before the campsite at the beginning of the portage to the right around Attean Falls. Scout Attean Falls. Often a boat has been pinned on the rock at the foot of the falls, blocking the exits. A paddle of 3.5 miles from Attean Falls to and across Attean Pond brings one home to the starting point of the Bow Trip on the north shore of Attean.

ATTEAN LANDING ➤ LONG POND   19.0 MI

Description:	Lakes, quickwater
Navigable:	Medium water
Scenery:	Forested
Maps:	Attean, Jackman, Heald Pond,
	Churchill Stream 15, DL 39 and 40

The western shore of Wood Pond at Jackman is built up, but east of US 201 the river and lakes along it are mostly wild. Long Pond has an alder- and willow-lined shore that suggests a dam long since washed out. The shoreline of Brassua Lake typifies that of a flooded lake: dry-ki, a few exposed sand banks, and green trees with dead limbs that died when these trees were within a forest, not along a lake. Both lakes are, for the most part, undeveloped.

From the landing on Attean Pond you come upon 0.75 mile of flat water on the river and another 2.5 miles across Wood Pond to the outlet. On the short river segment between Attean and Wood Ponds, the remains of a steamboat and barge rot away on the left. At Wood Pond, you can find an excellent campsite on the left. Access at Jackman is from a public landing on Wood Pond or at the US 201 bridge.

Except for the riffle under the bridge, it is 6.5 miles of smooth and somewhat winding river to Long Pond (11.0 miles), an 8-mile paddle with 2 narrow guts between the 3 separate sections. You can reach the river at the outlet by a dirt road leading north off of ME 6/15 just west of the Long Pond-Sandwich town line. At the east end of the clearing by the railroad tracks, follow a well-worn path to the river.

LONG POND ➤ MOOSEHEAD LAKE   15.5 MI

Description:	Lakes, quickwater, Class I, II, III, IV
Navigable:	Spring, summer, fall
Scenery:	Forested
Maps:	Churchill Stream, Brassua Lake West,
	Brassua Lake East, DL 40
Portages:	2.5 mi L ledge/falls 200 yd
	12.5 mi R Brassua Dam 200 yd
Campsite:	5.0 mi L Brassua Lake (on point where lake
	opens)

Between Long Pond and Brassua Lake, the Moose River drops steadily through wooded hills. Here, you travel several miles of challenging rapids when the water is high. Because this is a large river, the rapids are passable in lower water when they are easier to negotiate and when the harder pitches can be lined.

Below Long Pond, the intermittent rapids of Class I and II extend for 2.5 miles to a bridge at the site of the former Long Pond Dam on a well-used logging road that comes in from ME 6/15. **Caution!** Under the bridge is a ledge, which should be scouted. Landing on the left to scout, line, or carry can be difficult because the current is fast. You can also take out here. A short distance below is a low waterfall that you can portage or line on the left.

Below these two ledges are nearly continuous rapids for 1.75 miles. At the start, they are Class III, but soon they moderate to Class II. A sharp left turn 0.5 mile from the bridge is followed by a short stretch of quick water. Soon you come upon more Class II rapids and one more, larger section of quick water. This is followed by more Class II and another Class III section, which starts just above a quick S-turn that begins to the right. Intermittent Class II rapids continue to slack water, which soon opens into Brassua Lake (5.0 miles).

It is 7.5 miles across Brassua Lake to the dam (12.5 miles), the road to which might be closed. Portage on the left. Below the dam are Class I rapids and quick water for 1.0 mile. The last 2.0 miles to Moosehead Lake (15.5 miles) are flat, highly developed, and mostly close to the highway.

Roach River

The headwaters of the Roach River consist of a complex of mountain ponds east of Moosehead Lake, of which it is the largest tributary. It combines a variety of lake and whitewater paddling with good views of mountains that range from 2,500 to 3,500 feet.

Access to Third Roach Pond is public, on the northeast arm reached from a private logging road. Always remember to ask for and obtain permission before crossing property lines.

THIRD ROACH POND ➤ KOKAD-JO   12.5 MI

Description:	Lakes, Class I, II
Navigable:	High water: mid-May to mid-June
Scenery:	Forested
Maps:	Jo-Mary Mountain 15, First Roach 15, DL 42 and 41
Portages:	0.75 mi R dam 50 ft
	5.75 mi L dam
	(12.5 mi dam 100 ft)

Roach River begins 0.75 mile from the road access to Third Roach Pond. It is marked by an old log crib at the western end of the pond. The washed-out dam is full of spikes.

Fallen trees are the major hazard, especially at the start; the river is narrow and fast. Second Roach Pond is 1.5 miles beyond an old bridge abutment.

You might need to line the dam at the outlet of Second Roach Pond (5.75 miles). The next 1.75 miles are continuous, fast, with easy riffles and some mountain views. From the northern inlet of First Roach Pond (7.5 miles), it is a 5.0-mile paddle down the lake to the outlet at Kokad-jo (12.5 miles).

Description:	Lake, Class II, III
Navigable:	High water: May ice must be out on Moosehead
	Annual draw-down in October
Scenery:	Wild
Maps:	First Roach Pond 15, Moosehead Lake 15, DL 41
Campsites:	6.5 mi R high bluff MFS
	6.5 mi L small island MFS

The most interesting aspect of the Roach, other than the scenery and the continuous Class II rapids, is the shuttle. From Kokad-jo, proceed 2.5 miles toward Greenville. Take a right on a logging road and follow it 4.5 miles to a junction. Take a right and go 1.0 mile to Jewett Cove on Moosehead Lake. This is an MFS campsite.

The rapids are intermittent for 1.0 mile until Lazy Tom Stream enters on the right. From this point, the rapids are continuous. After 2.5 miles of fairly continuous Class II, you come upon 0.25 mile of quick water. Slightly harder Class II–III rapids for 1.0 mile, featuring several easy ledge drops, give way to Class II to the lake. The total drop is 200 feet. You don't have to deal with any dangerous spots here, but you also find no sections of flat water until you reach the lake. You find your car parked near the first deep cove on the left, after a 1.0 mile of pleasant lake paddling.

Dead River

The not-so-Dead River flows from Flagstaff Lake to the upper Kennebec River. It is one of New England's most outstanding whitewater rivers, and you can run it from early spring to late autumn. You paddle through nearly continuous rapids for hour after hour along a 15.0-mile section of wild river where the gradient averages 20 feet per mile.

The river takes its name from the flatwater section that now lies beneath Flagstaff Lake. The main discharge on the Dead is controlled by the dam at Flagstaff Lake. Seven high-water (3,500 to 7,000 cfs) releases are scheduled each summer, and eleven low-water (1,500 cfs) releases are scheduled. Call Central Maine Power's toll-free river-information line (800-557-3569) and follow the touch-tone menu. For early May releases, the actual river flow tends to be higher than those announced because of additional flow from the Dead River's tributary streams. For more information on the Dead, see the *AMC Classic Northeastern Whitewater Guide* by Bruce Lessels.

You can reach the head of the rapids at the mouth of Spencer Stream via a confusing road network from US 201 near West Forks. For transportation to the Spencer Stream put-in, call Webb's Store (207-663-2214).

Above Grand Falls the Dead River flows slowly through meadows, where you can enjoy good views looking back at the Bigelow Range. Below Grand Falls, a spectacular drop of about 30 feet, the narrow river valley is very attractive, although you spend most of your time looking at the river itself. At a medium water level (1,000 cfs), it takes 2.5 to 3 hours to reach Spencer Stream from Big Eddy, and 3 to 4 to run the rapids to The Forks.

FLAGSTAFF LAKE   18.0 MI

Flagstaff Lake is formed by a dam that floods the "dead" part of Dead River and backs up the North and South branches. The lake is 18.0 miles long. The shores are wild, and the views of the jagged peaks of the Bigelow Mountains 0.5 mile above are spectacular.

The first half has enough points and islands to break the wind, but a strong wind would be troublesome for paddlers on the wide eastern half. Take the northern channel around the high island 2.0 miles east of Jim Eaton Hill.

Over the years, stumps of the old forest have pulled free of the bottom and become stranded in coves and shallows. The end of the southern channel around the island is blocked by thick rafts of stumps from shore to shore.

At Flagstaff Dam, you should land as close to the left as possible. Either drag across the stumps and dam or use a short trail around them. Carry 0.75 mile, around unrunnable Long Falls. Much of the carry is on a good road accessible by a paved road from New Portland.

BIG EDDY ➤ SPENCER STREAM   7.75 MI

Description:	Flatwater, Class I, II
Navigable:	Spring, summer, fall: controlled release
Scenery:	Wild
Maps:	Little Bigelow Mountain 15, DL 29
Portage:	7.0 mi L Grand Falls 0.5 mi
Campsites:	0.5 mi R Big Eddy MFS car
	7.75 mi L Spencer Stream permit car

On the western side of the river at the foot of Long Falls, you find an observation point below the road to Spring Lake. You can lower a boat to the river here for 0.5 mile of easy Class II rapids that extend under the bridge to Big Eddy Campsite.

Below Big Eddy (0.5 mile) flat water extends for 6.5 miles to Dead River Dam. The portage around Grand Falls begins on the left bank above the washed-out dam, following a dirt road, and turning right onto another in about 0.25 mile. The portage ends at a pool, below and out of sight of the falls.

Below the end of the portage, the current is strong as it passes an island at the mouth of Spencer Stream (7.75 miles).

SPENCER STREAM ➤ THE FORKS   16.0 MI

Description:	Class II, III
Navigable:	Spring, summer, fall: controlled release
	Medium water (1,000–1,300 cfs)
Scenery:	Wild
Maps:	Pierce Pond 15, The Forks 15, DL 29, 30, 39,
	and 40

This is the classic Dead River run. The river is generally wide and boulder strewn, offering many choices of routes. The first 7.0 miles of the run are a good warm-up. After Enchanted Stream enters on the left just above Elephant Rock Rapid, the rapids are generally steeper and require solid Class III skills. Normally, the water depth is 2 to 3 feet.

Shortly below the put-in at Spencer Stream, the fun begins at Spencer Rips (0.25 mile), the first set of rapids. Stay in the middle of the waves going down the drop and eddy out on the left. You come upon a nice pool here to pick up the pieces, should that be necessary. Unless you go with someone who is familiar with the river, it seems to be an indistinguishable succession of Class II and III rapids, broken occasionally by pools and easier drops.

At 2.0 miles, a long rapid begins and culminates in the section known as the Minefield, which ends at a big, deep pool with an old log chute high on the right (2.75 miles). Hayden's Landing, marked by some log cribwork, is on the right (3.0 miles). Just below is Hayden's Landing Rapid, also known as Humpty-Dumpty. This is a short, intense rapid. The Basin, 3.5 miles from the start, is a long section of quick water.

At 4.5 miles, you can see the gravel pit put-in on the left if you look carefully. Unless you know it is there, it is difficult to spot. This put-in is an alternative to going all the way to Spencer Stream. It is just above the confluence of Stony Brook Stream and the Dead.

Next you come to a section of quick water that lasts about 0.75 mile, and then the rapids begin again. Enchanted Stream (7.0 miles) enters on the left and marks the beginning of Elephant Rock Rapid. Elephant Rock is a large rock on the right at the bottom of the rapid. It is a good play spot; the eddy below the rock is often full of boaters waiting for their chance to play in the holes on either side of the rock.

The rapids are fairly continuous from Elephant Rock to a short section of quick water (8.5 miles), when the river makes a sweeping bend to the left. Shortly below this, Mile Long Rapid begins. This rapid offers many choices, but the best routes are on the left, especially near the bottom, because of a wide pile of boulders on the right.

As the river finishes another sweep to the left at a short rapid, you can look up on the left and see Spruce Ledge. Upper Spruce Ledge Rapid (10.5 miles) is an excellent rapid with a good pool below. Near the bottom, on the left side, is a hole that can keep boats and boaters for a period of time. Shortly, Lower Spruce Ledge Rapid begins and carries the boaters around a bend to the left.

At 11.5 miles, Little Poplar Hill Falls begins. This rapid is tough in low water because it is very rocky. In higher water, waves and holes form, giving the river a very turbulent look. At the bottom of the rapid on the left is a hole formed by a basket of rocks. Stay away from this spot. A big pool stands at the bottom to make rescues, if necessary, but be aware that Poplar Hill Falls (12.0 miles) begins immediately below the pool. These rapids can be scouted on the right. The most difficult section is at the top. You can find a variety of routes through the rocks and holes. The left side is the most difficult. You encounter three or four large waves and drops in the first third of the rapid that happen fast, one after the other. You don't have time to think, only time to react. The middle is easier and still fun; the right is rocky, but the current is slower. Old bridge abutments on both shores mark the end of the difficult rapids. Class I rapids continue until the Dead reaches The Forks.

A public parking lot is on the left, north of The Forks. This takeout has been provided to relieve some of the traffic congestion in The Forks.

SPENCER STREAM ➤ THE FORKS   16.0 MI

Description:	Class III, IV, V
Navigable:	Spring: high-water releases
	High water: 3,500–5,500 cfs
Scenery:	Wild
Maps:	Pierce Pond 15, The Forks 15, DL 29, 30, and 40

At high-water levels, the Dead changes its character from a boulder-strewn Class II–III run to a strong Class IV, with a few rapids approaching Class V. The river is characterized by waves of up to 6 feet and innumerable holes. The water is brown, and at times it can be difficult to differentiate waves from holes.

Because the water is up to the alders, you might have some problems eddying out. The current is strong and quick, and when you do catch an eddy, it can be difficult to stay in it. Therefore, a swim at this high level can be very long and dangerous. **Caution!** Canoeists should have good self-rescue skills, and decked boaters should have a strong roll; a strong party of boaters is a must. The river at high water is for properly equipped experts only. If you doubt your abilities, do not do the run, or leave a car at the gravel pit as a backup. If you have had any trouble from Spencer Stream down to the gravel pit, take out. The run from Elephant Rock to Poplar Hill Falls is much heavier than the first 4.5 miles to the pit.

Another aspect of high-water days on the Dead River is that the releases have been set up for the rafting industry. You end up sharing the river with a very large number of rafts. The put-in gets crowded, so be prepared to wait your turn to get on the river. You also might wait and put in after the rafts have launched. Remember, too, that rafts move more slowly than canoes and kayaks, that they hamper visibility, and that they often go into large holes that individual boaters would choose to avoid.

You can notice right away that Spencer Rips looks very different. At this level, you can run it on the left, but the best ride is still on the right-hand side, right down the wave train. Catch the eddy on the left, and you can go back up and play in the wave train.

At 1.25 miles, a good surfing spot can be found on the right side of the river. Decked boaters can surf to their hearts' content on a good series of standing waves. The best play spots at high water tend to be above Elephant Rock; just remember to save some energy for the end of the run.

A fairly long rapid starts 0.75 mile below the surfing spot. The rapid culminates in a section called the Minefield, just above a big pool. You need to avoid two dangerous holes here. One is left of center near where the river turns to the left and the big pool becomes visible for the first time; the other is on the right, near the right banks just above the pool.

Hayden's Landing (3.25 miles), the next major rapid, contains several large holes than can recirculate boats and boaters. The one on the left at the bottom is particularly notorious. The route here is down the center through the wave trains.

The gravel pit put-in/take-out is 4.5 miles from the Spencer Stream put-in. If you are planning to take out here, it is a good idea to tie a flag to the trees to mark the spot. On high-water days, this take-out has a festive air from the many brightly colored markers that blow in the wind.

Elephant Rock is the next big rapid. At high water, you find a large hole at the top, just a bit right of center. Holes pepper the right side all the way down. The best run is to enter a little left of center and then move over to catch the wave train at the bottom just left of Elephant Rock. Do not catch the eddy below Elephant Rock. At this level, a large hole is behind the rock, and a very large whirlpool that can suck you back up into the hole.

Mile Long Rapid is full of holes and big waves. If you are in a canoe, you want to run this dry, if possible. The rapid is very long and can be tiring, but you have several places to eddy out behind rocks in the center of the river. When you can see the pool below the rapid, the best route to get there is not obvious because the entire end of the rapid is a huge wall of waves. A run left of center (about halfway between left and center) takes you through safely. Catch the eddy on the left and take a breather.

Upper Spruce Ledge has a nice series of waves, and the hole that is bad at lower water becomes a big wave here. Little Poplar is turbulent, with many large waves and several holes to avoid. A run just a bit right of center is a conservative route. Remember that a swim here could mean a swim through Big Poplar because the pool at the bottom of Little Poplar has a quick current and does not leave much time for a rescue.

Poplar Hill Falls is a Class IV–V rapid, depending upon the water level and where you run it. The left side is the most difficult because of its 6-foot waves and a number of very large holes. The middle is less arduous but is still quite thrilling. If you run the middle, be aware that it is the easier run for the first third of the rapid; then it becomes quite difficult. At this point, it is best to move toward the left. The far right-hand side also can be run at this level because most of the rocks are covered. Do not relax until you have reached the old bridge abutments, because even the last section of Poplar has holes, cross-currents, and barely submerged rocks waiting to catch boaters who let their guard down too early.

After you have run Poplar, you might realize that you are smiling. It's been a great run, you've made it, and you are already looking forward to the next high-water release.

Dead River (South Branch)

The South Branch of the Dead River flows out of Saddleback Lake on the northern side of Saddleback Mountain northward for some miles and then turns northeast. The river then travels through an open valley with many farms to Flagstaff Lake, which it reaches at its southwestern corner near the town of Stratton. South Branch offers a fine variety of paddling; a steep and difficult gorge, a long stretch of mostly smooth water, and a great whitewater run. All of these are in a beautiful setting between the Saddleback Range on the one side and East Kennebago Mountain on the other, much of it through green farming country that offers fine views to the river traveler. It is a small river, and the water runs off quickly after the snow is gone. Most of the rapids, therefore, are very shallow after the middle of May.

DALLAS SCHOOL ➤ LANGTOWN MILL   5.75 MI

Description:	Class II, II, IV
Navigable:	Spring: April
Scenery:	Forested
Maps:	Kennebago Lake 15, Rangeley 15, Quill Hill,
	Tim Mountain, Stratton 15, DL 28 and 29

Put in at the ME 16 bridge in Dallas and paddle 2.0 miles of smooth water to a few small rapids near a state picnic area. Below this, the river enters a deep gorge, a portion of which you can see from the highway. An alternate put-in is available about 0.5 mile above the entrance to the gorge. A short dirt road (75 yards) leads right down to the river's edge. You also find a wide shoulder for parking vehicles where the dirt road turns off ME 16. The gorge is difficult to scout, but you can see much of it by walking through the woods and peering down into the gorge.

The gorge has four ledge drops. Each has a break in the ledge that allows a defined, but tricky, passage. Depending on water level, these rapids are Class III or IV. At lower water, you face a lot of rocks; at higher water, more rocks are covered, but the current can be pushy. If you catch an eddy before each drop and you are a solid Class III boater, you should be able to read the drops and run them. The last drop is best run on the left. As you approach it, catch the large eddy on the left above it; you drop over a small ledge on your way to the eddy. After you are in the eddy, you can see the rooster tail and wave train clearly. If you line up with them when you leave the eddy, you are sure to have a good run.

After 1.0 mile in the gorge, the river comes near the road, where paddlers who wish to avoid the difficulties of the gorge above can choose to put in. The rapids for the next 3.0 miles to Langtown Mill gradually become easier (Class II). The take-out is on river right about 50 yards before a green iron bridge across the river. The bridge is posted as private property. Ask for and obtain permission to take out here.

LANGTOWN MILL ➤ GREEN FARM BRIDGE · 6.5 MI

Description: Flatwater, quickwater
Navigable: High water: April
Scenery: Forested, rural
Maps: Kennebago Lake 15, DL 29

Below Langtown Mill the river flows slowly, with many meanders and views of Bigelow and East Kennebago Mountains. A thin veil of trees lines the banks.

GREEN FARM BRIDGE ➤ FLAGSTAFF LAKE (ME 27) · 7.5 MI

Description: Lake, quickwater, Class II, III
Navigable: High water: May
Scenery: Forested, rural
Maps: Quill Hill, Stratton 15, DL 29

This bridge is about 1.0 mile off ME 16 on a gravel road that leaves the highway at Green Farm; it makes a good put-in spot for the lower section of the river. The first 4.0 miles below the bridge are quick water with frequent Class I rapids. Most of the boulders in the riverbed were dynamited years ago for log runs. About 1.0 mile above Lutton Brook, the rapids begin abruptly; for the next 1.5 miles to Nash Stream, they are continuous and difficult (Class III).

As the river burrows into the bedrock, the scenery becomes outstanding: ragged cliffs, rocky portals, and sunlight slanting through the hemlocks. The riverbed is mostly shallow ledge with a few deep pools. The last 1.5 miles of rapids below Nash Stream are not as difficult. About 0.3 mile below Nash Stream, the river doubles around a rock spine with a little beach shelving into a deep pool.

As the river nears Flagstaff Lake, the current tapers off. After entering Flagstaff Lake, you find a dirt road on the right is passable to four-wheel-drive vehicles. In the last mile, you can see Bigelow Mountain. When the lake is full, the ME 27 bridge is too low to pass under, but boats can slide through a culvert on the right. Stratton is another 1.0 mile.

Dead River (North Branch)

Much of the waterway that Benedict Arnold and his men struggled with on their way to Canada in the fall of 1775 has been flooded, and little remains of the wilderness through which they traveled. It was on the North Branch of the Dead River that Arnold's party was beset by floods late in October 1775.

Today, this river still flows relatively freely in a rugged setting. The river is followed by ME 27, but only occasionally is the highway close enough to be visible from the water. Except for a few cabins, you see hardly a building above Eustis. From the head of Chain Lakes, the narrow valley frames a view of the Bigelow Range.

The North Branch has some challenging rapids, but most of it is flat; more than 17.0 miles of the route described here is runnable in all but low water.

CHAIN LAKE ➤ EUSTIS   19.0 MI

Description:	Lake, flatwater, quickwater, Class II, III
Navigable:	High and medium water: mid-May through June
Scenery:	Forested
Maps:	Chain of Ponds, Jim Pond, Tim Mountain, Stratton 15, DL 38, 28, and 29
Portages:	5.0 mi L Chain Lakes Dam 10 yd
	7.25 mi R Sarampus Falls 15 yd
	(19.0 mi Dam at Eustis)
Campsites:	0 mi Chain Lakes (NW end) car
	13.5 mi R Alder Stream (upstream 0.5 mi) MFS car
	21.5 mi R Cathedral Pines private $ car

Portage the dam (5.0 miles) at the outlet of Chain Lakes on the left. The North Branch begins with 0.75 mile of quick water, which slackens at an abrupt left turn just above the ME 27 bridge (5.75 miles). Then travel 1.5 miles of good current to Sarampus Falls (7.25 miles), which is a short ledge drop beside a roadside picnic area. Usually, it must be lifted around.

Little Sarampus Falls, just around the next right turn, is a shorter drop. It is followed by 4.25 miles of flat water to Shadagee Falls (11.75 miles), which is flanked on both banks by low ledges; Shadagee Falls should be scouted. Beyond, flat water continues for another 4.25 miles to Upper Ledge Falls Dam.

The washed-out log-driving dam (16.0 miles) is usually run on the left, and it is followed by 150 yards of Class II rapids. After about 300 yards of flat water, you reach Ledge Falls, a Class III set of rapids (roughly 300 yards long) that begin with a sharp drop by a large boulder on the left. These rapids should be scouted before running. Flat water continues for 2.25 miles to the dam at Eustis (19.0 miles).

When the water level in Flagstaff Lake is low, you encounter a few riffles below the dam, and the river banks are exposed for several miles. You come upon a bridge and a causeway 2.0 miles south of Eustis. At the northeastern end of the lake, the Dead River begins below Long Falls Dam (40.0 miles).

Spencer Stream

Spencer Stream rises on the slopes of Kibby Mountain just west of Spencer Lake and flows south and west to the Dead River below Flagstaff Lake. It passes through some beautiful and wild country. The stream is usually too low for paddling by the end of June, but it does come up after heavy rains. It is difficult to reach the headwaters of the river. The old access road to Baker Pond is at times flooded by beavers. Flying in might be the most sensible option.

BAKER POND ➤ LOGGING BRIDGE   **13.75 MI**

Description:	Lake, quickwater, Class I
Navigable:	High water
Scenery:	Wild
Maps:	Spencer Lake 15, Pierce Pond 15, DL 39 and 29

From the inlet, it is a 1.5-mile paddle down the point to the outlet at the south end and then 1.5 miles down Baker Stream to Spencer Stream. Baker Stream is small, with many shallow rapids that might have to be lifted over. From the mouth of Baker Stream you travel 2.0 miles of pleasant quick water in Spencer Stream. Slack water follows for 3.0 miles to Spencer Dam (7.25 miles), a logging dam of which only the foundation remains. Below the dam are 4.5 miles of continuous rapids to a logging road bridge that offers access on weekdays but is gated on weekends.

LOGGING BRIDGE ➤ DEAD RIVER   7.5 MI

Description:	Class I, II, III
Navigable:	High water
Scenery:	Wild
Maps:	Pierce Pond 15, DL 29
Portage:	4.5 mi L falls

Below the bridge are more Class I rapids to Spencer Gut (4.25 miles), which is a 0.5-mile gorge with high rock walls. From these walls, the stream plunges in a series of falls and pools. The portage is on the left bank over a high ridge. On the right is the grave of a logger who drowned in the Gut in 1905. Below the Gut you see sporty rapids past smaller cliffs. Heavy rapids continue for 1.0 mile to the mouth of Little Spencer Stream (5.25 miles); below, 2.0 miles of Class I rapids lead to the Dead River.

Little Spencer Stream

Little Spencer Stream flows out of Spencer Lake south to Spencer Stream about 2.0 miles from its confluence with the Dead River. It provides an alternate route to Spencer Stream and the Dead River. In high water, Little Spencer is a pretty stream to pole down. However, usually it is low, and you have to lift over the shallow places.

WHIPPLE POND ➤ FISH POND   5.5 MI

This is a chain of wilderness ponds just to the north of Spencer Lake, separated by short pitches that are too small and steep to run. The scenery, especially on Hall Pond, is outstanding.

Put in from the jeep road from US 201 to Spencer Rips on Moose River, at the eastern end of Whipple Pond. Follow the narrow arm west to the rocky outlet, where an old trail is blazed to Hall Pond. The glacier dropped great boulders in clumps and rows, nearly blocking the pond at one point. The remains of an old logging dam mark the start of a short, rocky pitch to the next pond. Drag and paddle through several more ponds to the marsh above Fish Pond.

FISH POND ➤ SPENCER STREAM   **12.75 MI**

Description:	Lake, quickwater, Class I, II
Navigable:	High water, medium water: scratchy
Scenery:	Wild
Maps:	Spencer Lake 15, Pierce Pond 15, DL 39 and 29

The Spencer Lake–Rock Pond road crosses Clark Stream, the inlet to Fish Pond, which is 1.0 mile of narrow, winding stream above the pond. With a high-clearance vehicle, you can drive to Fish Pond, passing through a beautiful stand of white pine 0.25 mile before the inlet. It is 1.5 miles down Fish Pond to the narrows, 400 feet into Spencer Lake, which is 5.25 miles to the southern end. The old dam (7.75 miles) at the outlet was burned; lift over.

Little Spencer Stream is a delightful paddle, with intermittent rapids in a narrow stream for the 5.0 miles to the confluence with Spencer Stream. Because Spencer Stream is wider, it is too low when it is still possible to paddle Little Spencer Stream; in that case you can take out at the confluence.

Austin Stream

Austin Stream drains a number of small swamps and ponds northeast of Bingham. You find some easy paddling where the stream follows Dead Water Road north of the falls. The real attraction, though, is the continuous rapids between the pool below the falls and the Kennebec River. The gradient is unusually uniform—it has no steep ledge drops, but rather many short, steep rapids.

FALLS POOL ➤ SIDE ROAD BRIDGE   **5.25 MI**

Description:	Class II, III, IV
Navigable:	Medium-high water: April or after heavy rain
Scenery:	Wild
Maps:	Bingham 15, DL 30

The stream drops 360 feet in the first 4.0 miles below the falls pool. Short, steep, boulder-strewn rapids alternate with gentler, gravelly rapids, but you have no slack water in which to catch your breath. Stopping requires catching shore eddies; the ability to do this is critical, as there always seems to be at least one tree blocking the river somewhere in this upper part. Strainers formed by trees are normally the greatest hazard on this stream. However, in high water, a capsized boat could result in a long and bruising swim, as rescue would be very difficult.

The take-out is under a side-road bridge about 1.25 miles from US 201. Take the first left heading north on Route 16 to get to the take-out.

You can find the put-in by heading north on ME 16 another 0.25 mile to the Dead Water Road on the left. About 6.0 miles up the road, the stream comes right beside the road and is nearly at road level. This is just above the falls. Turn around and head back down the road about 0.3 mile (about 100 yards below where the old road comes in). About 200 yards into the woods and 150 feet down the side of the hill is a small pool a few hundred yards below the falls, which is the best place to launch boats. You find no trail here, but the woods are quite open. The pool is near the 820-foot contour line on the topographical map. If you have any doubts about running the stream, remember that taking out anywhere before the bridge requires pulling boats through the woods and up similar (or worse) hills.

Trees could be in the river here, and extra caution is advised. Constant maneuvering is required to thread a path down the riverbed. After several miles of naturally formed rapids, the riverbed becomes channelized just above where Chase Stream enters on the right (4.0 miles). From this point down, the riverbed is gravel and the rapids are Class I, II. When the water is high, an interesting trip might be to put in at the side road bridge over Chase Stream and run the rock-free waves down to the Kennebec.

SIDE ROAD BRIDGE ➤
KENNEBEC RIVER BOAT LANDING   1.75 MI

Description:	Class I, II
Navigable:	Medium-high water: April
Scenery:	Rural, towns
Maps:	Bingham 15, DL 30

Put in at the side-road bridge on Austin Stream (or about 1.25 miles farther up on the Stream Road bridge over Chase Stream) and enjoy some rock-free rapids. In higher water you might encounter some Class III waves and eddy lines. Take out at the boat landing on the Kennebec behind the mill in Bingham (Lander Street).

Carrabassett River

The Carrabassett River rises in the mountains of northwestern Maine on the northern side of Sugarloaf Mountain. It is a wild and tumultuous mountain brook above Carrabassett Village, but from there down it offers fine whitewater paddling and in its lower stretches some smooth-water travel. The valley is settled, and the stream is rocky and clear. After rain, the river rises and falls quickly. The best time for running is probably early in May, when the snows are still melting on Sugarloaf.

SUGARLOAF ACCESS ROAD ➤
CARRABASSETT (VALLEY CROSSING)   6.0 MI (Upper Carrabassett)

Description:	Class II, III, IV, V
Navigable:	High water is in April, but high water is not recommended
Scenery:	Forested
Maps:	Stratton 15, Little Bigelow Mountain 15, DL 29
Portages:	1 or more

This section of the river can be run by a team of experts at the right water levels. Several drops must be scouted, lined, or portaged. Boats should have full flotation, and rescue lines should be set up below the more difficult drops. Several of the most difficult drops are visible from ME 27 in the 2.0-mile stretch of river that starts 1.5 miles north of Valley Crossing.

Put in where the river is close to the road, a little south of the Sugarloaf Mountain Ski Area entrance. The river should be somewhat scratchy Class II–III near the start if the water level is right for the gorge below.

The first 2.0 miles are generally Class I, II, and III, with a few more difficult spots. Then the rapids become progressively harder, and the number of big drops increases as you approach the start of the gorge.

In the gorge, the river is very rocky, the current very pushy, the eddies very small, and the area in which to maneuver minimal. The gorge is definitely a Class IV–V section. Three drops in the gorge stand out from the rest. The first, which is visible from the road, falls 15 feet in three stages, with the last stage being about 8 feet straight down. The second big drop is just out of sight of the road, behind some camps. The river forms a 13-foot-wide chute between two rock walls and drops about 10 feet into a river-wide hole, which is a keeper. The third, the Pinnacles, is beside a high rock island at the end of the gorge, where you have a complicated approach to a 10-foot slanted drop. Below this drop, the rapids are Class I–II for the last 1.5 miles to the ledges just above the Valley Crossing Bridge. Take out on the left above the bridge or the right, just below the bridge.

CARRABASSETT ➤ KINGFIELD   10.0 MI (Middle Carrabassett)

Description:	Class I, II, III
Navigable:	High and medium water: April, early May, or after heavy rain
Scenery:	Forested, towns
Maps:	Little Bigelow Mountain 15, DL 29 and 30
Portage:	10.0 mi L dam

The put-in at the Valley Crossing Carriage Road Bridge is on river left, above the bridge. Parking is on river left in the general vicinity of the Kingfield Fire Department substation. A gauge is on the upstream side of the right bridge abutment. Minimum level is 1, but more water is definitely better. The river is Class I at the start at the 1 level and continues steadily to a left turn away from the road. The rapids on the corner where the river bends back to the right

(0.5 miles) can be tricky, especially in low water; there, the riverbed is very rocky with few channels.

At 1.0 mile, you reach the bridge above Packard's Pool. This should be scouted because a change in water level affects the rapid. At 1 on the Valley Crossing gauge, it can usually be run at river left. For the next 2.5 miles, the river is mostly Class I with occasional Class II and easy Class III sections.

At 3.5 miles, the river again turns away from the road. Then you arrive at the Elbow, which is a Class II–III rapid ending in a pool by a log cabin. The river continues with stretches of Class I-II water and bends to the right to parallel the road again. At about 5.0 miles, the river sweeps to the left, with a Class III drop above a small island. Either side can be run, but the left is better in low water. You find a nice pool at the bottom of the rapid. Rock Garden (5.5 miles) starts just after the pool and continues for about 1.0 mile. The river is filled with rocks that appear to offer many routes; however, some are dead ends, so you should choose carefully. From here, the river continues as a Class I-II with occasional quickwater sections. Take out can be at either on river left just below the Clay Brook Road Bridge or further down stream on river right at the State Highway Garage.

Below the Garage

This section of the Carrabassett has been run at flood stage when no rocks were showing. A run at this level is for experts only. A swim at this level can be long and dangerous. If the water is too high, do not run it.

KINGFIELD ➤ NEW PORTLAND   **6.5 MI (Lower Carrabassett)**

Description:	Class I, II
Navigable:	High water: late April and early May
Scenery:	Forested
Maps:	Little Bigelow Mountain 15, Kingfield 15, DL 30 and 20

This is an attractive stretch; the river is wider and the rapids are not as difficult as the section above. Put in on river right either behind Longfellows Restaurant in Kingfield or, to skip that flatwater section, put in further downstream across from Twitchell Fuel (yellow building with green metal roof) on ME 27. You find a nice rock garden above the take-out, which is on river left at the sandy beach, just below the wire bridge in New Portland. A stop at Gifford's Ice Cream in Farmington completes the trip.

The valley is more open. Take out at the wire bridge in New Portland.

NEW PORTLAND ➤ NORTH ANSON   13.5 MI

Description:	Flatwater, quickwater
Navigable:	Spring, wet summers
Scenery:	Forested, rural, towns
Maps:	Kingfield 15, DL 20
Portages:	5.5 mi ledge
	9.5 mi L Cleveland Rips
	(13.5 mi falls)

The views improve as you reach East New Portland. Take out above town, because under the bridge is an impassable drop.

Put in on the right bank below the drop. This section is mostly quick water, but halfway down is Cleveland Rips. You see some open pastureland, but it is mostly wooded until you get close to North Anson. Take out above the village of North Anson, because you come upon an impassable falls in town. It is then 1.0 mile to the Kennebec River.

Sandy River

The Sandy River rises in the Sandy River Ponds a few miles south of Rangeley and flows east to the Kennebec River, which it reaches a few miles south of Anson. Its upper reaches are a tumultuous mountain torrent and unrunnable until Smalls Falls, about 4.0 miles above Madrid. In the 52.0 miles from here to the junction with the Kennebec, the river drops 700 feet and offers a variety of runs for all tastes. Because of the many dams, paddling on weekdays is better, because more water is in the river, and the season is prolonged, lasting even into the summer. For weekend paddling, the spring is better, when the snows are still providing water from the melting on Saddleback and Mount Abraham.

SMALLS FALLS ➤ SOUTH BRANCH   5.5 MI

Description:	Class II, III, IV
Navigable:	High and medium water
Scenery:	Forested, towns
Maps:	Rangeley 15, DL 19
Portages:	3 mi R ledges
	3.5 mi R ledge
	4.25 mi e falls
	4.75 mi e falls

The Sandy River is small here, but it can rise quickly when the snows are melting in the mountains. Then the rapids become very heavy. In high water, it is an interesting kayak run; in medium water, it can be run by open canoes. Four ledges are particularly difficult. The action you take at them depends on the water level.

Put in below Smalls Falls from a track on the left bank. The first 1.0 mile is continuously difficult, with some fallen trees, especially at a sharp S-curve. Below the first US 4 bridge, the going is easy away from the road. As the river turns back toward the road, and just below a long island, a series of four ledges starts, with the last one being the highest. These are best scouted/lined on the right and run on the left, and they are more ledgy compared to the rounded boulders above. The rapids become easier as they follow the road to the bridge in Madrid (3.5 miles).

The second ledge below the bridge should be scouted as it is full of sharp rocks. The river swings away from the road, and 0.25 mile above the second US 4 bridge is a small gorge, which should be inspected in advance. Below the second US 4 bridge is another falls (the steepest) with a large boulder below, which makes an island in the gorge. The rapids gradually ease to the third US 4 bridge, just above the confluence with the South Branch.

SOUTH BRANCH ➤ PHILLIPS   5.75 MI

Description:	Class II, III
Navigable:	High water: early May
Scenery:	Forested, rural
Maps:	Phillips 15, DL 19

This run is somewhat less difficult than the section above, but only experienced paddlers should attempt it, because it has a number of Class III rapids. From the ME 4 bridge 2.0 miles south of Madrid, it is only 200 yards to the confluence of the South Branch. About 1.0 mile below here, Orbeton Stream (which flows out of Redington Pond on the east flank of Saddleback) enters on the left. The junction is a fine lunch spot. You leave the brawling mountain stream behind at this point and travel on a wide river, with open pastures providing many fine views of the mountains to the north and west. The rapids are nearly continuous although not difficult, but at almost every bend you come upon heavy waves, which must be avoided. Take out on the left 1.0 mile upstream of Phillips at Davenport Flats where the road comes close to the river.

If for any reason you are considering running through Phillips, be aware that both the ME 142 and the ME 149 bridges have unrunnable gorges above them. If you attempt the gorge above ME 142, you should scout carefully from above and below, as the height is deceptive. The best approach is from directly upstream through a 3-foot-wide chute on the left of the rock island. You can take out at a railroad park on the left bank, 1.0 mile above the next waterfall.

PHILLIPS ➤ FAIRBANKS BRIDGE   17.25 MI

Description:	Class I, II
Navigable:	High and medium water
Scenery:	Forested, rural
Maps:	Phillips 15, Kingfield 15, DL 19 and 20

Below the ME 149 bridge, put in on the left to run the Class III rapid within sight downstream and another Class III rapid 0.25 mile downstream, where the river makes a sharp turn to the right. You can also put in on the left below these. The remainder of the 8.0 miles to Strong is quick water and riffles, with lovely mountain views.

Above Strong 0.5 mile is a Class II rapid that runs for 0.25 mile. A ballpark on the right below the bridge in Strong offers good access.

At Strong, the river turns south; several Class II rapids occur. The river is constantly changing in depth from shoal water to deep pools. Above the Fairbanks Bridge, ME 4, 1.0 mile is an easy ledge drop that can make things sporty. Access is downstream on the right.

FAIRBANKS BRIDGE ➤ FARMINGTON FALLS   10.25 MI

Description:	Quickwater, Class I, II
Navigable:	Medium and low water
Scenery:	Rural, towns
Maps:	Kingfield 15, Farmington DL 19 and 20

The river is smooth for the remaining 3.5 miles to Farmington. At 0.5 mile below, Farmington Temple Stream enters on the right. Another 0.5 mile brings an interesting ledge drop; then the river is smooth and winding for the next 6.0 miles to Farmington Falls. Just above the ME 156 bridge Wilson Stream enters on the right. If you wish to avoid whitewater, you should take out well above the bridge or a mile farther upstream, where the river comes close to the road on the right.

FARMINGTON FALLS ➤ NEW SHARON   6.0 MI

Description:	Class I, II, III
Navigable:	Medium water
Scenery:	Rural
Maps:	Farmington, New Sharon, Farmington Falls, DL 20

The remains of a washed-out dam are visible above the bridge as the river begins to pitch for 200 yards of Class I–II water. Then the river smoothes out and winds through farm country to the town of New Sharon. Here the river turns sharply to the left and under the US 2 bridge.

Rapids start well above the bridge, increasing in intensity to a sharp right-hand turn that generates 5-foot waves. These should be avoided except by experts in high water and scouted carefully in medium water. The rapids end in 0.75 mile; a campground is on the left bank.

NEW SHARON ➤ KENNEBEC RIVER   **20.25 MI**

Description:	Flatwater, quickwater
Navigable:	Medium and low water
Scenery:	Forested, rural
Maps:	New Sharon, Norridgewock 15, Anson 15, DL 20
Portage:	16.0 mi dam

The river flows smoothly with good current below the rapids in New Sharon. A USGS gauging station is near Mercer, and in 5.0 miles you come upon a dam below Sandy River. Below the dam are 3.5 miles of winding river to the junction with the Kennebec River. Take out 1.0 mile downstream on the left bank or 5.75 miles downstream at Norridgewock, at a boat ramp.

Sandy River (South Branch)

The South Branch is a very small stream that can be run in medium water as an alternate start to the Sandy River. It has been run from above the confluence of the branches 2.7 miles above ME 4 on Number Six Road, but this is too small and obstructed to be recommended. A better start is after 1.5 miles, where the river comes close to the road. It is a fast Class II to an abutment on a private road 1.0 mile above ME 4, where the difficulty gradually diminishes.

Temple Stream

Temple Stream rises in Avon and flows southeast to the Sandy River at West Farmington. It is small, with several dams, and the running is mixed smooth water and rapids.

DRURY POND ➤ SANDY RIVER   **8.5 MI**

Description:	Class I, II, III
Navigable:	High water: early spring
Scenery:	Forested, rural, towns
Maps:	Farmington, DL 19
Portages:	1.5 mi dam at Temple
	7.5 mi dam at West Farmington

If the water level is high enough, you can put in just below the outlet of Drury Pond north of Temple. The first 2.0 miles to the dam are all smooth. The next 2.5 miles below the dam to the first bridge have Class II rapids. In the next 1.5 miles to the millpond the rapids become steeper, Class III. Then it is 1.5 miles down the pond to the dam at West Farmington. Below the dam the river is mostly smooth for the remaining mile to the Sandy River, 1.0 mile below Farmington.

Wilson Stream

Wilson Stream rises on the northern side of Saddleback Mountain but does not become runnable until Wilson Pond in Wilton. The 15.0 miles from there to the junction with Sandy River at Farmington Falls offer a variety of rapid and smooth water with only two dams to carry.

You encounter a sharp rapid through the town for 0.75 mile to the lower dam, so it is well to put in below this dam. In another 0.75 mile, a fall requires a carry, so most paddlers decide to put in below this fall.

WILTON ➤ EAST WILTON   3.5 MI

Description:	Class II
Navigable:	High water: early spring
Scenery:	Forested, rural, towns
Maps:	Farmington, DL 19
Portage:	(3.5 mi dam East Wilton)

Put in below the lower dam in a parking lot on the right just below the bridge, 1.5 miles below Wilton. From here to East Wilton the river is mostly Class II rapids. In East Wilton, take out on the left above a broken dam. Carry on the road across the bridge, and put in on the right.

EAST WILTON ➤ NORTH CHESTERVILLE   10.0 MI

Description:	Quickwater
Navigable:	Medium water: May
Scenery:	Forested, towns
Maps:	Wilton, Farmington Falls, DL 19 and 20
Portages:	1.0 mi low dam
	(11.0 mi broken dam North Chesterville)

After a short Class II rapid below the dam, it is mostly quick water to the dam at North Chesterville. A small dam 1.0 mile below the start can be lifted over.

NORTH CHESTERVILLE ➤ FARMINGTON FALLS   4.0 MI

Description:	Smoothwater, Class II
Navigable:	Medium water: May
Scenery:	Forested, towns
Map:	DL 20

You travel a short rapid below the dam. The following 4.0 miles to Farmington Falls and the junction with the Sandy River at Farmington Falls are all smooth water.

Sebasticook River

The Sebasticook River rises in North Dexter and flows south for a long distance, paralleling the Kennebec before finally joining that river at Winslow, opposite Waterville. Because most of the drops have been dammed for power purposes, you can experience a long river run, even in the summer, through a section of rural Maine in which urbanization has hardly begun. The upper section should probably be run in the spring, when you have plenty of water.

NORTH DEXTER > GREAT MOOSE POND   22.0 MI

Description:	Flatwater, some rapids
Navigable:	High water: early spring
Scenery:	Forested, rural
Map:	DL 31

Put in at North Dexter from ME 23, or if the water is low, from a side road that leaves the main road south of North Dexter and reaches the river 0.5 mile lower down, where it is somewhat larger. This section of river is still somewhat small and best run at high water. It is mostly smooth and is the only rapid that can be lined or carried. The river runs through mountainous country that has fine views in all directions. For 13.0 miles from the start, the river runs through marshes in a general southwesterly direction to Mainstream Pond. Then 3.0 miles of paddling takes you to its southwestern end and the town of Mainstream. Below the town you come upon 0.5 mile of rapids followed by 1.0 mile of easy river to Lake Como. The outlet leaves the lake at its southwestern corner; in 0.25 mile you face a sharp rapid, after which the river is easy for 2.0 miles to Great Moose Pond. You can take out at Castle Harmony just before entering the lake or continue southwest across the lake 3.0 miles to the boat launch on Great Moose Drive on the west side of the outlet.

GREAT MOOSE POND ➤ PITTSFIELD   10.0 MI

Description:	Flatwater, some rapids
Navigable:	Spring, summer
Scenery:	Forested, rural, towns
Maps:	DL 31 and 21
Portages:	2.0 mi dam at Hartland 0.5 mi
	9.0 mi dam at Waverley Ave (Pittsfield)
	10.0 mi dam at Mill Pond (Pittsfield)

From the boat launch upstream of the outlet of Great Moose Pond it is only 2.0 miles to the dam at Hartland. It is best to make the 0.5-mile carry around this dam, the remains of a lower dam, and a very rocky set of rapids that is difficult to traverse in low water. Below this point the river transitions to flat water at the upstream end of Douglas Pond, upstream of the ME 2 bridge. Douglas Pond is a large impoundment fringed by vast wetlands that is an important nesting area for black terns. A 2.0-mile paddle south on Douglas Pond brings you to the dam at Waverly Avenue in Pittsfield. A boat launch sits just upstream of the dam and the Waverly Avenue bridge, on river right. Below this dam is a 1.0-mile stretch of flat water through the Mill Pond to a second Pittsfield dam, just downstream of Main Street.

PITTSFIELD ➤ BURNHAM   9.0 MI

Description:	Quickwater, Class I, II, III
Navigable:	Spring, most summers
Scenery:	Forested, rural, towns
Map:	DL 21
Portage:	9.0 mi dam

Access below the second Pittsfield dam, downstream of Main Street, is somewhat difficult. Most paddlers launch in Manson Park, which is less than 1.0 mile downstream of the dam. From Manson Park it is 2.5 miles to the confluence with the East Branch of the Sebasticook River, and another 1.0 mile to the small boat launch just downstream of the Peltoma Avenue (Horseback Road) bridge on river right. You can take out here or continue for another 2.5 miles of mostly flatwater paddling to the Eel Weir Road bridge. Just upstream of the bridge, a small rapids marks the upstream influence of the backwater from the dam near the Pittsfield-Burnham line. The large impoundment of this dam is 2.0 miles long. A small take-out area beside ME 100, on river right, sits just upstream of this dam.

BURNHAM ➤ CLINTON   10.0 MI

Description:	Some rapids, Class I and II, and long pools
Navigable:	Spring and most summers. Flows subject to hydropower regulation.
Scenery:	Forested, rural, towns
Map:	DL 21

Presently you find no convenient access immediately below the dam near the Pittsfield-Burnham line. Eventually, federal relicensing of the dam will require a boat portage and access below the dam. Flows can be highly variable in this stretch, depending on operation of the dam. Most paddlers choose to skip the 2.0-mile stretch below the dam and put in near the intersection of Troy Road and ME 100 in Burnham Junction, just downstream of the confluence with Twenty-Five Mile Stream. From here it is 8.0 miles downstream to Clinton, where you come upon an unimproved boat access area on Main Street (river right) at the site where an old woolen mill was torn down.

Description:	Flatwater, Class I, II, III
Navigable:	Spring and most summers. Flows subject to hydropower regulation.
Scenery:	Forested, rural, towns
Map:	DL 21
Portages:	5.0 mi dam at Benton Falls
	10.0 mi dam at Winslow

Below the boat access area in Clinton, at the site of the former woolen mill, is a steep rapid that some paddlers might choose to portage around. From here it is mostly gentle rapids and pools to the impoundment at the Benton Falls dam. You can use the boat launch upstream of the dam, on river left, or you can portage around the dam. Below the dam tailwater, with its ledge outcroppings, is the upstream end of the backwater influence of the dam in Winslow. The dam in Winslow has an impoundment that is approximately 5.0 miles long. The boat launch just upstream of the dam on river left is where most paddlers take out. Below the dam it is less than 0.5 mile to the Kennebec River in Winslow.

Sebasticook River (East Branch)

The East Branch of the Sebasticook River rises in Martin Bog in the southern part of Dexter, but is hardly runnable until it reaches Corinna. From here, it provides an alternative and somewhat shorter start for the trip down the main Sebasticook River. It flows through open, rolling country in which the banks are largely wooded. The East Branch has a number of spots for access, so the trip can be matched to the stage of water. Below Corinna it can probably be run in any but a dry summer.

MOODY ➤ NEWPORT   11.0 MI

Description:	Lake, quickwater
Navigable:	Spring: high water
Scenery:	Forested, towns
Maps:	DL 32 and 22
Portages:	6.0 mi dam at Corinna
	6.25 mi second dam at Corinna
	6.75 mi third dam at Corinna

When you have sufficient water, you should be able to put in at the bridge on the side road off ME 7 in the northern part of the town of Corinna. This bridge is just west of Moody and below a dam on the river. The river is small for a few hundred yards. Then it opens up to a wider stream for the 3.0 miles to the millpond above Corinna, passing a bridge at Lincoln Mills, 2.0 miles down (an alternative starting point). Then travel 1.0 mile of deadwater to the upper dam at Corinna. Below the upper dam is 0.25 mile of millpond to the middle dam and then 0.5 mile of millpond to the lower dam.

The area between the upper and lower dams is a federal Superfund site, because of ground water contamination by an old woolen mill. This stretch of river might not be navigable for many years on account of the extensive cleanup and the physical relocation of a stretch of the East Branch. You should take out above the upper dam and put in below the lower dam, thereby avoiding the Superfund site in downtown Corinna. After river restoration is completed, you will be able to paddle through Corinna again.

You then travel 3.0 miles of river below the lower dam to the entrance to Sebasticook Lake. Then 3.0 additional miles take you across the lake to the town of Newport at the southwestern corner, where the river flows out, and where you find a small park and boat launch.

NEWPORT ➤ SEBASTICOOK RIVER   9.0 MI

Description:	Quickwater
Navigable:	Spring, summer
Scenery:	Forested, towns
Maps:	DL 22 and 21

Two dams are located at Newport: the first at the lake and the second 0.5 mile below, across the millpond. The second dam eventually will be removed to allow fish passage. If you start here, put in below these dams. Then you have 9.0 miles of good current, the last half through a large bog to the main Sebasticook River 3.0 miles below Pittsfield. Those not wishing to go farther can take out 1.0 mile down that river at the Peltoma Bridge on Horseback Road. Beware of woody debris jams that sometimes create obstructions on the East Branch.

Stetson Stream

Maps: Stetson 15, Pittsfield 15

Stetson Stream is the outlet of Pleasant Lake in Stetson and flows west to Sebasticook Lake, thus providing an alternate means of access to the East Branch of the Sebasticook River. It runs largely through swamps and is sluggish, losing most of its altitude at the dam at Stetson. It can be run in the summer if not too low, but is better in the spring.

PLEASANT LAKE ➤ NEWPORT   12.0 MI

You can put in at the east end of Pleasant Lake from a side road off ME 222. It is then 2.0 miles west across the lake to the outlet, which is located in a bay on the north side near the western end. Some 1.5 miles of travel down the river through a swamp bring you to the ME 143 bridge and the dam at Stetson. Then you travel 2.5 miles of river, again largely through swamp, to Sebasticook Lake. Down the arm of Sebasticook Lake 1.0 mile, you pass under Durham Bridge into the main lake. Some might wish to take out here. It is then 5.0 miles across the lake to the town of Newport at the southwest corner, where the East Branch of the Sebasticook flows out and where you find a small park and boat launch.

Martin Stream

Martin Stream rises in Troy and Thorndike and flows north and west into the East Branch of the Sebasticook 1.0 mile below Newport. It becomes runnable in Dixmont and is a pleasant trip on a small stream with good current through relatively wild country.

The spring migration of suckers up Martin Stream is most impressive, sometimes carpeting the bottom with masses of fish.

DIXMONT ➤ NEWPORT   16.0 MI

Description:	Lake, flatwater, quickwater, Class I, II
Date checked:	1986
Navigable:	High water: spring
Scenery:	Wild, forested, rural
Maps:	Dixmont, Plymouth, Newport, DL 22
Portages:	1.5 mi R Dixmont Falls 20 yd
	9.75 mi R Plymouth dam 150 yd

Put in at Mitchell Road just west of ME 7 between Dixmont and North Dixmont. The stream is small. It is 1.5 miles to Dixmont Falls, then 150 yards to the ME 7 bridge in North Dixmont. After 0.5 mile, the river enters an alder jungle thick enough to impede all but the most determined paddlers.

At 7.0 miles you reach the backwater from the dam in Plymouth. Paddle down the lake to the dam and falls in Plymouth (9.75 miles). Just below is a nice Class II rapid.

At 13.0 miles you come upon a sharp ledge drop to look over. The bridge at Ridge Road in Newport is 14.5 miles, the last before the confluence with the East Branch (16.0 miles).

TWENTY-FIVE MILE STREAM   8.0 MI

Description:	Flatwater, mild rapids
Navigable:	Spring: high water
Scenery:	Forested, rural, wetlands
Map:	DL 21
Portages:	Beaver dams, woody debris jams

Twenty-Five Mile Stream flows from the outlet of Unity Pond 8.0 miles before joining the Sebasticook River in Burnham Junction. The stream is mostly slow-moving water through wetlands, with beaver dams and woody debris jams that can shift from year to year, making passage difficult. The stream can be accessed from the outlet of Unity Pond on the Horseback Road, or 2.0 miles farther downstream at ME 139 by dragging your boat 50 yards down Bog Brook. Just upstream of the confluence with the Sebasticook is a curving section of rapids that flows past an old dam site. If you want to avoid the rapids, you can take out at the Troy Road bridge in Burnham Junction.

Belgrade Lakes Trip

Maps: Norridgewock 15, Augusta 15, Waterville 15, DL 12 and 20

The Belgrade Lakes offer a variety of trips. The usual trip is a circular one starting from East Pond and ending at Messalonskee Lake only 3.0 miles from the starting place. You can then return to the start or descend Messalonskee Stream to the Kennebec River at Waterville.

EAST POND   2.5 MI

This is the highest of the chain and the usual starting point. You find access at a public picnic spot off East Pond Road, just south of Alden's Camp.

THE SERPENTINE   2.0 MI

This is the outlet of East Pond. It is wide and smooth, and in 1.5 miles you come to a sharp left turn. The channel to the right can be explored but is only the outlet of Sucker Brook. Just beyond on the right is a picnic site. In another 0.5 mile, the dam at Smithfield is reached. Either you can carry this, if you have enough water in the brook below, or you can put in 300 yards farther at the beach on North Pond.

NORTH POND   2.0 MI

From Smithfield on the eastern shore it is only 2.0 miles to the outlet, Great Meadow Stream, which takes off at the center of the southern shore. But you have many more miles of lake to explore, including a trip into Little Pond through the Narrows at the southern end of the western shore.

GREAT MEADOW STREAM   4.0 MI

Great Meadow Stream is the outlet of North Pond, and it leaves that pond near the center of the southern shore. It twists and turns for 4.0 miles to Great Pond, marking the boundary between Rome on the right and Smithfield and Belgrade on the left.

GREAT POND   5.0 MI

This is located in Belgrade, although the northern and part of the western shores are in Rome. It is a very large lake, and you should be on the alert for sudden squalls. You can find public campsites on Crooked and Oak islands. It is only 5.0 miles southwesterly across the lake to the outlet at Belgrade Lakes on the western shore, but you have many bays and inlets to explore. The outlet is really only an extension of the lake for 0.5 mile to the dam. Take out at the cement bridge and carry 50 yards around the dam and into Long Pond.

LONG POND   6.0 MI

Although the northern end of the pond in Rome is worth exploring, the usual route crosses the pond to the western shore, where it turns south and passes under the bridge at Castle Island in 2.0 miles. Paddle another 4.0 miles south on a constantly narrowing pond to the outlet, Belgrade Stream. About 1.0 mile above the outlet, Ingham Stream enters on the right.

BELGRADE STREAM   9.0 MI

It is 2.0 miles down the stream to Wings Mills. After going under the bridge, keep to the right to avoid the sluiceway on the left. Boats can be hauled over the old fish ladder on the right. It is then only 6.0 miles more to Belgrade and another 1.0 mile to Messalonskee Lake.

MESSALONSKEE LAKE   8.0 MI

This is an Abenaki name meaning Snow Pond. The lake is long and narrow and provides an 8.0-mile paddle to its northern end, where at Oakland you are only 3.0 miles from the starting place at East Pond. You can terminate the trip here or continue down Messalonskee Stream to the Kennebec River.

MESSALONSKEE STREAM   9.0 MI

This is the outlet from the Belgrade Lakes; consequently, the water level holds up well, and the stream can be run in the summer. The banks are a mixture of wooded and open land, and the river flows in a pleasant valley. Because of three dams and an impassable cascade in Oakland, you cannot go directly into the river from Messalonskee Lake. It is best to make a 2.0-mile carry around all these obstructions and put in at the pond below town. Below Oakland 1.5 miles is a dam and a 0.5 mile carry on the right. It is then 4.0 miles to the first dam in Waterville and then 1.0 mile of backwater to the second dam. From this last dam it is 1.0 mile to the Kennebec River.

Cobbosseecontee Stream

The upper Cobbosseecontee Stream is a series of lakes and streams, starting with Torsey Lake in Mount Vernon and descending through Maranacook Lake and Lake Annabessacook to Cobbosseecontee Lake, from which Cobbosseecontee Stream flows to the Kennebec River at Gardiner. The trip can be made in either direction as most of the way is lakes or backwater from dams, with easy paddling through gentle, rolling country. Only the 0.8 mile of rapids between the dams below Cobbossee Dam requires high water. The trip can be extended for many miles of additional paddling on the lakes.

TORSEY LAKE ➤ GARDINER   40.5 MI

Description:	Lakes, flatwater
Navigable:	Spring, summer, fall
Scenery:	Forested
Maps:	Augusta 15, Gardiner, DL 12
Portages:	Numerous on connecting streams; see text below

TORSEY LAKE   3.5 MI

You can put in at the north end of the lake from a side road about 1.0 mile off Cobbs Hills Road, or at the southern end at the very tip of the lake, where you find a public boat launch. The lake is long and narrow, twisting about in its course southward.

TORSEY LAKE OUTLET   2.0 MI; 3 DAMS

You encounter a dam at the outlet and then 1.0 mile of millpond to Readfield, where you come upon two dams. Carry these both together. The final 1.0 mile to Maranacook Lake is meandering meadow brook. If the water in this stream is too low, the entire 2.0 miles can be easily carried by road.

MARANACOOK LAKE   5.5 MI

From the inlet stream, crossed by ME 41 almost at the lake shore, it is 5.0 miles down the lake. You pass the town of Maranacook halfway to Winthrop, where you find a public launch area at Norcross Point with toilets and water. At Winthrop the outlet is Mill Stream.

MILL STREAM   0.75 MI; 1 DAM

This provides the connection from Maranacook Lake to Lake Annabessacook or vice versa. At the Maranacook Lake end, enter the stream under Memorial Drive, lift over the small dam at the other side of the bridge, and descend to the Main Street bridge. Here, you must portage across the street 100 yards to the water just beyond the Carlson Woolen Mill building. Then you can paddle the remainder of the distance and enter Lake Annabessacook through a large culvert under US 202.

LAKE ANNABESSACOOK   4.0 MI

It is 4.0 miles down this lake to the outlet stream and about 2.0 miles to the narrows. From here, you should head for the southeastern corner, where the outlet is located.

If the season is not too dry, you can paddle up the outlet stream to Lower Narrows Pond, passing under a road and through a culvert.

JUGGERNOT STREAM   1.25 MI; 1 DAM

This stream, the outlet of Lake Annabessacook, provides unobstructed travel to Cobbosseecontee Lake, except for a short carry over the outlet dam.

COBBOSSEECONTEE LAKE   6.5 MI

Cobbosseecontee means Sturgeon Lake in the Abenaki language (*contee* meaning "lake"). Rightfully, the word *lake* should not be repeated in the name, but because so few people know the Indian languages, the usage will probably continue. The dam at the outlet raised the level of the lake 9 feet, enlarging the lake area but reducing the size of some of the islands. Although it is only 6.0 miles north up Cobbosseecontee Lake to the outlet, Cobbosseecontee Stream, on the eastern side, you have another 3.0 miles to the head of the lake at East Winthrop and 2.0 miles from the inlet to the southern end of the lake at Dismal Swamp in Monmouth. Many islands here invite exploration.

COBBOSSEECONTEE STREAM   11.0 MI; 2 DAMS

It is only 0.25 mile from the bridge near the lake shore to the outlet dam, which must be carried on the western end. You travel a 0.8-mile set of Class II rapids at high water, but they must be carried in low water, on the western side. The Collins Mill Dam is another short portage (on the west) 2.25 miles below Cobbossee Outlet dam. Some 6.0 miles below the dam, Oxbow Pond is reached, and in another 1.0 mile Horseshoe Pond. The river is wide all the way to Pleasant Pond, after the Collins Mill Dam.

PLEASANT POND   2.0 MI

Although it is only 2.0 miles down Pleasant Pond from the inlet to the outlet (Cobbossecontee Stream) at the northern end, you can paddle 4.0 miles to the south into Upper Pleasant Pond and enjoy considerable mileage of lake travel.

COBBOSSEECONTEE STREAM ➤ GARDINER 4.0 MI

From Pleasant Pond it is an easy paddle for the 4.0 miles to Gardiner. Take out above the first dam, because in the last 1.5 miles to the Kennebec River you face three more dams and some difficult Class III–IV rapids.

Chapter 4
Penobscot Watershed

Penobscot River (Headwaters)

The Penobscot River has two major tributaries, the East Branch and the West Branch, which offer a variety of paddling trips through a vast semiwilderness area of Maine. The West Branch is itself formed by the confluence of the North Branch and the South Branch, two small streams that drain a wild and densely forested area that is accessible only by private logging roads.

The North Branch was formerly the principal means of access to the headwaters of the St. John River. Carry trails to 5th St. John Pond and Baker Lake were popular routes before modern logging roads and airplanes.

The West Branch from Seboomook Lake to Millinocket is a large river with good paddling throughout the summer. However, during spring runoff, the high water can cause dangerous conditions in some places. The West Branch is one of the most scenic sections of the Penobscot. Its banks are heavily forested, with little evidence of civilization, and the spectacular views of Mount Katahdin

PENOBSCOT WATERSHED

Scale in miles

0 10 20 30 40

along the lower section add to its wilderness character. Roads from Greenville and Millinocket allow easy access at several points along the river.

The East Branch of the Penobscot flows from Grand Lake Mataga-mon at the northeastern corner of Baxter State Park to Medway, where it joins the West Branch, forming the main river. The East Branch, al-though not as large as the West Branch, offers good paddling through-out most of the season and, like its western sister, affords good views of the mountains of Baxter State Park. Webster Stream, a tributary of the East Branch, flows from Telos Lake to Grand Lake.

Penobscot River

This is a large river paralleled by highways, often on both sides, and bordered by a mixture of forests, farms, cities, and towns. It is quite dif-ferent from the East and West branches, which join it downstream.

Because most of the drops have been harnessed for power, this river consists primarily of smooth water, with some quick water. In many sections, it is more like a long, thin lake than it is like a river.

MEDWAY ➤ BANGOR   70.0 MI

Description:	Flatwater, quickwater, Class I, II
Navigable:	Spring, summer, fall: controlled release
Scenery:	Forested, rural, towns
Maps:	Millinocket 15, Mattawamkeag 15, Winn 15, Lincoln 15, Passadumkeag 15, Orono 15, Bangor 15, DL 43, 44, 33, and 23
Portages:	7.0 mi L Mattaseunk dam
	36.0 mi R West Enfield dam
	60.0 mi L Old Town dam
	61.0 mi L Veazie dam
	(70.0 mi R Bangor dam)

From Nicatou Island at the confluence of the East and West Branches, the Penobscot River flows for 7.0 miles to Mattaseunk Dam, carried left. From there, it is 4.5 miles to the mouth of the Mattawamkeag River (11.5 miles) at Mattawamkeag. In another 1.75 miles is the beginning of Five Island Rapids, which are 0.5 mile long. They are easy Class II, and the principal drop (frequently bony in low water) is at the end of the islands as you approach Winn. Flat water predominates for the next 16.0 miles past the North Lincoln bridge (20.0 miles) to Mohawk Rapids, a 0.75-mile section with some rocks and a good current. In another 5.5 miles the West Enfield Dam is reached and carried right.

Below the West Enfield Dam (36.0 miles) the Penobscot passes the mouth of the Piscataquis River (37.0 miles) on the right, the ME 6/155 bridge (37.25 miles), and the Passadumkeag River (41.25 miles) on the left. In the next 18.75 miles to Old Town, the river flows through somewhat wider bottom lands and spreads into several channels with many islands.

About 2.0 miles above the first dam at Old Town, you should take the left channel if you wish the most direct route. On the right, the Stillwater River (actually a western channel of the Penobscot) leaves, headed northwesterly.

The first dam at Old Town (60.0 miles) is located upstream of the highway bridge connecting Old Town with Milford. It is carried left. Flat water for 1.0 mile brings you to (61.0 miles) the second dam at Old Town, also carried left. You find a Class II rapid below this dam. Downstream 2.0 miles, where the Stillwater rejoins the Penobscot, you come to a Class III rapid, the most difficult on the lower river. Scouting from the right side might be warranted for those with loaded boats. On the right you find an easier passage. Below 4.0 miles (all Class I) you come to the Veazie Dam (67.0 miles), carried left. Downstream 3.0 miles you encounter the remains of the Bangor Dam (70.0 miles). If the tide at Bangor is high or nearly high, you can paddle through this breach. Otherwise, avoid its powerful currents.

BANGOR ➤ BUCKSPORT   21.0 MI

Description:	Tidal
Navigable:	Spring, summer, fall
Scenery:	Forested, rural, towns
Map:	DL 23

The Penobscot is tidal below Bangor and a large river. Take note of tide and weather. A number of launching ramps are available.

The section below the breached Bangor Dam, 1.5 miles upstream of the mouth of the Kenduskeag River, is very urban and has strong currents when the water level in the river is high. From East Hampton to South Orrington, the river generally is scenic and flat except when wind and tide are opposed. The river then opens up and becomes over 1.0 mile wide in places.

Experienced paddlers can go down the main (western) channel from Bucksport and then back up East Channel for an 11.0-mile circuit of Verona Island. The combination of ebbing tide and upstream wind can create large rolling waves in the main channel. Current patterns near the northern end of the island can also be confusing.

The tidal range at Bangor is 13 feet; high water is 4 minutes later than it is at Portland.

Penobscot River (West Branch)

The West Branch of the Penobscot is formed by the junction of the North and the South Branches at the western end of Seboomook Lake. It flows generally east for 108.0 miles through well-wooded valleys and unpopulated lakes to Medway, where it joins the East Branch.

Its upper waters were formerly the most traveled waterways in Maine because they were the access not only to the West Branch itself, but also to the East Branch, the Allagash, and the St. John. Today, private logging roads provide easy access to many points along the river. Remember to ask for and obtain permission before crossing property lines.

The river is large enough to be run at any season, but some of the more difficult rapids must be carried at high water.

PITTSTON FARM ➤ SEBOOMOOK DAM   **12.5 MI**

Description:	Lake, flatwater, Class I
Navigable:	Spring, summer, fall
Scenery:	Wild
Maps:	Seboomook Lake 15, North East Carry 15, DL 48 and 49
Portage:	(12.5 mi L Seboomook Dam)
Campsite:	12.0 mi R Seboomook Dam $ car MFS permit

Put in at the Ranger Station at Pittston Farm at the western end of Seboomook Lake. It is a 12.5-mile paddle across the lake to Seboomook Dam. Take out on the left. If you have a loaded boat, you want to skip the run from below Seboomook Dam to Roll Dam Campsite. You can start your trip again at the campsite, which is right beside the last drop of the ten or so Class III-IV drops that are collectively called "The Roll Dams."

SEBOOMOOK DAM ➤ ROLL DAM CAMPSITE   3.5 MI

Description:	Class III, IV
Navigable:	Spring, summer, fall: controlled release
Scenery:	Wild
Maps:	Seboomook Lake 15, North East Carry 15 DL 49
Campsites:	0 mi R Seboomook Dam $ car MFS permit
	4.0 mi R Roll Dam $ car MFS permit

Put in on the left below the dam. The gauge is chiseled into a large rock on the left just downstream from the put-in. This is a fun run with a reading from 1 to 3. It can be run lower (a 0 reading corresponds to 300 cfs), but some of the ledges might be scratchy. At levels higher than 3, some of the hydraulics are keepers.

You travel flat water for 0.75 mile below the dam. The first ledge, Double Hydraulic, sets the mood for the more difficult section below. At a reading of 3, this rapid has a keeper in the middle. The best run is on the extreme right.

Another 0.5 mile of flat water leads to a more continuous section of ledges. The ledges range in height up to 5 feet with a clean chute through each one. Generally, the ledges can be scouted on the right side, if desired. The exception to the scout-right rule is a line of rocks that seems to block the river. The best route here at low water is on the extreme left, while higher water opens up a route on the extreme right.

The maze section follows. It features huge rocks in the center and a choice of routes, with the most exciting surfing and ender possibilities on the left. A pool leads to the last ledge in this section, which features a pour-over in the center. Go right. The take-out is just below on the right, either before or after a final small ledge.

At low water, the ledges might look intimidating, but a good rescue pool is below each one. The run is considered Class III at low levels. Higher levels result in more powerful holes and cross-currents and are considered Class IV.

ROLL DAM CAMPSITE ➤ RIPOGENUS DAM   43.5 MI

Description:	Lakes, flatwater, Class I
Navigable:	Spring, summer, fall
Scenery:	Wild
Maps:	North East Carry 15, Caucomgomoc Lake 15, Chesuncook 15, Ragged Lake 15, Harrington Lake 15, DL 49 and 50
Portage:	43.5 mi R Ripogenus Dam 2.5 mi by car
Campsites:	8 sites between Roll Dam and Pine Stream BPR
	21.0 mi R Pine Stream
	24.0 mi R Boom House
	8 sites on Chesuncook Lake
	41.5 mi R Chesuncook Dam $ car

This is the smoothwater section of the West Branch. Below Roll Dam Campsite the river continues with moderate current to North Easy Carry (4.25 miles).

Lobster Stream enters on the right in 2.5 miles. Sometimes it flows backward into Lobster Lake when the West Branch is rising.

Lobster Lake, which has several attractive campsites, makes a good side trip. The lake is an easy 2.0-mile paddle via Lobster Stream. The bridge for the private road from North Easy Carry crosses Lobster Stream just above the confluence with the West Branch.

In the remaining 17.25 miles you find a variety of campsites, some of which are listed above. The current slows, becoming flowage from the lake for the last several miles. The bridge on the Ragmuff/Caucogomoc private road crosses at 11.0 miles. Look for Lone Pine campsite on river right and Ouellette's campsite on river left as you approach Big Island (16.0 miles). At Boom House campsite (24.0 miles), the river opens up into Chesuncook Lake. The main issue to be reckoned with on Chesuncook Lake is the wind. Use good judgment in dealing with it.

Chesuncook Dam (41.5 miles) near the southeastern end is a convenient take-out point. You find no dam there, just the site of a dam flooded out by the present Ripogenus Dam (43.5 miles) 3.0 miles to the east at the end of Ripogenus Lake.

If you are continuing down the West Branch, you must portage 2.5 miles along the road on the southern bank from Rip Dam to Big Eddy because Ripogenus Gorge is impassable to loaded canoes. See the *AMC Classic Northeastern Whitewater Guide* by Bruce Lessels for further information.

RIPOGENUS GORGE ➤ MCKAY STATION   1.5 MI

Description:	Class III, IV
Navigable:	Spring, summer, fall: controlled release
	recommended level 800 to 2,000 cfs only
Scenery:	Wild
Maps:	Harrington Lake 15, DL 50

This run begins just below the dam with a short but exceedingly difficult portage. This is a run for experienced decked boaters only after thorough and complete scouting. The most difficult drop is the last one.

MCKAY STATION ➤ BIG EDDY   2.5 MI

Description:	Class IV, V
Navigable:	Spring, summer, fall: controlled release
	cfs below 1,000 is dangerous
	cfs from 1,500 to 2,300 is recommended
	cfs above 2,300 becomes very pushy
	cfs above 4,500 approaches Class VI
Scenery:	Wild
Maps:	Harrington Lake 15, DL 50

This is a difficult whitewater run and is only for expert boaters. The access road to the river is now gated, and a fee is being charged per vehicle. The fee includes camping, too, unless you choose to camp in a privately owned campground.

The gorge is about 220 yards long and is a series of 30-foot standing waves, which ends in Exterminator, a Class IV set of very large waves ending in a hole. You can run the left side of the gorge and avoid most of the waves and Exterminator (a good idea). But even on the left side, you must cross a number of small diagonal holes that tend to draw you toward the center of the river. You come upon an eddy on the left opposite Exterminator and another eddy farther down on the left, right before the drop into Staircase Rapid. Staircase is a Class IV+ rapid that consists of a series of four very large holes. It is important to note that the character of Staircase changes dramatically with a change of water level.

Just after Staircase is an eddy that gives you a chance to catch your breath. Here you can decide whether you want to run Little Heater, a Class IV cascade that is 7 feet high, on the right of the island, or Big Heater, a Class III rapid on the left. Shortly afterward, you leave the gorge and enter Little Eddy which can be a take-out or a put-in on the left.

Below Little Eddy is a Class II–III rapid about 220 yards long. You also gain an excellent view of the Katahdin skyline. In about 330 yards, you come to Troublemaker Rapid (Class IV), which contains several small holes and a very strong breaking standing wave. Next are 220 yards of Class II rapid before the last eddy ahead of Cribwork Rapid. You can see Telos Bridge. Take out before the bridge on the right to portage Cribwork; take out on the left to scout Cribwork before deciding whether to run it.

Cribwork Rapid is long (about 660 yards). It is a very heavy Class V rapid with no way to stop in the middle. It must be scouted. (Watch someone else run it first if possible.) As you pass under the bridge, you pass Telos Hole, which guards the rapid. From here, it is a wild and rocky rapid, dropping more than 25 feet. Do not underestimate the difficulty of the entrance to the rapid. If you get off your line at the top, the rest of the run could easily become disastrous. **Caution!** If you feel any hesitation, do not run it! Remember that better paddlers than you have walked this rapid!

You barely have time to recover after Cribwork before you enter Bone Cruncher (2.0 miles), a Class IV rapid with large holes and waves. The remaining distance is Class I to Big Eddy Rapid, Class III.

Description:	Class II, III, IV, V
Navigable:	Spring, summer, fall: controlled release up to 3,000 cfs recommended
Scenery:	Forested
Maps:	Harrington Lake 15, Katahdin 15, Norcross 15, DL 50 and 42
Portages:	2.25 mi R Big Ambejackmockamus Falls
	6.0 mi L Nesourdnahunk Falls
	11.0 mi R Pockwockomus Falls
	13.75 mi L Debsconeag Falls, on a dirt road
Campsites:	0 mi Big Eddy private $ car
	Many additional campsites

This section is one of the most scenic along the Penobscot's many branches. It also contains some heavy rapids that are separated by considerable lengths of deadwater. Many paddlers set up mini-shuttles along the river to cut out the flatwater stretches.

The regular text is for boaters who wish to run rapids up to Class III. The text in italics is for experts in whitewater boats.

It is 1.0 mile to Little Ambejackmockamus Falls, a Class II or III drop, depending on the water level. Beyond 1.0 mile and past some rapids, take out on the right where the road is close to the river at a sharp left turn (2.25 miles) in order to carry around Big Ambejack-mockamus Falls (Big A).

Big A is 0.25 mile of standing waves leading to a Class IV drop with a very large, dangerous keeper in the center. At the second drop, run right or left because another hole is in the center. The third drop has a large wave with a pool at the bottom. Each drop should be scouted on the right.

A short distance below Big A, the Horserace begins, a long rocky Class II–II+ rapid. If the water level is not right, or if you are inexperienced, carry 1.5 miles around both Big Ambejackmockamus Falls and the Horserace to Nesourdnahunk Deadwater.

After 2.0 miles of deadwater, take out above the ledge on the left and carry Sourdnahunk Falls (6.0 miles).

Nesourdnahunk Falls is another Class IV. As you turn left in Class III rapids, the river goes over a falls with an 11-foot drop. The right is rocky, although at the correct water level the water covers a smooth rock that can be used as a slide to make the drop. The left is a very heavy run over the drop into a large hole with about ten standing waves below, followed by 330 yards of Class II rapids. You can carry back up and do the drop several times.

At the end of the carry around Nesourdnahunk Falls is the 3.0-mile Abol Deadwater, which extends to some Class I rips under the Abol bridge (0.5 mile above Abol Falls). An easy Class II is above Abol Falls (10.0 miles). Stay along the right bank; the portage begins at a small beach right after a large one, and close to the falls. Follow the roads and take a left. A cabin faces the falls, which is visible from above.

Abol Falls is another Class IV rapid. It is 275 yards long and full of very large rocks and waves. The right has smaller waves and many rocks. The center has bigger waves and holes and fewer rocks. The run behind the island on the right is very narrow with large rocks.

Quick water continues for 0.5 mile; then easy Class II rapids lead to a cabin on the right, marking Pockwockamus Falls (11.0 miles). Portage along the road on the right and then take the third left to the bottom of the falls. A shorter trail begins close to the top of Pockwockamus Falls.

Big Pockwockamus Falls (Class IV) is characterized by large rocks and many standing waves. Scout from the right, and locate the large hole on the right about 100 yards into the rapids. Find a good marker on shore so that you have something to sight from to miss this hole.

Pockwockamus deadwater extends for 2.5 miles to Debsconeag Falls (13.75 miles), which can be portaged on either side. The portage on the left begins 100 yards above the falls in a small cove and is about 0.5 mile long. The portage on the right is below a large island in a tiny clearing where the bank is steep but only 3 feet high. The portage is 620 yards up a hill and down to the end of the falls.

Debsconeag Falls is a very dangerous Class V rapid that starts off with two huge holes (keepers) at the top. It is necessary to make the move around these holes. You come upon several other large holes before the rapid ends. This is the hardest rapid in this section of the river; if you attempt to run it, scout on the left and run it in several sections.

You face a drop with a big wave; then it is a 3.0-mile paddle across Debsconeag Deadwater to Passamagamet Falls (17.0 miles), a

Class III rocky drop with two chutes. In 1.75 miles, you reach Ambejejus Falls, although high water in the lake below might flood them out. The river soon opens into Ambejejus Lake (19.0 miles).

In Spencer Cove, 3.25 miles to the east, the road to Baxter State Park comes close to the lake (22.25 miles).

SPENCER COVE ➤ ME 11 (QUAKISH LAKE)   11.0 MI

Description:	Lakes
Navigable:	Spring, summer, fall
Scenery:	Forested
Maps:	Norcross 15, Millinocket 15, DL 43

From Spencer Cove it is 4.0 miles across Ambejejus Lake and the end of Pemadumcook Lake to Nicks Gut, where you pass into North Twin Lake, and an additional 5.0 miles down that to Elbow Lake. You can make a detour here into South Twin Lake, which is about the same size. It is 1.0 mile across Elbow Lake to the dam, which must be carried. Then travel 1.0 mile of river, passing under ME 11 halfway down, to Quakish Lake.

ME 11 ➤ SHAD POND, VIA WEST BRANCH   6.5 MI

Description:	Flatwater, Class III, IV
Navigable:	Spring: sometimes
Scenery:	Forested, towns
Maps:	Millinocket 15, DL 43
Portage:	1.0 mi Quakish Dam

The distance from the boat-launching ramp at ME 11 to Quakish Dam is 2.0 miles. The dam diverts most of the water to power plants, but during spring runoff this stretch is sometimes possible. This historic stretch contains Blue Rock Pitch and Grand Falls, 3.0 miles below the dam, and runs into Shad Pond.

QUAKISH DAM ➤ SHAD POND   3.5 MI
(ALTERNATE ROUTE VIA MILLINOCKET STREAM)

Description:	Lakes, quickwater
Navigable:	Spring, summer, fall
Scenery:	Towns, forested
Maps:	Norcross 15, Millinocket 15, DL 43

When no water is in the West Branch, through travelers might be able to paddle the mile to the outlet of Ferguson Pond and portage through the Great Northern Paper Company mill to Millinocket Stream. Millinocket Stream is followed for 2.25 miles to Shad Pond.

SHAD POND ➤ EAST BRANCH PENOBSCOT   5.5 MI
(ALTERNATE ROUTE VIA MILLINOCKET STREAM)

Description:	Flatwater, quickwater
Navigable:	Spring, summer, fall
Scenery:	Towns
Maps:	Millinocket 15, DL 43
Portages:	1.75 mi 60-foot dam
	3.5 mi dam at East Millinocket
	5.0 mi dam at Bethel Church

You can put in or take out at Rice Farm on the left, at the entrance to Dolby Flowage. At the end of this is a 60-foot-high dam. In another 1.5 miles you reach the somewhat lower dam at East Millinocket. It is then only 1.5 miles more to the last dam at Bethel Church; 0.5 mile below, the West Branch meets the East Branch to form the main Penobscot River. Few people paddle the West Branch below Millinocket because of the numerous dams and the presence of heavy industry (paper mills).

Penobscot River (South Branch)

The South Branch flows from the border mountains northwest of Jackman to Seboomook Lake. Its upper part is too steep and too small for paddling even in high water. The lower part, below Canada Falls Dam, has a series of ledges so that a portage along the road to Pittston Farm is recommended. Although the middle section provides a fast run in high water, it is not worth the effort of getting to the put-in point, especially because you can find better and more accessible rivers in the same general area. The upper part of the watershed contains only a few ponds, so the water level drops rapidly after spring runoff.

BRIDGE ➤ CANADA FALLS DAM   17.5 MI

Description:	Lake, Class I, II
Navigable:	High water: May
Scenery:	Wild
Maps:	Andy Bay, Penobscot Lake 15, Seboomook Lake 15, DL 47 and 48
Portage:	(17.5 mi ledges 3.0 mi [by car])
Campsite:	17.5 mi L Canada Falls Dam MFS $ car

A private road from US 201 about 12.0 miles northwest of Jackman follows the southern bank of the South Branch for 8.0 miles until it crosses the river 3.0 miles downstream from Little Canada Falls. The bridge is out, however.

Shallow rapids flow for about 2.0 miles to Kellher Falls, a sharp ledge drop that cannot be run and is difficult to line. This section can be carried on the left. Always remember to ask for and obtain permission before crossing property lines.

The next 9.5 miles to Canada Falls Lake (11.5 miles) are mostly good current with shallow rapids. It is 6.0 miles across the lake to Canada Falls Dam (17.5 miles) at the end of the northeastern arm.

The remaining 3.5 miles to Seboomook Lake contain several severe ledge drops that cannot be run or lined through. It is recommended that this section be portaged using the road to Pittston Farm on Seboomook Lake.

CANADA FALLS DAM ➤ SEBOOMOOK LAKE   3.5 MI

Description:	Class IV, V
Navigable:	Spring: May–early June
Scenery:	Wild
Maps:	Seboomook Lake 15, DL 48
Portage:	1.0 mi R 20-foot waterfall 150 yd
Campsite:	Canada Falls Dam MFS $ car

Put in below Canada Falls Dam at the campground there. You can find a gauge painted on a rock at the put-in. High water is over 1 on the gauge, medium is 0 to 0.75, and low is below 0. **Caution!** If the water is over 1, do not run it! If you cannot easily handle Class IV rapids, do not run at any level. This is a Class IV+ run at medium water and a Class III+ at low water, with some shallow spots. It has one mandatory carry around a 20-foot waterfall and five difficult Class IV+ drops that are very difficult to portage.

The first 0.25 mile is quick water, followed by a Class III drop. Another 0.25 mile below this is a Class IV gorge about 400 yards long. Another 0.5 mile (1.0 miles) below this gorge is a small island in the river. Be extremely careful here because the waterfall is just 20 feet below the island. Take the channel on the right side of the island and portage to the bottom of the falls.

The next 0.75 mile contains two Class II rapids. After this, watch carefully at every river bend for a rocky cliff on the right shore and a cabin across from it on the left bank. As soon as you can see the cabin, eddy out immediately; this is the start of Cabin Rapid, a Class III+ with very heavy current that flows into a nasty souse hole. Scout and/or carry on the left. Most boaters catch the eddy on the right just yards above the hole, then ferry to an eddy on the left from where they can take the left channel. If you have had any problems getting downriver to this point, take out at the cabin. This is the closest the road comes to the river; the rapids below are much more difficult and dangerous.

After Cabin Rapid, you enter a gorge with sheer rock cliffs. Into the gorge 0.25 mile is the first of three Class IV+, V drops within a 40-yard distance. The first drop is marked by a large rock outcropping in the middle of the river. It has been run on both sides; take a long, hard look at both sides because a swim here means a swim through the next two drops. A carry trail is on the left from which you can also scout the next two drops. The second drop is just like the first—a large rock outcropping in the middle of the river that can be run on either side. The third drop is marked by a near river-wide hydraulic that is a keeper. The only soft spot is on the left side of the hole, but it requires a very difficult approach only a few feet from a drop into the reversal.

After the gorge is a short Class III+ S-turn, then a Class II+, III and finally flat water to the bridge and the take-out.

Penobscot River (North Branch)

The North Branch flows from Little Bog south to Seboomook Lake where it joins the South Branch to form the West Branch. Because few lakes and swamps are here to provide headwater storage, this section can be run only during early spring runoff. The lower position contains broad sandbars; usually after May low water makes paddling impossible.

Access to Little Bog is by private logging road. The trip can also begin at Big Bog. You can find several bridges out on the private logging roads in this area, but it is usually possible to ford the river.

BIG BOG DAM ➤ PITTSTON FARM   **20.75 MI**

Description:	Class II, III
Navigable:	High water: May
Scenery:	Wild
Maps:	Norris Brook 15, Penobscot Lake 15, Seboomook Lake 15, DL 48

Most of this river has good current with shallow rapids. You come upon a bridge 4.5 miles below the put-in point at Big Bog Dam, and in 4.25 miles you reach the mouth of Dole Brook (8.75 miles). You travel easy rapids and smooth water for the 7.25 miles to Leadbetter Falls (16.0 miles). This is a short rapid under a bridge, which can be run in medium water but which is difficult in high water. In 4.0 miles, the river opens into a bay at the end of Seboomook Lake (20.0 miles), with Pittston Farm beyond on the right (20.75 miles).

It is a 12.75-mile paddle down Seboomook Lake from the mouth of the North Branch to Seboomook Dam (32.75 miles).

Nesowadnehunk Stream

Nesowadnehunk Stream (locally spelled *Sourdnahunk* and pronounced "sourdihunk") originates in Little Nesowadnehunk Lake on the Penobscot side of the divide south of Telos Lake and in a steep 1.0 mile of travel runs into Nesowadnehunk Lake. Below this lake, enlarged by the lumbermen to run logs down the river below, the stream flows south for 17.0 miles to the West Branch of the Penobscot about 0.5 mile below the Sourdnahunk Falls, in the Abol Deadwater. Because the water level is controlled at the dam, it can be run almost anytime down to the

Daicey Pond Brook (about 13.0 miles), but Baxter State Park authorities discourage running more than the first 5.0 miles down to Campground 5 at Sourdnahunk Field. The lower end of the stream is a tumultuous descent over falls and cascades to the Penobscot; unrunnable, but well worth a visit on foot.

NESOWADNEHUNK LAKE ➤ CAMPGROUND 5   5.0 MI

Description:	Class I, II
Navigable:	Medium water
Scenery:	Wild
Maps:	Telos Lake 15, DL 50

Nesowadnehunk Lake is a large body of water 5.0 miles long and 1.5 miles wide. The Sourdnahunk Tote Road from Baxter Park reaches the lake at the outlet dam. You can put in below the dam and enjoy a fine 5.0-mile run down easy water (mostly Class I and II rapids with numerous pools in between) to Sourdnahunk Fields where the road from Ripogenus Dam crosses. This is a delightful and easy run that offers fine views of Mounts Veto and Doubletop on the right and Katahdin with its subsidiary peaks on the left.

CAMPGROUND 5 ➤ DAICEY POND BROOK   8.0 MI

Description:	Class I, II, III
Navigable:	Spring, summer, fall
Scenery:	Wild
Maps:	Harrington Lake 15, DL 50
Portages:	2.0 mi L Ledge Falls 100 yd
	Lower river impassable

This is a considerably more difficult section and should be undertaken by experts only, as the river drops sharply with pools in between the drops. Ledge Falls is a natural rock falls. Then it is Class I–II for 1.75 miles to the washed-out Slide Dam, with 250 yards of Class III below; scout from the left. The river is then easier for the 2.0 miles to the road crossing for the Kidney Pond Camps. This is an easy spot to take out. About 2.0 miles below here is the Appalachian Trail crossing, about 0.25 mile above the Daicey Pond Brook. You can take out here and carry a short distance to the Daicey Pond Camp road.

River travel is possible for another 1.0 mile, but you have no way to take out except by poling back upstream. The old toll dam there marks the beginning of the wild plunge down to the Penobscot.

Nahmakanta Stream (via Debsconeag Lakes)

Nahmakanta Stream is a tributary of the Penobscot River (West Branch) at Pemadumcook Lake. It flows from Mahmakanta Lake, a medium-sized lake situated among the low mountains southwest of Baxter State Park. The beginning of this stream can be reached from Debsconeag Deadwater on the West Branch via the Debsconeag Lakes.

A circuit trip from Spencer Cove on Ambejejus Lake, up the West Branch, through the Debsconeag Lakes, and down Nahmakanta Stream to Pemadumcook Lake is a 3- or 4-day trip through relatively isolated country. The Debsconeag Lakes are clear and in rugged settings, but you face several long portages on this approach to Nahmakanta Lake. Nahmakanta Stream provides a short but enjoyable run in May.

PENOBSCOT RIVER (WEST BRANCH) ➤
NAHMAKANTA LAKE   **10.25 MI**

Description:	Lakes
Navigable:	Spring, summer, fall
Scenery:	Wild
Maps:	Abol Pond, Rainbow Lake East, Rainbow Lake West, Wadleigh Mountain 7.5, DL 42 and 50
Portages:	2.5 mi L into Second Debsconeag Lake 0.75 mi
	4.75 L toward Third Debsconeag Lake 400 yd
	5.0 mi into Third Debsconeag Lake
	7.5 mi R into Fourth Debsconeag Lake 0.5 mi
	9.0 mi R into Nahmakanta Lake 1.25 mi
Campsite:	0.5 mi R First Debsconeag Lake (beach at eastern end) permit

Keep to the west of the island that encloses the northern end of Debsconeag Deadwater and follow the short passage westward into First Debsconeag Lake. The latter is 2.0 miles long. At the western end (2.5 miles), a 0.75-mile portage leads to Second Debsconeag Lake. (The portage trail forks near the middle; go right.)

On the southern shore of Second Debsconeag Lake near the west end, a small brook enters the lake. The portage (4.75 miles) begins just east of this brook and ends at a small pool above an abandoned driving dam. A 100-yard paddle leads to the third portage, a 30-yard scramble into Third Debsconeag Lake.

Third Debsconeag Lake (5.0 miles) is the largest of these lakes and is roughly horseshoe-shaped. The portage to Fourth Debsconeag Lake leaves a short distance before the end of a narrow western arm.

The portage to Nahmakanta Stream follows a dirt road to a bridge over the stream just below Nahmakanta lake. Begin this portage at a landing on the western shore a short distance from the southwestern end of the lake.

Nahmakanta Stream

NAHMAKANTA LAKE ➤ PEMADUMCOOK LAKE   5.25 MI

Description:	Quickwater, Class I, II
Navigable:	High water: May
Scenery:	Wild
Maps:	Harrington Lake 15, Jo-Mary Mountain 15, Norcross 15, DL 50, 42, and 43
Campsites:	9.0 mi R shelter on Appalachian Trail
	5.0 mi R
	7.75 mi L 2 sites
	9.5 mi R
	12.0 mi R Pemadumcook Lake car

Nahmakanta Stream begins at the southeastern end of Nahmakanta Lake. At the right-hand bend below the bridge is a narrow 200-yard Class III rapid that can be scouted or portaged most easily on the right bank. Following a 0.25-mile deadwater, you come to a succession of short, easy Class I and II rapids, which are all separated by pools. These extend for about 1.0 mile.

Then you reach a second 0.25-mile section of flat water (1.5 miles), followed by more short rapids and a nice 0.5-mile Class II rapid that extends through about a half dozen bends in the river before it ends at a pool (2.75 miles). Then you come upon another 1.0 mile of short, easy Class I and II rapids with pools or quick water between them. The last 1.5 miles are mostly quick water with a few easy rapids.

From the mouth of Nahmakanta Stream (5.25 miles), it is 10.25 miles down Pemadumcook Lake and across Ambejejus Lake to Spencer Cover (15.5 miles) on the road from Millinocket to Baxter State Park.

Millinocket Stream

Millinocket Stream is the outlet of the Millinocket Lake north of Baxter State Park and a tributary of the Aroostook River. It should not be confused with another Millinocket Stream, which is the outlet of another Millinocket Lake and a tributary of the West Branch of the Penobscot. Millinocket Lake can be reached by a short portage from a branch road from the Grand Lake Road. Inquire locally for directions.

MILLINOCKET LAKE ➤ LIBBY CAMP   6.0 MI

Description:	Lakes, flatwater, Class I, II
Navigable:	Spring, summer, fall: controlled releases
Scenery:	Wild
Maps:	Millinocket Lake 15, DL 57

Portage the dam at Millinocket Lake. It is a short distance to Round Pond, with an old logging dam at the outlet. Just below is Millinocket Falls, a short Class I–II rapid, which should be scouted from the left bank. This is followed by 1.5 miles of Class II rapids to Millimagassett Stream. You can ascend 0.5 mile of stream and 0.5 mile of log sluice to Millimagassett Lake, which features beautiful islands and a view of Baxter Park mountains.

Below are 1.5 miles of deadwater and 0.5 mile of Class I water to the bridge at Moosehorn Crossing. This is followed by 1.0 mile of quick water to Devil's Elbow, a 0.5-mile series of Class II ledge drops. It is then 0.5 mile to Libby Camp, where Munsungan Stream joins up to form the Aroostook River.

Mooseleuk Stream

The swift Mooseleuk Stream, which rises in Mooseleuk Lake just off the American Realty Road in T10 R9, is one of the major tributaries of the upper Aroostook River. The trip can make an excellent weekend in the wild. Beware of being swept into the bushes in the many bends.

MOOSELEUK LAKE ➤ OLD FIRE WARDEN'S CAMP 18.0 MI

Description:	Lake, quickwater, Class I
Navigable:	High water: spring
Scenery:	Wild
Maps:	Mooseleuk Lake 15, Millinocket Lake 15, Grand Lake Seboeis 15; DL 56 and 57

It is a very pretty 2.0-mile paddle down Mooseleuk Lake to the outlet and the remains of an old logging dam. At once you enter a swift stream (Class I) with many sharp bends. At 10.0 miles the large, heavily used Pinkham Road bridge crosses just above Chandler Stream. In 2.0 more miles, you negotiate a sharp right bend in the stream to Boars Head Falls, where the river narrows into Class II rapids. Boars Head Falls is an excellent camping spot. It is only 3.0 more miles to the Aroostook River, in a large deadwater just below the privately owned (old) fire warden's camp.

Saint Croix Stream

The Saint Croix Stream rises in Saint Croix Lake in T8 R4 and flows north to the Aroostook River at Masardis. Although the Bangor and Aroostook Railroad parallels the stream, it is a very wild area full of history of past logging days. The stream is a large one and drains a large swamp above the Saint Croix River, so it makes good paddling in all but the lowest water season. The stream varies from smooth to very rough water in the middle section.

HOWE BROOK ➤ AROOSTOOK RIVER   18.0 MI

Description:	Lake, quickwater, Class II, III+
Navigable:	High water: difficult
	Medium water: excellent
	Low water: scratchy
Scenery:	Wild
Maps:	Howe Brook 15, Oxbow 15, DL 58

You have about 1.0 mile of lake-like river below the lake before you enter Saint Croix Stream. From here, it is 5.0 miles of slow swampy paddling to a bridge where the water quickens, with several sets of Class II rapids and a falls, which is a Class III+ stretch of water with ledges. This can be run, lined, or carried on the right side. In 0.5 mile, you reach Pride; then 4.0 miles of Class II whitewater take you from Pride to Griswold (9.5 miles). In Griswold are the remains of an old mill site with a very nice chute (Class II+). Below Griswold are 7.0 miles of flat swampy stream, until the Blackwater River enters on the right (16.5 miles). Below is a section filled with rocks, which can be hard going in low water. In another 1.5 miles, you reach Masardis and the US 1 bridge, below which is the confluence with the Aroostook River.

Squa Pan Stream

Squa Pan Lake, south of Castle Hill, is a dogleg-shaped lake about 15.0 miles long and 1.0 mile wide, for the most part wild and unspoiled. The outlet stream is short but swift and flows into the Aroostook River above Ashland.

SQUA PAN LAKE ➤ AROOSTOOK RIVER   3.0 MI

Description:	Flatwater, quickwater, Class I, II
Navigable:	Whenever dam is open; call WPS New England
	(207-493-4589) for information.
Scenery:	Wild, rural
Maps:	Ashland 15, Presque Isle 15, DL 58

When the water is low, you can see the remains of the original dam a few miles up the lake.

The dam and bridge at the outlet must be carried about 100 yards on either side. Below the bridge are continuous Class II rapids for 2.5 miles. In this distance, the river drops 63 feet through wild, wooded country. Then you go under several railroad bridges and, finally, the ME 11 bridge into a deadwater for the last 0.5 mile to the Aroostook River.

Sandy Stream

Millinocket Lake has one major tributary: Sandy Stream. It drains the southeastern flank of Mount Katahdin. The upper sections of Sandy Stream are too steep to paddle, but the lower part, reachable by Togue Stream, is runnable. These streams are remote, and they are only occasionally run. Access to Togue Stream is possible only after the ice has gone out of Lower Togue Pond; that usually occurs in early May.

The first 1.0 mile of Togue Stream is the hardest. Where you have drops in elevation—you cannot really call them rapids—you also have a combination of large rocks, overhanging trees, and jackstrawed logs that requires you to line the boat. Portaging is not an easy alternative, so you must resign yourself to working the boat slowly downstream, snaking around some obstructions here and sawing some logs there. Improvements made one year are likely to be undone in the high water of the next. Patience, determination, and about 2 hours bring you to a large beaver pond. From that point, the river is virtually unobstructed, and for the next 2.0 miles you find yourself in a very wild section of Baxter State Park.

The flow in Sandy Stream is subject to rapid fluctuations because of the steepness of the upper watershed. The stream has only a few ponds and swamps in its headwater, so the water level is responsive to a heavy rain fall or a rapid melting of the snow.

Description:	Lakes, quickwater, Class I, II
Navigable:	High water: heavy rain or rapid snowmelt
	Medium water: May
Scenery:	Wild
Maps:	Katahdin 15, Norcross 15, Millinocket 15, DL 51
Campsite:	10.5 mi L mouth of Sandy Stream permit

Lower Togue Pond lies just inside of the southern boundary of Baxter State Park, and the road from Millinocket to the park goes along the western shore. The entrance of Togue Stream (1.25 miles) is on the northeastern shore of the pond, but the exact location is difficult to see unless you are close to it.

In the first 100 yards of Togue Stream is a short, lineable drop; in the middle of the drop is an old, rotting bridge that you can just sneak under in medium water. For most of the next mile, short navigable sections alternate with others where lining and some clearing is necessary. After a couple of hours of slow progress, you reach a large beaver pond (2.25 miles) that is several hundred yards long. It is located along the northernmost portion of the stream.

For the next 2.75 miles, you travel a mixture of flat water, quick water, and Class I rapids. Then you come upon a 50-yard, Class II rapid immediately above the confluence with Sandy Stream (5.0 miles).

Sandy Stream is much larger than Togue Stream. The first half consists mostly of quick water over small stones with gravel bars and wide, sweeping turns. An occasional overhanging tree constitutes Sandy Stream's primary hazard.

In 3.0 miles, you reach a 50-yard, Class II rapid that begins at a washed-out driving dam (8.0 miles). After 1.0 mile of flat water, you come to Red Pine Rapids (9.0 miles), a 0.25-mile pitch that is Class II in medium water and Class III in high water. It extends through an S-turn, and it can be easily scouted from or portaged along the left bank. The final 1.25 miles to Millinocket Lake (10.5 miles) are smooth.

Take out at the dike between Millinocket Lake and Spencer Cove on Ambejejus Lake (15.0 miles).

Penobscot River (East Branch)

The East Branch drains the region north and northeast of Mount Katahdin. It has also been the recipient of part of the Allagash drainage since the construction of Telos Dam in 1841. In that year, three other dams were constructed along the Allagash, making it possible to drive logs from the upper Allagash region down the East Branch rather than north to the St. John River. Today, Telos and Grand Lake Matagamon Dams store water for use in power generation farther downstream.

Generally you find sufficient water in Webster Stream through early June. The East Branch is navigable for much of the season. The lakes are usually drawn down from mid-September to mid-October, providing a good flow at that time.

You can travel by canoe or kayak from the West Branch to the East Branch using the two access routes described in Chapter 5, "Allagash Wilderness Waterway."

GRAND LAKE DAM ➤ MEDWAY   47.5 MI

Description:	Class I, II, III
Navigable:	Spring, summer, fall: controlled release
	High water difficult, medium water
	recommended, low water passable but thin
Scenery:	Wild
Maps:	Traveler Mountain 15, Shin Pond 15, Stacyville
	15, Millinocket 15, DL 51 and 43
Portages:	Many, depending on water level
Campsites:	0.75 mi L Grand Lake Road (bridge) private $ car
	9.75 mi L Grand Pitch permit
	23.5 mi L Lunksoos Camp MFS car
	27.25 mi L Whetstone Falls (between rapids)
	MFS car

From just below Grand Lake Matagamon Road bridge, where you find a few rapids, smooth water for 4.5 miles takes you to Stair Falls (5.25 miles), a series of shallow ledges. They are best run on the left if water level permits; if it does not, you can also use a portage on the left. Then for 1.25 miles, you travel quick water to Haskell Deadwater, below which is Haskell Rock Pitch (7.0 miles), the first of four falls on the East Branch. (The USGS Traveler Mountain

Sheet shows Haskell Rock Pitch in the wrong location.) You find a 0.5-mile portage on the right. In the next 1.0 mile to Pond Pitch (7.75 miles), the second falls, you go through three sets of rapids. A portage is on the left.

Below Pond Pitch, in 0.75 mile, you reach Grand Pitch (9.75 miles), the third and most spectacular of the Grand Falls of the East Branch. The portage is on the left. About 0.5 mile beyond is Hulling Machine Pitch, the fourth falls. Stop above the rapids just above the falls, and portage on the right. Less than 1.0 mile below these falls is Bowline Falls, a short Class II rapid. If you run it, starting on the far right is recommended. Mostly smooth water continues for the remaining 9.0 miles to the mouth of Sebeois River (21.0 miles).

Flat water continues for the next 6.0 miles to Whetstone Falls (27.0 miles). These consist of two sets of rapids separated by fast water. The upper section, Class III, can be run by experienced paddlers in medium water. The lower part is easier in medium water. It can be difficult in high water. At Lunksoos Camp (23.5 miles), as well as above the bridge at Lower Whetstone Falls, the MFS campsites offer good access to the river.

The next rapids are in 9.0 miles at Crowfoot Falls, Class II or III, depending on the water level. After another 2.25 miles, below a railroad bridge, is Grindstone Falls. This is a Class III–IV rapid, which should be run empty. The first drop is best run on the left; the remainder (about 0.5 mile of heavy rapids even at medium water) is runnable between the shore and the main current.

The last 9.0 miles to the confluence with the West Branch (47.5 miles) in Medway are mostly smooth, except for Meadowbrook Rips (40.5 miles) and Ledge Falls (45.0 miles). The latter are difficult in high water. You pass under the ME 157 bridge (47.0 miles) 0.5 mile before reaching the West Branch.

Webster Stream

Webster Stream flows from Telos Lake through a human-made canal to Webster Lake and then on to Grand Lake Matagamon. Because most of the stream and much of Grand Lake lie within the boundaries of Baxter State Park, campsites must be arranged and paid for in advance with the park office.

TELOS LANDING ➤ GRAND LAKE DAM   24.0 MI

Description:	Class I, II, III
Navigable:	Spring, summer, fall: controlled release
	High water (over 600 cfs) difficult, dangerous
	Medium water (300-500 cfs) recommended
	Low water (100-150 cfs) skinny but runnable
Scenery:	Wild
Maps:	Telos Lake 15, Traveler Mountain 15, DL 50, 56,
	57, and 51
Portages:	2.0 mi R Telos Dam 25 yd
	14.5 mi R Grand Pitch 0.5 mi
Campsites:	0 mi Telos Landing AWW $ car
	4.5 mi R Webster Stream lean-to
	8.0 mi R Little East Branch Grand Lake (5 sites)
	24.75 mi L Grand Lake Road (below dam) private
	$ car

From the end of the Allagash Wilderness Waterway access road at Telos Landing, it is 2.0 miles to Telos Dam. Below the dam, a 1.0-mile canal leads to Webster Lake. The flow is controlled at the dam, and you can often arrange for water to be let through for paddling. It is a fast run in medium water. From the end of the canal, it is 3.0 miles across the lake to the outlet (6.0 miles).

The first 6.5 miles from Webster Lake to Indian Carry (12.5 miles) are mostly shallow rapids and fast current. Indian Carry in medium water is a Class III rapid that can be run by experts. However, it requires very difficult maneuvering, and it is recommended that this drop be carried on the right bank.

The next 2.0 miles to Grand Pitch (14.5 miles) contain several very difficult Class III ledge drops, which can be run by experts in medium water. At Grand Pitch, obscure portage trails on each side of the stream require considerable effort to carry this falls. A 0.5-mile alternative on the right bank follows a trail that leads to a logging road. It bypasses the main falls as well as two more severe ledge drops 0.5 mile below these falls.

You reach Grand Lake Matagamon (15.75 miles) 0.5 mile below the last drop, and 8.25 miles down the lake is the dam (24.0 miles), which you portage on the right.

Seboeis River

The Seboeis River flows from Grand Lake Seboeis south to the East Branch of the Penobscot, joining the latter 21.0 miles below the Grand Lake Matagamon Dam. It offers a good alternative to the upper section of the East Branch. Because it has no difficult rapids and only one short carry around a pretty, though impassable, falls, it is particularly suitable for inexperienced paddlers. It has a continuous, moderate current to its junction with the East Branch and flows through an unspoiled valley. You can find some nice unmarked walks up the hills that flank the river.

The usual starting point is the MFS campground on the Grand Lake Matagamon Road and ME 159 from Patten. Above there, the river has very steep and difficult rapids with poor access and is not recommended for paddling. The first place to take out on the East Branch is at the MFS campsite at Lunksoos Deadwater, 2.5 miles below the mouth of Seboeis River.

The flow drops fast after the spring runoff, and the trip should not be attempted after the second week in June. Good campsites can be found along most of the river, although with good water the river can be run easily in one day.

GRAND LAKE ROAD ➤ EAST BRANCH   17.25 MI

Description:	Class I, II
Navigable:	Spring
Scenery:	Wild
Maps:	Shin Pond 15, Stacyville 15, DL 57 and 51
Portage:	0.25 mi L Grand Pitch 100 yd
Campsite:	0 mi L Grand Lake Road MFS car

Travel 1.25 miles of Class II rapids to Grand Pitch, an unrunnable drop with a 100-yard portage on the left. The approach to the falls is marked first by a small ledge drop and then by a very large, high ledge on the left bank of the river. The remaining 16.0 miles to the East Branch (17.25 miles) contain fairly continuous Class I rapids.

Mattawamkeag River

The Mattawamkeag River is a large tributary of the Penobscot that flows through a big area southwest of Houlton. The West Branch drains two large lakes in addition to extensive swamps; in late spring or early summer, its water level is more dependable than that of the East Branch. Below Island Falls, the river is apt to be runnable after other rivers in northern Maine have become too low.

The Mattawamkeag flows through several small towns, a factor that calls into question the drinkability of the water.

The longest trip on the Mattawamkeag described in this book—some 90.0 miles—begins in Patten on Fish Stream. Unfortunately, you find few established campsites on this trip.

HAYNESVILLE ➤ KINGMAN   34.25 MI

Description:	Flatwater, quickwater, Class I, II
Navigable:	Spring, summer, fall
Scenery:	Forested, rural, towns
Maps:	Amity 15, Danforth 15, Wytopitlock 15, DL 53, 54, and 55
Campsite:	28.25 mi L Meadow Brook permit permission

Here you find two large deadwaters, one below Haynesville and the other beginning at Wytopitlock. They total 19.0 miles in length. The balance is a mixture of smooth and quick water with some rapids. The stretch between Bancroft and Wytopitlock becomes very shallow during dry spells in August possibly necessitating dragging canoes through the scratchiest sections.

In two places, local highways more or less parallel the river for a total of 15.5 miles. Although it is not a wild river in these sections, it is attractive. Below the ME 171 bridge in Wytopitlock, the river flows slowly for 9.75 miles through a large hardwood swamp with almost no evidence of humans.

Rock cribs in the river at Wytopitlock are all that remain from the days of the log drives, which ended about 1950.

Below the US 2A bridge in Haynesville you travel 7.5 miles of deadwater. The deadwater ends 1.0 mile below the Ferry Bridge, where the current picks up to Ledge Falls (9.5 miles), which is wide and about 100 yards long (shallow, but passable in medium water).

As its name implies, it is all ledge. A short distance beyond is a brief, easy rapid.

You find a good current most of the way from Ledge Falls to Wytopitlock. Occasionally, sections are Class I. Below the falls 4.75 miles Baskahegan Stream enters left (14.25 miles), and 4.25 miles farther is the Bancroft railroad bridge (18.5 miles).

The easy traveling ends 1.0 mile above Wytopitlock; after 2.0 miles of deadwater the river flows under the ME 171 bridge (23.25 miles). The Wytopitlock Deadwater continues for another 9.75 miles and ends at a series of Class I–II rapids that last for 1.25 miles and end at the ME 170 bridge in Kingman (34.25 miles). Look for the massive red oak trees near the oxbow.

KINGMAN ➤ MATTAWAMKEAG   12.5 MI

Description:	Flatwater, quickwater, Class II, III, IV, V
Navigable:	Passable at most water levels
Scenery:	Wild, forested
Maps:	Wytopitlock 15, Winn 15, Mattawamkeag 15, DL 44
Portages:	7.25 mi L Heater 300 yd
	8.25 mi L Upper Gordon Falls 50 yd
Campsites:	4.0 mi R First Pitch permit permission
	4.75 mi L Third Pitch $ car

The Mattawamkeag is one of central Maine's outstanding rivers. The best whitewater is found in this section, with five distinct rapids, ranging from Class II to Class IV–V. The Heater involves a difficult 300-yard portage; the portage around Upper Gordon Falls is an easy 50 yards. The description that follows is for springtime levels; the vast watershed of the Mattawamkeag ensures adequate levels for less intense boating in most summers. The Heater and Upper Gordon always demand respect.

Mattawamkeag Wilderness Park, P.O. Box 5, Mattawamkeag, ME 04459 (888-724-2465 or 207-736-2464), abuts the southern bank of the river for 1.0 mile from Scatterack Rapid down. The park offers camping and hiking trails. You can also cut out the flat water at the beginning and end of the trip by putting in at the park above Scatterack and taking out below Lower Gordon Falls. You miss only

Ram's Head Falls. The park road opens in the middle of May. The best 3.0 miles with the easiest shuttle involves putting in at the park gate, above the Heater, and taking out below Lower Gordon Falls.

Put in at the bridge in Kingman or downstream, river left. You can drive a short distance down a gravel road on the left in order to cut out some flat water. You find Ram's Head Falls (Class II–III) after 4.0 miles of paddling. The start is a small gorge with heavy waves. A short pool leads to the second half of Ram's Head.

Scatterack (Class II–III) begins after 0.75 mile of flat water. The heaviest waves are on the left. A sand beach follows, marking the Mattawamkeag Wilderness Park camping area. Slewgundy Heater (Class III–IV at spring levels) follows.

The entrance to the Heater is a series of standing waves. Eddy out left before entering the gorge. The Mattawamkeag is a large river that is narrowed down tremendously at this point. High water finds large exploding waves. You can portage 300 yards on the left, but this is difficult. Medium water finds more manageable waves in the gorge. Eddy right at the end of the gorge and avoid the left side, which contains large holes. A succession of ledges and holes follow, best run on the right side.

Below the Heater 0.75 mile is Upper Gordon Falls (8.25 miles). The easiest portage is on the left bank. Upper Gordon Falls is a difficult Class IV–V drop. It is a classic horseshoe-shaped drop of about 11 feet, with a good rescue pool below. Scout either side. The center run hits the huge waves at the bottom. You can sometimes sneak on the left side. Large holes and abrupt drops await if you fall off your line.

Around the corner to the left is Lower Gordon Falls, Class II–III. Enter left and move to the center, through the heavy waves. Quick water continues to the US 2 bridge in Mattawamkeag (12.5 miles). You can take out on River Road on the right, avoiding a portion of this section. The Penobscot is 0.5 mile below.

Wassataquoik Stream

The stream flows from Baxter State Park to the East Branch of the Penobscot River.

KATAHDIN STREAM ➤ WHETSTONE FALLS   8.5 MI

Description:	Class III
Navigable:	High or medium water: after heavy rain
Scenery:	Wild
Maps:	Stacyville 15, DL 51

Take the unmarked road to Katahdin Brook. Put in on Katahdin Brook and paddle 100 yards to Wassataquoik Stream. This is a wild river flowing out of the heart of Baxter State Park into the East Branch of the Penobscot River.

You have three alternate take-outs: the first is 4.0 miles downstream at the bridge before the confluence with the East Branch; the second is at Lunksoos Pool on the East Branch at 5.5 miles; and the third is at 8.5 miles at the Whetstone Falls Campground. This take-out allows you to run Whetstone Falls, Class III, III+.

Mattawamkeag River (West Branch)

Below Mattawamkeag Lake, the West Branch, already a large river, is mostly rapids and quick water for 12.5 miles. It is a pleasant and easy paddle in medium or high water, and it is similar to the lower Allagash. Like the latter, some places are scratchy in low water, requiring you to walk your boat down. It is wild, although about a dozen cabins line the river.

The West Branch above Island Falls is passable in high water, except in a few places, from ME 11 in the township of Moro.

ISLAND FALLS ➤ HAYNESVILLE   24.5 MI

Description:	Lakes, flatwater, quickwater, Class I, II
Navigable:	High and medium water: mid-May to July
	Medium water: Fall
Scenery:	Wild
Maps:	Island Falls 15, Sherman 15, Mattawamkeag Lake 15, Amity 15, DL 52 and 53
Portage:	0 mi R
Campsite:	11.25 mi L Mattawamkeag Lake (small) MFS

Anyone approaching the US 2 bridge in Island Falls should land above or under it, right bank, and lift around the ledges at the old broken dam. Below, right of the island, a short pitch is followed by 6.5 miles of flat water to Upper Mattawamkeag Lake. Upon entering the latter, turn right and southeast through a thoroughfare for 1.5 miles.

It is 3.5 miles southeast across Mattawamkeag Lake to the outlet (11.5 miles), after which you travel 0.5 mile of Class II and 1.5 miles of Class I rapids. The remaining 10.5 miles are mostly quick water, with some easy rapids in the last 0.5 mile before the confluence with the East Branch (24.0 miles).

Another 0.5 mile beyond is the US 2A bridge in Haynesville (24.5 miles).

Fish Stream

Fish Stream flows eastward to the West Branch of the Mattawamkeag River at Island Falls. It is an easy paddle through wild country, where you can also find good fishing.

PATTEN ➤ ISLAND FALLS   16.5 MI

Description:	Flatwater, quickwater
Navigable:	High and medium water: May–June
Scenery:	Wild
Maps:	Sherman 15, Island Falls 15, DL 52

A side road reaches Fish Stream from ME 159 about 1.0 mile east of Patten and downstream from a lumber mill. The upper part is all flat, with a few fallen trees blocking the way. After 6.75 miles you come upon a ledge, passable in high water, 0.25 mile before the stream swings around the southern end of an esker, a prominent ridge of glacial material that extends north for several miles. The rest of the way to the ME 159 bridge (13.5 miles) is mostly flat, but a few riffles are scratchy in low water. In the remaining 2.25 miles to the West Branch (15.75 miles), you encounter quick and flat water.

Below the confluence 0.75 mile, and past the ME 159 bridge, is the US 2 bridge (16.5 miles). Take out on the right at or above it; beyond it, at the old dam site, some ledges are not passable.

Mattawamkeag River (East Branch)

The East Branch is seldom run in comparison to the West Branch. The rapids in the upper part have to be run in high water, and you have no convenient access at the end of the rapids to run the quick water of the lower end.

SMYRNA MILLS ➤ RED BRIDGE   7.0 MI

Description:	Flatwater, quickwater, rapids
Navigable:	High water
Scenery:	Rural, towns
Maps:	Smyrna Mills 15, Mattawamkeag Lake 15, Amity 15, DL 52

This section is small and is runnable only at high water. Both the beginning and end can be reached from US 2. The river is mixed rapid and smooth and offers an interesting run early in the season.

RED BRIDGE ➤ HAYNESVILLE   20.0 MI

Description:	Class II and more difficult rapids
Navigable:	High water
Scenery:	Wild
Maps:	Mattawamkeag Lake 15, Amity 15, DL 52 and 53

Below Red Bridge are intermittent Class II rapids to the outlet from Pleasant Lake. Below here, around the foot of Outlet Mountain, the going becomes very rough. Paddling becomes easier after that. The remaining distance is open going with a slow current. Local people commonly motor up to Nickerson Brook when fishing.

Baskahegan Stream

Baskahegan Stream, a tributary of the Mattawamkeag River, drains a flat region in eastern Maine. It consists almost entirely of flat water and large lakes. The shorelines are predominantly lined with hardwood forests, and, except near Danforth, you see few cabins or houses. The water is very dark.

Description:	Lakes, flatwater, Class I, II
Navigable:	High or medium water: first 5.75 mi
	Passable at most levels below 5.75 mi
Scenery:	Wild, town
Maps:	Scraggly Lake 15, Danforth 15, DL 45
Portages:	0.5 mi R dam at Danforth 50 yd
	39.0 mi R ledges in South Bancroft 150 yd
Campsite:	17.75 mi R Baskahegan Lake Dam (poor) permit

Begin on ME 6 at Lindsey Brook. You might encounter beaver dams in the 1.25 miles before the Lindsey Brook enters Toman Deadwater on Baskahegan Stream. At the end of this deadwater, 1.0 mile of easy Class I–II rapids end with a short narrow Class II drop. You come upon a bridge at the beginning of Middle Deadwater (3.25 miles).

Middle Deadwater is 1.75 miles long, and at its end (5.0 miles) is 0.75 mile of rapids that begin as Class I–II. **Caution!** About 0.5 mile after leaving Middle Deadwater, the river widens somewhat where you come upon quick water. Then you encounter a blind right turn before a narrow sluice, where you find a series of sharp drops between sloping ledges. A short distance beyond, a dirt road on the right provides a better starting point in low water.

Below the dirt road (5.75 miles), the river meanders for 7.75 miles to Baskahegan Lake (13.5 miles). The river is passable at low water, but some wading might be necessary.

The washed-out dam on Baskahegan Lake (17.75 miles) is runnable. The next 9.25 miles to Crooked Brook Flowage are flat water, with the current being stronger in the last 4.0 miles. It is a 3.5-mile paddle on Crooked Brook Flowage northwards to the dam in Danforth.

Below Danforth (30.5 miles), Baskahegan Stream has flatwater for 8.5 miles. Pass a bridge near South Danforth, land on the right, and portage along the edge of a field past a series of ledges. Easy rapids continue to the Mattawamkeag River (39.5 miles). You come upon a highway bridge over the Mattawamkeag just above the mouth of Baskahegan Stream.

Wytopitlock Stream

Wytopitlock Stream rises in Wytopitlock Lake in Glenwood and flows south to the Mattawamkeag River at Wytopitlock. It is a relatively small stream but navigable in high water from the lake down. It is mixed rapid and smooth, but most of the rapids are runnable. Wytopitlock Lake can be reached from US 2A at Glenwood.

WYTOPITLOCK LAKE ➤ US 2A   9.25 MI

Description:	Flatwater, quickwater, Class I, II
Navigable:	Medium water: late spring
Scenery:	Wild
Maps:	Mattawamkeag Lake 15, Wytopitlock 15, DL 44 and 52

The stream leaves Wytopitlock Lake just to the east of the launching ramp and takes a hard right. Shortly after that right, a Class III drop in the center of the stream should be scouted prior to any trip. Past the bridge are rapids, a short deadwater rapids, another deadwater above the third bridge, and then 0.5 mile of rapids to Thompson Deadwater. There, the river is wide and deep through an open marsh, with much wildlife visible. The deadwater ends at an old dam site (6.25 miles) and rapids continue the next 3.0 miles to the US 2A bridge.

US 2A ➤ MATTAWAMKEAG RIVER   8.5 MI

Description:	Flatwater, quickwater, Class I, II
Navigable:	Medium water: late spring
Scenery:	Wild
Maps:	Mattawamkeag Lake 15, Wytopitlock 15, DL 44

Wytopitlock Stream flows into one of the largest hardwood swamps in Maine. The confluence with the Mattawamkeag is 1.2 miles below the ME 171 bridge.

Molunkus Stream

Molunkus Stream rises in Thousand Acre Bog in Crystal just west of Patten and flows south through Sherman Mills and Macwahoc to the Mattawamkeag River just below Kingman. It is navigable from Sherman Mills, or with good water from Sherman Station. The upper part is best run with high to medium water, but much of the stream can be run at any time. It is entirely through woods, and no public campgrounds are available.

SHERMAN STATION ➤ SHERMAN MILLS   3.0 MI

Description:	Quickwater
Navigable:	High and medium water
Scenery:	Towns
Maps:	Sherman 15, Mattawamkeag Lake 15, Wytopitlock 15, DL 52

You can put in at the crossing of the West Branch just below Sherman Station. Then you can run 1.0 mile down to the main stream and 2.0 miles down that stream to Sherman Mills. This is largely through swamp with a good current but no rapids.

SHERMAN MILLS ➤ MACWAHOC   20.0 MI

Description:	Flatwater, quickwater, rapids
Navigable:	High and medium water
Scenery:	Wild
Maps:	Sherman 15, Mattawamkeag Lake 15, Wytopitlock 15, DL 52 and 44

Just below the put-in spot a short rapid goes down to a deadwater and then another rapid below the deadwater, 1.0 mile in all. The next 6.0 miles to the road crossing 1.0 mile south of Monarda are mostly smooth water. This spot might be a better place to put in if the water is low up above. Below here are 2.0 miles of mixed rapid and smooth water and then mostly smooth water with a fast current for the next 10.0 miles to Macwahoc. For much of this latter part of the run, the river is paralleled by nearby US 2. At Macwahoc US 2 crosses the river.

MACWAHOC ➤ MATTAWAMKEAG RIVER   10.0 MI

Description:	Flatwater, quickwater
Navigable:	Medium water
Scenery:	Wild
Maps:	Wytopitlock 15, DL 44

Just 100 yards below the US 2 bridge Macwahoc Stream enters on the left. You travel a short rapid for 0.5 mile below the start. Then the river meanders through a swamp for the rest of the way to the Mattawamkeag River, which it enters 2.0 miles below Kingman, where the only convenient take-out spot is located.

Alternatively, you can paddle downstream through the rapids on the Mattawamkeag to Mattawamkeag Wilderness Park.

Macwahoc Stream

Macwahoc Stream starts in Macwahoc Lake in Sherman and flows first southeast, then south and slightly west to join the Molunkus Stream at Macwahoc. You can paddle from its headwaters at Macwahoc Lake all the way to the mouth, but high- to medium-stage water would be best for the upper portions. Macwahoc Lake can be reached easily from US 2 in Sherman, and, if the water is low, Lower Macwahoc Lake, which would provide a better starting place, can also be reached from this road in Silver Ridge.

MACWAHOC LAKE ➤ LOWER MACWAHOC LAKE   6.0 MI

Description:	Lakes, rapids
Navigable:	High and medium water
Scenery:	Wild
Maps:	Sherman 15, Mattawamkeag Lake 15,
	Wytopitlock 15, Mattawamkeag 15, DL 52

You have several possibilities for the start of this trip. If the water is high, you can put in from a road off US 2 north 2.0 miles of Woodbridge Corner on the inlet stream to Macwahoc Lake and run down the stream 0.5 mile to the lake, 1.5 miles south down the lake to its outlet, and then 0.5 mile down the outlet, Macwahoc Stream. Here,

a bridge crosses where a road comes in from US 2 closer to Woodbridge Corner. In somewhat lower water, this would be a better put-in
spot. The next 4.0 miles to Lower Macwahoc Lake are largely rapids
with small ponds or backwaters between them. The inlet to Macwahoc Lake enters at the center of the northern shore; from here, it is
0.5 mile east to the landing on the eastern shore.

LOWER MACWAHOC LAKE ➤ MACWAHOC   20.0 MI

Description:	Quickwater, rapids
Navigable:	High, medium, and low water
Scenery:	Wild
Maps:	Sherman 15, Mattawamkeag Lake 15,
	Wytopitlock 15, Mattawamkeag 15, DL 52 and 44

You can put in at the landing on the eastern shore of Lower Macwahoc
Lake reached by a dirt road from the southeast. After about 1.0 mile
down the lake, you enter Macwahoc Stream, which descends with
a good current for the next 3.0 miles. Then steep rapids begin for
1.0 mile to a swampy area. After about 0.5 mile of easy going, rapids
start again and continue for 1.0 mile to a long swampy area, Reed
Deadwater. This continues for nearly 8.0 miles to the mouth of Reed
Stream. Below Reed Deadwater you come upon a small but sharp
ledge drop that might need to be carried around depending on water
level after which is slower water. There follows a rapid that should
be scouted or portaged depending on water level. Scout and carry on
right under power lines. The rest is just fast water, which is best run
early to mid May in high water. It is 5.5 miles from Reed Stream to
the junction with Molunkus Stream at Macwahoc.

Piscataquis River

The Piscataquis River is one of the major tributaries of the Penobscot.
Both of its two branches, the East Branch and the West Branch, rise
south of Moosehead Lake and join at Blanchard to form the main
stream, which then flows eastward to the Penobscot River at Howland.
The West Branch has some miles of good paddling below the crossing
of the Shirley Mills–Lake Moxie road. But this is followed by a deep and
very difficult gorge north of Breakneck Ridge with no way to leave the

river. The East Branch has some easy paddling above Shirley Mills, but no good way exists to reach it. Below, it is too steep and rapid for some distance; then it is a good run, but inaccessible. In effect the river is runnable only below the junction of the two branches or from Blanchard on down, except for a team of expert paddlers. From Blanchard, the river is mixed rapid and smooth, with some sections practically all smooth water. Above Dover-Foxcroft, it is usually too low for summer travel, although usable until late in the spring.

Piscataquis River (West Branch)

The West Branch of the Piscataquis is a very difficult but rewarding river to explore. No access to the river exists other than two logging-road bridges. Paddlers who wish to explore the wild flatwater areas must line and portage many difficult rapids and ledge drops, while expert whitewater paddlers must paddle several miles of slow water on each end in order to challenge the ledge drops and rapids. **Caution!** The difficulty of the ledge drops, combined with the isolation of the river, means that extreme caution must be used when running the river.

SHIRLEY MILLS ROAD ➤ OAKES BOG   2.75 MI

Description:	Flatwater, Class I, II, III
Navigable:	Medium to high water: May
Scenery:	Wild
Maps:	Greenville 15, DL 31 and 41
Portages:	Ledges

Put in at the bridge at the outlet of West Shirley Bog. Most of this section is long stretches of quick water, separated by short, steep ledge drops or rapids. Several of these have to be scouted, and one ledge drop needs to be portaged, as an undercut ledge sticks out from the right side at the bottom of the drop. In one unique spot the river seems to end, but you can actually take a wide slot through a ledge. Take out just above Oakes Bog, where the logging road crosses. This upper section is much easier than the section below Oakes Bog.

OAKES BOG ➤ BLANCHARD 8.75 MI

Description:	Flatwater, Class I, II, III, IV, V
Navigable:	Medium to high water: May or after heavy rains
Scenery:	Wild
Maps:	Greenville 15, DL 31
Portage:	5.25 mi L 15-foot falls 100 yd

This section of the river is recommended for experts only. After you put in the river, you must be prepared to face Breakneck Ridge Gorge. This gorge is Class IV at low to medium water levels, and Class V at high water levels, with one falls that is normally portaged.

Put in at the bridge just above Oakes Bog. It is about 1.0 mile down the bog to the old dam remains, which now form an easy rapid. Hatch Falls (2.25 miles) is the first major landmark after the bog. When you see the river fall out of sight through granite ledges and pine trees, you should land on the right shore and scout. This is a four-stage ledge drop, which is of Class III–IV difficulty, depending on the water level. Below Hatch Falls 100 yards is another sharp 4-foot drop that can take you by surprise. Below this is a 2.5-foot ledge and a 5-foot ledge (2.75 miles). The 5-foot ledge is below a cabin on the right and should be scouted.

After Bald Mountain stream enters on the right (5.0 miles), the rapids build from Class I to continuous Class II–III, with occasional small ledge drops. The walls of the gorge also start to rise. The river drops 320 feet in the next 3.0 miles. You can recognize the beginning of the most difficult section by a Class III rapid leading into a 100-foot-long sloping ledge (5.0 miles) that forms a tricky Class III–IV drop. Both river banks are all ledge at this point, as the walls steepen. (This point is just above "neck" in "Breakneck" on the topographical map.) It is critical to scout and set up rescue bags at this rapid, as a 15-foot falls is just around the corner. The easiest portage is to the left side of the falls. Below the falls is a pool. Around the next corner are Class II–III rapids leading into a 10-foot sloping ledge, followed by a 7-foot straight drop. The straight drop has a bad hole at the bottom at certain water levels. The next 1.0 mile is a very tight, rocky Class III–IV rapid. This is followed by a mile of quick water, through an island maze in which you should generally stay left. The last 1.0 mile is on the Piscataquis

River formed by the junction of the East and West branches. Take out at the bridge in Blanchard.

Piscataquis River (East Branch)

BLANCHARD ➤ UPPER ABBOTT   8.0 MI

Description:	Class II, III, IV
Navigable:	High water: spring or after heavy rains
Scenery:	Forested
Maps:	Greenville 15, Kingsbury 15, Guilford 15, DL 31
Portage:	3.0 mi e Barrows Falls (optional)

Put in above the bridge in Blanchard, where you find a Class II–III rapid. Rapids continue for 100 yards below the bridge. The remaining distance to the bridge above Barrows Falls is largely flat water.

The bridge makes an alternate put-in, but Barrows Falls starts immediately. Barrows Falls is a beautiful slate gorge that is normally rated heavy Class III. High water results in violent deflection waves and a Class IV rating. Scout right, and carry either side.

Class II rapids follow almost continuously to Upper Abbott. You travel some slightly harder rapids, but the difficulty never exceeds Class III. The final rapid is located under the old bridge in Upper Abbott. Run on the left side of the right chute.

UPPER ABBOTT ➤ DOVER-FOXCROFT   13.0 MI

Description:	Quickwater, Class I
Navigable:	Spring or unusually wet summer
Scenery:	Rural
Maps:	Guilford 15, Dover-Foxcroft 15, DL 31 and 32
Portages:	5.0 mi R Guilford 1.25 mi
	(13.0 mi R Dover-Foxcroft 2 dams 0.75 mi)

Travel a shallow riffle from the old to the new bridge at Upper Abbott. The riffles and current diminish and disappear as you draw nearer to the dam in Guilford. No convenient take-out exists at the dam in town; take out at the senior citizens' housing where the river nears ME 6/15 less than 1.0 mile upstream on the left.

From the town athletic field below the mills on the left bank you travel quick water and occasional Class I rips for about 3.75 miles to Lowe's covered bridge. This bridge marks the beginning of Class I–II rapids that are rocky in low water and consist of wide expanses of low, choppy waves in high water. The first two rapids are easier than the rest. Rapids 50 to 100 yards long alternate with longer, smooth stretches until you reach a washed out dam marked by the remains of a masonry millhouse on the left. This drop is usually run on the left, but varying water levels might allow other routes. You can carry on the right if you wish. The current is almost gone below the railroad trestle, and from there it is 1.0 mile of flat water to the handy take-out and parking spot at "the cove." You come upon two dams in Dover-Foxcroft, each about 20 feet high. Portage by car 0.75 mile from the cove to Brown's Mill (also called the Tannery).

DOVER-FOXCROFT ➤ DERBY   18.5 MI

Description:	Flatwater, quickwater, Class I, II, III
Navigable:	Spring, summer
Scenery:	Rural
Maps:	Dover-Foxcroft 15, Boyd Lake 15, Schoodic 15, DL 32

Below Brown's Mill are two ledges, each 1 to 1.5 feet, followed by a rocky rapid around a long left turn. Both the ledges and rapid are Class II at moderately high water. You find a good current and easy rapids for 3.0 miles to the bridge at East Dover, below which is a 100-yard-long rapid, which is a fast, wavy, Class I on the left and a mild Class II on the right at most water levels. Smooth river for 7.0 more miles brings you to the bridge at South Sebec, and 8.5 miles farther is the confluence of the Sebec River and the bridge near Derby.

Just above the confluence with the Sebec is a railroad bridge. Under the bridge is a steep and rocky rapid 100 yards long, Class II at low runnable level and potentially heavy when the river is high. Downstream 0.25 mile is the ME 11 bridge, which has a shorter and easier rapid under it.

Description:	Flatwater, quickwater, Class I, II, III
Navigable:	Medium water
Scenery:	Forested, towns
Maps:	Schoodic 15, Lincoln 15, Passadumkeag 15, DL 32 and 33
Portage:	(24.5 mi L dam)

The beginning and end of this section is smooth, broken in the middle by 5.0 miles of rapids, which can be portaged by car. This is a large river, and the rapids generate heavy waves even in medium water.

Downstream from the ME 6/11/16 bridge 4.0 miles, the Pleasant River enters on the left. It flows over several easy rapids and then drops over a steep Class II rapid. Occasional easy rapids continue to the high former railroad bridge (9.0 miles). If you wish not to run the heavier rapids below, take out at a dirt road just above, on the left. This is the last reasonable access, as the banks become steep and high.

Easy rapids start immediately and run to Schoodic Point (10.75 miles), where the Schoodic River enters left in an impressive rapid. The Piscataquis River turns sharply right and begins dropping more steeply, creating large waves (Class III in medium water). The rapids decrease in difficulty for the next couple of miles. If you portaged the long rapids, you can start again 3.5 miles from Schoodic Point, where the river comes close to the road near the Medford-Maxfield town line.

Seboeis Stream enters left 0.5 mile above the I-95 bridge (21.75 miles). The river gradually slows to flat water. Take out at a launching ramp above the dam at Howland. The confluence with the Penobscot is just below.

Kingsbury Stream

Kingsbury Stream drops 600 feet in the 16.0 miles between Kingsbury Pond and Abbott Village with only one unrunnable waterfall. Although it is small at the outlet of Kingsbury Pond, the stream picks up over a dozen small feeder streams from the large east-west ridge along ME 16, between the pond and where Thorn Brook enters. The two major tributaries, Thorn Brook and Carlton Stream, each carry nearly as much water as Kingsbury Stream just above Cole's Corner. This additional flow makes the waves much bigger and current more powerful below Cole's Corner. The water is best on warm days during the last of the snow melt, as the land it drains is quite steep and water levels drop quickly after the snow is gone.

KINGSBURY POND ➤ THORN BROOK 8.5 MI

Description:	Class I, II, III
Navigable:	High water: mid-April
Scenery:	Wild
Maps:	Kingsbury 15, DL 31
Portage:	3.75 mi L 30-ft waterfall 100 yd

The upper part of Kingsbury is an interesting run of short, steep rapids, followed by stretches of quick water when the water level is high. Unfortunately, the water level is right only a few days each year. You are committed to do the entire section after you put in, as the stream does not come near the road again until just before the normal takeout. Put in just below the outlet of Kingsbury Pond on river right. After going under the bridge, you come to a narrow Class I rapid. If this rapid is scratchy, you will not have enough water in the wider rapids for the next 4.0 miles, and they will require wading.

The stream flows through a peaceful swampy area for about 1.0 mile and then starts its descent to the Piscataquis River. You face occasional trees blocking the river, but no ledge drops until the falls (3.75 miles). The falls are located near the word "Stream" on the topographical map. A quick current continues up to the lip of the falls, but no difficult rapids. Pull out on the left bank well above the falls where you find a rough portage trail. The portage trail ends at a 20-foot slanting cliff over which the boats must be lowered. The falls cannot be safely run because the water makes a 90-degree turn off a ledge halfway down the falls.

Kingsbury Stream takes on the character of a larger stream below the falls, as it has picked up a number of small feeder streams by this point. In high water, some moderate-sized waves and holes can develop in several of the tougher spots. Take out where Kingsbury Stream comes beside ME 16 and Thorn Brook enters.

THORN BROOK ➤ COLE'S CORNER ROAD BRIDGE   2.25 MI

Description:	Class II, III, IV
Navigable:	Medium-high water: April
Scenery:	Forested
Maps:	Kingsbury 15, Guilford 15, DL 31
Portage:	0.10 mi e ledge

This section of Kingsbury Stream makes a nice ending to the upper part of the stream, or a good start to the lower part of this stream if you have planned a medium-length day of paddling. Just below where Thorn Brook enters Kingsbury Stream, a Class III–IV ledge drop can be run at the right water levels. This ledge drop can be scouted quite easily from ME 16 by walking downstream about 150 yards from the bridge across Thorn Brook and then going into the woods about 100 feet.

The portage is normally over the rocks on the right shore. The rest of the run down to the Cole's Corner Road bridge is almost continuous Class II–III. The waves are bigger and the current more powerful than they are above Thorn Brook, because the stream has nearly doubled its drainage area. Just above Cole's Corner Road bridge, the river narrows into a short, more difficult stretch, with a rock wall on the right bank. This is best scouted from the left bank. Take out at the bridge or about 0.25 mile downstream from the bridge on river right.

COLE'S CORNER ROAD BRIDGE ➤ ABBOTT VILLAGE   5.25 MI

Description:	Quickwater, Class II, III
Navigable:	Medium-high water: April
Scenery:	Forested
Maps:	Guilford 15, DL 31
Portage:	3.75 mi L 30-ft waterfall 100 yd

The Class II rapids below Cole's Corner Road bridge quickly mellow to Class I and quick water after the river swings away from the road. Carlton Stream enters on the right (1.0 miles) in the middle of a swampy area. About 0.75 mile below this is a Class II–III rapid (1.75 miles) where the river makes a wide, sweeping turn to the right. In another 0.75 mile, you come upon pine trees and granite ledges on river left (3.5 miles). Just around the corner is the most difficult rapid in this section. This double ledge drop should be scouted from the left. Watch out for the holes on the bottom drop. About 1.25 miles farther down is the last big drop (4.75 miles). This is a steep U-shaped rapid than can be run on the left after scouting. Take out about 0.5 mile downstream on the left, where a dirt road comes in from ME 16. **Caution!** Do not run down to the ME 16 bridge in Abbott, as the ledges under the bridge are very dangerous.

Pleasant River

The Pleasant River rises east of Greenville and Moosehead Lake. The West Branch flows out of Gulf Hagas to Katahdin Iron Works to Brownville Junction; there, it joins the East Branch, which flows out of lower Ebeemee Lake, northwest of Seboeis Lake. The combined river then flows south to Brownville, where it turns southeast to meet the Piscataquis east of Derby. The upper part is steep and should be run in moderately high water. The lower river is broad and shallow but can usually be run in the summer. The stream is clear and the banks wooded and attractive.

BROWNVILLE JUNCTION ➤ BROWNVILLE   5.5 MI

Description:	Flatwater, quickwater
Navigable:	High and medium water
Scenery:	Forested
Maps:	Sebec 15, Schoodic 15, Boyd Lake 15, DL 42 and 32

This section would primarily be paddled at the end of a trip on the East or West Branch. You can use a "water level" put-in on the left bank of the East Branch 1.0 mile above the confluence with the West Branch.

From the confluence it is 1.5 miles of easy paddling to Brownville Junction and another 4.0 miles to the dam in Brownville.

BROWNVILLE ➤ PISCATAQUIS RIVER   11.0 MI

Description:	Quickwater, Class I
Navigable:	Medium water
Scenery:	Forested
Maps:	Sebec 15, Schoodic 15, Boyd Lake 15, DL 32

A ledge is just below the dam in Brownville. The remainder of the
distance is very pleasant with easy rapids and quick water for 5.0
miles to the ME 16 bridge north of Milo and then another 6.0 miles
to the Piscataquis River, which is reached about 5.0 miles below the
bridge at Derby. No road is near the river at this point, but 1.0 mile
downstream at the Upper Ferry you can take out on either side of
the river.

Pleasant River (West Branch)

KATAHDIN IRON WORKS ROAD
(UPSTREAM OF SILVER LAKE) ➤
KATAHDIN IRON WORKS   4.0 MI

Description:	Quickwater, Class I
Navigable:	Medium water: mid-May to mid-June
Scenery:	Wild
Maps:	Sebec 15, DL 42

Put in near where Katahdin Iron Works Road first comes near the
river after crossing the log bridge. This is near "X609" on the topographical map. The river is narrow with good current. It is generally shallow with gravel riffles, downed trees, and forest debris
forming Class I obstacles. The stream becomes broader, deeper, and
slower in the last 1.0 mile above Silver Lake. You can take out at the
bridge on Katahdin Iron Works Road or continue 0.75 mile down
Silver Lake to Katahdin Iron (K.I.) Works. The old dam at K.I. is
completely gone, leaving a swift, shallow, and rocky rapid down
past the bridge at K.I.

Description: Flatwater, quickwater, Class II, III
Navigable: High water: can usually be run from mid-April
                    through May
Scenery: Forested
Maps: Sebec 15, DL 42

Put in at the bridge at Katahdin Iron Works or upstream at Silver Lake. The upstream put-in allows the running of 200 yards of Class III rapids to the bridge. Class II rapids continue to a more difficult spot. Billy Jack Rip (also known as Mud Cut) can be scouted either side (1.5 miles). The best route through this Class III rapid goes down the middle, threading the needle between a pour-over and a hole, through the large waves at the bottom. Other routes are possible.

Class II rapids continue for 3.0 miles, followed by quick water and flat water for the remaining 4.5 miles to the ME 11 bridge, where you find a good take-out on the left below the bridge.

Pleasant River (East Branch)

LOWER EBEEMEE LAKE ➤ WEST BRANCH   3.5 MI

Description: Class I, II
Navigable: Medium water: May
Scenery: Forested
Maps: Sebec 15, DL 42
Portage: Near start R 100 ft

Put in at the bridge at the foot of Lower Ebeemee Lake. The 2-foot drop just above this bridge would be runnable (Class II–III) in medium or high water if it were not blocked by a partially detached bridge timber. Drift down 50 yards to where a jumble of small boulders marks the site of an old dam. In high water, the extreme left might be runnable in decked boats (Class III–IV). Most paddlers carry 100 feet on the right. A 50-yard-long pool leads into a Class II rapid that quickly splits into two channels; 75 percent of the flow goes left. The first 50 feet of this channel are tight and fast, possibly Class III at some levels; the remaining 100 feet are technical Class II at medium water. You now come to a series of mild (Class I–II) rapids alternating with short stretches of quick water.

The river suddenly kinks to the right 1.5 miles below the put-in. At the apex of the kink, a 1-foot ledge divides the stream into two chutes. The left chute has most of the flow and forms an irregular souse hole of significant dimensions. The right chute is shallow and contains two 90-degree turns. Between the two chutes is dry ledge at medium or lower water. Just below this drop, which is the last one that should take your mind off the scenery, the river divides into multiple channels, with most of the water going to the left again. The extreme right channel comes close to a gravel pit just north of "the prairie," which makes an acceptable put-in for those wishing to avoid the rapids above. The remaining 2.0 miles to the high ME 11 bridge are very scenic, and the rapids are less frequent and diminish from easy Class II to Class I and then disappear.

The smaller Middle Branch enters a short distance below the bridge. A short side road comes near the left bank, making an easier take-out than the steep climb up to ME 11. The river is smooth for the remaining 1.0 mile to the West Branch.

Sebec River

The Sebec River drains Sebec Lake, located in Willimantic and Bowerbank, and flows east and south to the Piscataquis River at Derby. Together with the lake it provides an easy 20.0-mile trip on smooth water during most seasons of the year.

EARLEY'S LANDING ➤ DERBY   22.75 MI

Description:	Lake, flatwater
Navigable:	Spring, summer
Scenery:	Forested, rural
Maps:	Sebec Lake 15, Sebec 15, DL 32
Portages:	12.5 mi Sebec Lake Dam
	20.5 mi Milo Dam

Put in at Peaks-Kenny State Park on Sebec Lake or at the outlet, in Sebec. From the state park it is 4.0 miles to the Narrows, where the lake narrows to less than 0.25 mile. For the next 7.5 miles to Sebec the lake is generally less than 1.0 mile wide. At Sebec, you come upon a dam with a short rapids below. Approximately 4.0 miles farther along is about 100 yards of rocky Class II rips.

The dam in Milo is right in the middle of town, and the river splits into two channels just below it. The left channel has a small power-house put online in 1982. Choice of channel and portage route varies with the day of week and amount of water in the river. The rapids for the next 0.5 mile are bony Class I–II if one gate is open, heavy with more water. The confluence with the Piscataquis is 0.25 mile above the ME 11 bridge, which has an easy Class II rip under it.

Big Wilson Stream

Big Wilson Stream rises in Wilson Pond near the Kennebec-Piscataquis divide south of Moosehead Lake. It is a major inlet to Sebec Lake.

BODFISH CROSSING ➤ WILLIMANTIC   5.0 MI

Description:	Quickwater, Class I, II, III
Navigable:	High water: April, early May
Scenery:	Wild, forested
Maps:	Sebec Lake 15, DL 44 and 31
Portages:	3.5 mi L 10-ft waterfall
	3.6 mi L 12-ft waterfall

Just below the bridge near Bodfish Crossing is a formidable series of cascades. The easiest put-in is slightly below, on the right. Parking is limited. About 1.5 miles of quick water leads to a Class III rapid caused by three ledges. The first is best run right, with a quick move back left to set up for the center chute in the second. The third is easier with routes on the left and center.

The next 2.0 miles are quick water. Large boulders on the left, into which the river seems to disappear, mark the beginning of the best part of the run. The main flow turns left into a Class III rapid. A 4- or 5-foot drop over a ledge follows in 75 yards. Scouting reveals a good route on the right. Flat water leads to the brink of the first falls. Carry the 10-foot, downright scary, drop on the left.

The outflow of the first falls is a Class III rapid, which drops into a pool. Take out on the left after the pool, or run the Class II rapid that follows and eddy out left at the lip of a 12-foot falls. This drop is not as intimidating as the first, but most paddlers portage.

Class II rapids lead to some easy, 2-foot ledges in a small gorge. The 2-foot drop in the gorge is easily run left of center. Take out below the bridge on the left.

WILLIMANTIC ➤ SEBEC LAKE 4.0 MI

Description:	Class I
Navigable:	Spring, summer
Scenery:	Wild, forested
Maps:	Sebec Lake 15, DL 31
Portage:	4.0 mi falls at Earley's Landing

Below the Willimantic Bridge the river is Class I with fast, shallow riffles in mid-June. This section is passable almost anytime. From the bridge in Willimantic it is 4.0 miles to Earley's Landing on Sebec Lake. Portage around two waterfalls at Earley's.

Ship Pond Stream

Ship Pond Stream is the outlet of Onawa Lake and flows to Sebec Lake at Bucks Cove, from which point it is 2.0 miles of lake paddling to a road access.

During early spring the road access to the start is impassable, and the lake might also be frozen.

COW YARD FALLS ➤ SEBEC LAKE 3.0 MI

Description:	Flatwater, quickwater, Class I
Navigable:	Medium water: May–June, after heavy rains
Scenery:	Wild
Maps:	Sebec Lake 15, DL 41, 31, and 32
Portage:	2.75 mi e waterfall 50 yd

Cow Yard Falls can be reached by a private road (gate) that leaves ME 150 at Earley's Landing at Willimantic. Remember to ask for and obtain permission before crossing property lines. Cow Yard Falls is an 8-foot ledge. Put in below the falls or below the Class II ledges, if you prefer. After a few Class I rips, the stream flows quickly over a gravel bed for 0.5 mile. After 1.0 mile of meandering river, it spreads out over a shallow stretch, which might have to be waded for 0.25 mile at low water at summer levels. A short piece of deep flat water leads to the falls at Bucks Cove.

The falls is about 5 feet in several quick steps followed by a rocky pool and a 2-foot ledge drop at the apex of a bend to the right. The rocky out-run leads into Bucks Cove, an isolated arm of Sebec Lake, which contains three wooded islands and many glacial boulders.

It is 1.0 mile southeast to the mouth of the cove and another 1.0 mile west to Packard's Landing. South across the lake 3.0 miles is Peaks-Kenny State Park and a public landing. To the west of Bucks Cove 0.5 mile is the lower of the two falls at Earley's Landing on Big Wilson Stream.

It is not unduly strenuous to paddle Ship Pond Stream in the upstream direction as the finish of a trip on Big Wilson Stream or Sebec Lake.

Passadumkeag River

The Passadumkeag River rises in Lee and flows south for some miles, then southwest, and finally west to the Penobscot River at Passadumkeag. It has many miles of good paddling on it, but the upper part is best done at moderately high water.

WEIR POND ➤ PISTOL GREEN   18.0 MI

Description:	Flatwater, quickwater, marsh
Navigable:	Spring, summer, fall
Scenery:	Wild
Maps:	Springfield 15, Nicatous Lake 15, Saponac 15, DL 44 and 34
Campsites:	9.0 mi R Brown Brook
	12.75 mi L Cold Spring
	18.0 mi L Pistol Green

The stream is fairly small. The described put-in is at the bridge below Weir Pond.

You can put in at Weir Pond or at a road crossing just below the pond, both reachable by the same road off ME 6 west of Springfield. If you put in at Weir Pond, you travel 0.5 mile of pond and 0.5 mile of swampy stream to the lower put-in spot. The next 17.0 miles are all smooth water, with the river meandering through swampy areas all the way to the mouth of Nicatous Stream at Pistol Green.

An alternative start can be made via the West Branch (Passadumkeag) below Number 3 Pond. Blowdowns and beaver dams make for tedious going. High water in the spring might wash out a few of the beaver dams and downed trees, and might make it easier to get over or around them.

Rand Brook (3.75 miles) marks the start of the old portage across to Upper Sysladobsis and the Saint Croix drainage.

PISTOL GREEN ➤ PASSADUMKEAG   32.25 MI

Description:	Lake, flatwater, quickwater, Class I, II
Navigable:	Spring, summer, fall
Scenery:	Wild, forested, rural
Maps:	Saponac 15, Passadumkeag 15, DL 34 and 33
Portages:	4.5 mi L Grand Falls 0.75 mi
	18.5 mi R then L Lowell Dam
	(32.0 mi L dam at Passadumkeag)
Campsites:	5.0 mi L Grand Fall
	13.0 mi L Saponac Pond

The river is smooth for the first 4.0 miles. Grand Falls is a wild rapid in which the river drops 100 feet in a mile and should be carried. You can use a good carry road here. Also, you have good road access here from ME 188.

The river winds through flat bottom lands to Saponac Pond (12.25 miles). In high water, the river is hard to find in the maple swamp before the pond. A campsite is on the south shore; it is somewhat buggy. You travel 1.0 mile of river beyond the pond to Pond Rips and White Horse Rips, which some paddlers might wish to line or carry.

The river is smooth again for 3.0 miles to the broken dam at Lowell (18.5 miles). Portage right through a field, cross the river on the bridge, and take the trail along the left bank. The ledges make fearsome waves in high water. Except for Rocky Rips (25.5 miles), the river is smooth all the way to Passadumkeag.

The usual take-out is at an iron bridge 2.0 miles upstream of Passadumkeag.

Nicatous Stream

Nicatous Stream drains Nicatous Lake and flows northwest to the Passadumkeag River at Pistol Green. It is part of a major Indian canoe route.

Nicatous means "Little Fork" and applies to the junction of this stream and the Passadumkeag. At that point, a canoeist ascending the Passadumkeag has a choice of routes to follow. Nicatous Stream leads to Kiasobeak, now called Nicatous Lake, from which you can easily reach the headwaters of four major river systems.

NICATOUS LAKE ➤ PISTOL GREEN   7.75 MI

Description:	Flatwater, quickwater, marsh, Class I, II, III
Navigable:	Medium water
Scenery:	Wild
Maps:	Nicatous Lake 15, Saponac 15, DL 34
Portage:	0.25 mi dam

You can use a public landing at the small dam at the outlet. The river flows for 2.0 miles through boggy areas separated by short, boulder-strewn sections. Class I rapids commence after a long boggy stretch and increase without letup to Idiot Dog Falls, 50 yards of granite ledges and Class III if enough water is present (3.0 miles). At the bottom, a crumbling log bridge has posed some hazards in the past. The bridge is a good picnic spot; just upstream on the left at bank level is a cold spring.

Below the bridge is another short, sharp pitch; then rapids diminish quickly. The final 3.0 miles flow through a swamp with gravel bars and pools; this is good moose country. You can find a bridge and campsite 0.5 mile above the Passadumkeag.

Gassabias Stream

This stream is part of a major east-west Indian canoe route and also used to be the traditional approach to the Machias River in the days before roads. You can easily pole or paddle up and down Gassabias Stream with only a minimum of dragging in low water.

GASSABIAS LAKE ➤ NICATOUS LAKE   3.0 MI

Description:	Flatwater, quickwater, rapids
Navigable:	High, medium, and low water
Scenery:	Wild
Maps:	Nicatous Lake 15, DL 34 and 35
Campsites:	Red pine grove by the portage
	Outlet of Gassabias Lake
	North side of "Snakka"

The low bridge at the outlet of Gassabias Lake might have to be carried if the water is high. After a 1.0 mile of deepwater swamp comes 1.0 mile of mossy boulders, but no rapids, where you must be alert for the problems in the low water. This ends at the CCC road bridge, where marsh begins again and continues to Great Falls. At Great Falls, the stream narrows and plunges 5 feet vertically in the next 200 yards. Soon you reach Nicatous Lake, just south of the "Snakka," a long, undulating stone ridge that almost cuts the lake in two.

The 2.0-mile portage to Fourth Machias Lake starts on the east shore of Gassabias Lake just to the left of a large stand of red pine. The portage trail begins as a groove cut into the peat bog from heavy use. The trail is passable, but difficult.

Kenduskeag Stream

GARLAND ➤ FRENCH STREAM   7.5 MI

Description:	Quickwater, Class I, II
Navigable:	High water: spring runoff or pond drawdown)
Scenery:	Forested
Maps:	Dover-Foxcroft 15, Stetson 15, DL 32
Portages:	2.75 mi L dam at Twin Brook lift-over
	2.75+ mi L ledge lift-over

Just below the dam at Garland, ME 94 crosses the stream. Put in here at relatively high water levels only. The first 1.0 mile is mostly quick water, with sharp turns and minor alder tangles. After the first 1.0 mile, a rock-strewn channel requires quick maneuvering in spots, generally with stretches of quick water below each rapid. This continues for about 0.5 mile to a road crossing and another 0.5 mile to the backup of a small, washed-out mill dam at Twin Brook. Burnham Brook enters on the left in this area but might be missed in the meanders.

Another 0.8 mile brings you to the old dam at Twin Brook. It might be lifted over on the left or might be run after scouting if water level is advantageous. Within 0.1 mile of the dam is another road crossing. Beneath this bridge is a ledge drop of 2 to 3 feet over which the current takes a sharp S-turn. After scouting from above the bridge, and with careful execution, the stream can be run to the left bank above the ledge, and the boat lifted over. It is slightly more than 1.0 mile below the ledge to the next road crossing. Between the ledge and the crossing are more rapids interspersed with quick water, much like the section above the pond. The remainder of the run to the ME 11/43 bridge comprises occasional rapids with numerous beaver dams, blowdowns, and tangles. The crossing of ME 11/43 is just (30 yards) upstream of the confluence with French Stream, which at this point is approximately the same size as the Kenduskeag. Take out here on the right under the bridge.

FRENCH STREAM ➤ KENDUSKEAG   13.5 MI

Description:	Flatwater, quickwater, Class I, II
Navigable:	Medium to high water: April, May
Scenery:	Forested, rural
Maps:	Stetson 15, Bangor 15, DL 32
Portages:	11.5 mi ledge lift-over
	13.5 mi ledge lift-over

Below the ME 11/43 bridge, the river is doubled in size by French Stream entering right. The bridge at McGregor Mill is 1.25 miles, and it is another 1.25 miles to the second bridge. The current is fast, with some rapids up to Class II; then the river pools up for 2.0 miles or so. You find little current, and the water becomes deeper on its way to a rapid above a covered bridge at Robyville (7.0 miles). The bridge cannot be seen from the beginning of the rapid, but the change in terrain is obvious, as the river makes an S-turn over a ledgy drop, Class III.

The rapids for the next 0.75 mile are slightly harder. Just above the fourth bridge is a 3.5-foot drop over a ledge, which you might need to line or carry. The next ledge before the bridge in Kenduskeag is even more difficult.

KENDUSKEAG ➤ FLOUR MILL FALLS 15.0 MI

Description:	Quickwater, Class I, II, III
Navigable:	High water: March, April
Scenery:	Forested
Maps:	Bangor 15, DL 32, 22, and 23

The bridge in Kenduskeag is the start of the Kenduskeag-to-Bangor race. The first 10.0 miles are meandering quick water with a few riffles to Six Mile Falls, the only Class III rapid in this section. Six Mile Falls is a 200-yard Class III rapid at most water levels and is easily scouted and run on the left. The next 3.0 miles to Bull's Eye Bridge are mostly quick water.

A put-in can be made at Bull's Eye Bridge. The 2.0 miles to the park and parking area above Flour Mill Falls are Class I–II rapids. Most paddlers take out on river left above Flour Mill Falls.

FLOUR MILL FALLS ➤ SECOND VALLEY AVENUE BRIDGE 0.5 MI

Description:	Class IV
Navigable:	High water: March, April
Scenery:	Forested
Maps:	Bangor 15, DL 23

This is a favorite after-work run for local paddlers. Put in at Valley Avenue above Flour Mill Falls. Be sure to scout the drop from the observation platform. The farther upstream you put in, the longer the warm-up. Flour Mill Falls has two distinct drops. The cleanest route at high water involves running the top drop on the right and grabbing a micro-eddy on the right. Then peel out and run the second drop right down the middle. Lower water necessitates approaching the second drop from the left, as the upper drop becomes dry on the right.

A ledge halfway to the Valley Avenue Bridge provides fine surfing. Eddy out right above the bridge. The drop below the bridge is the most dangerous on the river. A pour-over on river right creates a nasty hole, which might recirculate a boat or boater for an extended time. The best route is just right of the central bridge abutment. Aim for the second guardrail support from the right and avoid the curler farther right and the smaller hole on the left. A short pool, offering excellent squirting, follows.

You can easily run the ledge at the old Maxfield Mill site on the left. The river then passes through Class II rapids to a Class III ledge, Shopping Cart. This area is the site of an annual slalom race. You can find good surfing and enders in the waves here.

Take out at a park on river right. The river then flows under the second Valley Avenue Bridge and through downtown Bangor. The Penobscot is 0.75 mile downstream. The lower portion of the river is tidal.

Souadabscook Stream

Souadabscook Stream (alternate spelling, Sawadapskook) rises in Etna Pond and flows east to join the Penobscot River south of Bangor. It was one of the major Indian waterways, connecting the Penobscot and Kennebec watersheds; a portage connected to the Sebasticook River.

BLACK STREAM ➤ VATIADES LANDING   **3.5 MI**

Description:	Lake, quickwater, Class I
Navigable:	High and medium water: mid-April to early June
Scenery:	Rural, towns
Maps:	Bangor 15, DL 22 and 23

Put in from US 2 at a culvert 3.75 miles west of Hermon. This culvert connects Black Stream, a tributary of the Kenduskeag River, to Souadabscook Stream in high water. Little parking is available here.

The 1.75 miles to Newburgh Road and the Maine Central Railroad crossings are all flat water, except for a Class II chute over what appears to be a sunken stone wall. Newburgh Road offers good parking, and this section can be paddled upstream.

The pond is another 0.25 mile, and the outlet of the pond is 1.5 miles to the southeast. Vatiades Landing on Bogg Road is an additional 0.5 mile.

Black Stream, while a tributary of the Kenduskeag, is more likely to be paddled as an extension of this trip. It can be ascended from the culvert at the start of this trip 0.5 mile to a washed-out culvert or descended 1.0 mile to Black Stream Road (an alternate start).

VATIADES LANDING ➤ HAMPDEN   9.0 MI

Description:	Lake, flatwater, quickwater, Class II, III, IV
Navigable:	High water: March, April
Scenery:	Forested, rural, settled
Maps:	Bangor 15, Bucksport 15, DL 22 and 23
Portage:	7.0 mi L Grand Falls and Dam 0.5 mi

The flatwater section begins at Vatiades Landing on a side road just north of I-95. The stream is smooth at the start, as it goes south under I-95, and then flows into Hammond Pond, which often is still frozen when the stream is at its best. The outlet is 0.5 mile east across the pond on the northeastern corner.

The current gradually quickens, flowing through a deepwater swamp, and passes under I-95 twice more. Some warm-up around scattered rocks prepares you for the ledge just above Manning Mill Road, a drop of 2 or 3 feet, cleanest on the right. Manning Mill Road is the usual put-in for whitewater paddlers. The property on both sides of the river is private.

A pool below the bridge leads to a good surfing hole, followed by a sharper drop that is best run right center. A harder ledge lies just above Emerson Mill Road. The exciting route is down the middle, although you can find a viable route on the extreme left.

Good surfing waves are found below the bridge. Scout from the right side. Crawford's Drop is often considered Class IV. The best route is on the far left, although an interesting route can be found on the right. The drop below Papermill Road often has high waves.

Below the bridge on river left is the take-out and the beginning of the portage around Grand Falls, a dangerous Class V drop. Put in below the dam that follows the drop. A series of ledges leads to quick water that continues to the take-out in Hampden. Take out on the right above the Route 1A bridge at the Hampden waterworks building. The Penobscot is 0.25 mile below.

Marsh Stream

Marsh Stream flows eastward from Monroe to tidewater on the Penobscot.

MONROE CENTER ➤ WEST WINTERPORT   9.5 MI

Description:	Flatwater, quickwater, Class I, II
Navigable:	High water: spring
Scenery:	Forested
Maps:	Brooks 15, Bucksport 15, DL 22
Portage:	9.25 mi e dam in West Winterport

You can use a good trail on the left to the put-in at the base of the falls. The Class I rips for 1.0 mile slow down through bottom farmland. The ME 141 bridge is passed at 3.0 miles. Just before the Marsh Stream Road bridge (5.75 miles) is Crooked Rip, a right-left-right ledge drop, Class II in low to moderate water. The junction with the North branch is another 0.25 mile.

The deadwater starts above the dam in West Winterport.

WEST WINTERPORT ➤ FRANKFORT   6.5 MI

Description:	Quickwater, Class I, II, III
Navigable:	High water: spring, after heavy rains
Scenery:	Forested
Maps:	Bucksport 15, DL 22 and 23
Portages:	5.0 mi L Flatrock Falls 100 yd
	(6.5 mi e dam)

This is a nice day trip with a variety of whitewater. Put in from Loggin Road in West Winterport just off ME 139. It starts with 2.0 miles of quick water, which is followed by three Class I rapids.

Just above a snowmobile bridge (3.25 miles) is a double ledge, running at 45 degrees to flow (Class II). In another 0.75 mile is a rock garden (Class I–II).

Beyond the railroad bridge (possible access) are Railroad Rip, which has complicated currents, and Pine Island Rip (Class II). Run left of the island; to the right is disastrous. Portage or line from the island if necessary. Scout before running.

Around another corner is Flatrock Falls (5.0 miles), Class IV–V. The runout is poor, as the river immediately becomes wider, shallow, and full of boulders and logs. One Class II drop comes before the final 1.5 miles mostly on flowage above the dam at Frankfort.

The last 1.0 mile on the North Branch of the Marsh River is tidal on the Penobscot River.

Chapter 5
Allagash Wilderness Waterway

Allagash River

Maine's best-known canoe route has attracted paddlers to the Allagash and its headwater lakes for more than a century. Since Thoreau ventured into the Allagash waters across Mud Pond Carry, the name Allagash has conjured up images of wildness and adventure by canoe. Today, the Allagash is one of few eastern U.S. rivers that can provide a remote paddling-trip experience of a week or more throughout the summer season. The legendary Allagash is Maine's only designated Wild & Scenic river, and since 1967 most of its shoreline has been owned by the state and managed as the Allagash Wilderness Waterway.

For some who do the Allagash trip, it symbolizes an achievement, the culmination of a series of trips, with the Allagash providing the finishing touch. For others, it is the beginning (maybe the first experience in a canoe or kayak), with other rivers to follow depending upon the individual's affinity for backwoods and blackflies, rain and rapids, winds and waves, and all the

ALLAGASH
WILDERNESS
WATERWAY

N

Scale in miles

0   10   20

St John River

Allagash

Allagash River

Musquacook Stream

First Musquacook Lake

Long Lake

Clayton Lake

Chemquasabamticook Stream

Umsaskis Lake

Third Musquacook Lake

Fifth Musquacook Lake

Clear Lake

Allagash River

Chemquasabamticook Lake

Churchill Lake

Eagle Lake

Allagash Lake

Chamberlain Lake

features of an extended paddling trip. People from all over the world come to Maine just to do the Allagash trip, and even for some Maine residents paddling the Allagash is the fulfillment of a lifelong dream.

Between ice-out and mid-June, fishing is the primary use of the Allagash waters. As the season progresses, paddlers are drawn to the wilderness setting for its traditional canoe- and kayak-camping experience. Heaviest paddle-tripping use occurs between mid-July and mid-August. In the middle of the summer, solitude can be hard to find, especially if you schedule your trip to run from weekend to weekend as most parties do. If you wish to encounter fewer people on the waterway, visit in mid- to late June, late August, or September.

You do not need to purchase USGS maps unless you are paddling into the Allagash Wilderness Waterway instead of using a vehicle access point. A map of the waterway is available free of charge from the Maine Department of Conservation, Northern Region, 106 Hogan Road, Bangor, ME (207-941-4014). Waterway rangers can also supply you with this map, and it is available at the North Maine Woods checkpoint as you drive in to the waterway. This official map shows the location of the 80-plus campsites, but does not show topography or all existing roads.

DeLorme mapping company publishes a Map & Guide of the Allagash/St. John Rivers, which shows campsites, roads, trails, and topographic features. It is for sale in many stores throughout the state and can be ordered from DeLorme at P.O. Box 298, Yarmouth, ME 04096 (800-561-5105).

If you plan to drive to the put-in, a current copy of the DeLorme *Maine Atlas and Gazetteer* is a must. The atlas shows every road and trail, and newer editions have topographic features. The maze of logging roads you have to negotiate can be confusing to those unfamiliar with the area, and road signs are rare. This atlas can be purchased directly from DeLorme (see above) and is available throughout Maine in most convenience stores.

Waterway land use and camping fees are collected at North Maine Woods checkpoints and electronic gates on the private roads leading to the waterway. In 2007, Allagash Wilderness Waterway day-use fees were $5 for adult Maine residents, and $8 for non-resident adults. Children under age 15 are free. Seniors' rates are reduced. Camping (overnight) fees are $8 per night in addition to the day fee for Maine resident adults, and $10 per night in addition to the day fee for non-Maine resident adults. Rates are lower for seniors. Children under 15 are free. Go to www.northmainewoods.org for current fee information.

North Maine Woods also can supply you with a list of outfitters, guides, and shuttle services that operate in the Allagash region.

For those who fly by floatplane into the Allagash, registration and camping fees are collected by the first waterway ranger encountered. Floatplanes are allowed to land only at certain designated locations within the waterway, so be sure to consult with your flying service when planning your trip itinerary. Flying services that provide flights to the Allagash are located in Greenville, Shin Pond, Millinocket, and Bangor.

From Chamberlain Bridge, the southernmost vehicle access point, the distance is 87.5 miles to the end of the Allagash Wilderness Waterway at West Twin Brook. Most parties continue on to Allagash Village, another 6.0 miles, before taking out. The trip from Chamberlain to Allagash will take 6 to 9 days (5 to 8 nights) depending on wind and water level and your paddling pace and daily mileage.

You find waterway Ranger Stations at Chamberlain Thoroughfare Bridge, on Allagash Lake, at Churchill Dam, on Umsaskis Lake Thoroughfare, and at Michaud Farm. A ranger is also usually present on Eagle Lake and at Round Pond.

Establishment of the Allagash Wilderness Waterway

A hydroelectric dam on the St. John River was first proposed in the 1920s. The site chosen was Rankin Rapids, 9.0 miles downstream from Allagash Village. A dam at that location would have wiped out the lower portions of both the Allagash and the upper St. John Rivers. The late 1950s saw renewed interest in damming the St. John, but public pressure ultimately prevented the construction of a high dam downstream from the mouth of the Allagash River.

In August 1962, the Natural Resources Council of Maine recommended land acquisition and management of the Allagash by the state or federal government. The following year, the Bureau of Outdoor Recreation in Washington recommended federal protection for the river. Pressure from the federal government for protection of the river through land acquisition led to the state's establishment of the Allagash Wilderness

Waterway on December 28, 1966. The act setting up the waterway authorized a bond issue of $1,500,000 ". . . to develop the maximum wilderness character of the Allagash Waterway," which was passed by Maine voters and matched by federal funds. The state acquired a corridor averaging 500 feet wide along the shore of the river and all the lakes it flows through from Telos Dam north to West Twin Brook, including Allagash Lake and Allagash Stream. The act also placed some restrictions on land use within 1.0 mile of the shorelines of the waterway.

One of the first projects undertaken by the state was the reconstruction of Churchill Dam to ensure that the flow through Chase Rapids could be regulated and maintained throughout the paddling season.

In 1970 the governor of Maine applied for and received federal Wild & Scenic river designation for the Allagash, and existing dams were grandfathered as historic structures. The Allagash was the first state-administered "wild" component of the Wild & Scenic river system.

The protection afforded the Allagash River applies to development, dam construction, and timber harvesting. Guidelines were established with the federal "wild" designation calling for strictly limited access points, temporary bridge crossings, relocation or discontinuation of roads, and restriction of the public use of private roads passing through the waterway. In 1999 a 10-year management plan for the waterway was developed that brought the Allagash under public scrutiny. The plan, adopted in 2000, authorized a number of new road access points. The increase raised concerns about possible negative effects on the wilderness experience of waterway users. One new access point in particular, John's Bridge, spurred much public debate over management of the Allagash, and remains controversial.

Camping use since 1973 has numbered approximately 45,000 to 50,000 visitor nights between ice-out and the end of September. While overall camping visitor numbers have remained flat in recent years, since 2001 the trend shows an increase in shorter visits and day use.

Early Logging along the Allagash

The Allagash is a river rich in human history, and the remnants of that history add to its appeal as a paddling trip. In 1835, logging began to have an impact on the Allagash region. As was the case all over the state, the early loggers built dams at the outlets of the lakes to store and release water into the rivers to drive logs downstream to a mill. Today, only a trace of old driving dams can be found at the outlet of Allagash Lake and Mud Pond. The remnants of Long Lake Dam still form a substantial obstruction that is mostly underwater.

Dams are of particular interest on the Allagash because of the diversion of much of its headwaters into the East Branch of the Penobscot. A dam at the site of Lock Dam raised the level of Chamberlain and Telos Lakes so that the water would flow east rather than north. Telos Dam was built to control the flow into the East Branch. A dam at the site of the present Churchill Dam raised the level of the water in Eagle, Churchill, and Heron Lakes. This allowed booming of logs on these lakes to another dam at the southern end of Eagle Lake that functioned as a lock. There, the logs were raised up to Chamberlain Lake, from where they were boomed down to Telos Dam and into the Penobscot watershed.

Unique to the Allagash were the Eagle Lake Tramway, used for 6 years from 1903, and the Eagle Lake and West Branch Railroad that operated over a 13.0-mile roadbed between Eagle and Chesuncook Lakes from 1927 to 1933. The remains of the tramway are still visible close to the old locomotives near Eagle Lake. You can still paddle through remnants of the railroad trestle crossing the north end of Chamberlain Lake.

Parties traveling the river stop to view the remains of two Lombard log haulers at Cunliffe Depot, the site of a long-gone logging settlement. Other evidence of lumbering history can be seen at campsite locations such as Long Lake Dam and Allagash Falls.

The history of the river is told in *The Allagash* by Lew Dietz (Holt, Rhinehart and Winston, 1968, and reprinted in 2000 by Down East Books). This book adds meaning to many of the places of interest along the river and gives you a picture of life in the Maine woods during the past two centuries. Another book, *Allagash* by Maine guide and author Gil Gilpatrick (self-published in 2003), gives a sense of the evolving human use of the area first as a hunting territory of Penobscot Indians and then by the river's logging history and the recreational paddling tradition.

The Allagash Wilderness Waterway Trip

The most popular vehicle access points at the southern end of the waterway are Chamberlain Thoroughfare Bridge and Indian Stream. Both are reached from Greenville or Millinocket by private logging roads that are open to the public. Be prepared to pay user fees to pass through gates on all these roads. From Ashland, you can use the American Realty Road to reach Long and Umsaskis Lakes and Churchill Dam. Churchill Dam and Umsaskis can also be reached by continuing north from Chamberlain Bridge.

CHAMBERLAIN THOROUGHFARE BRIDGE ➤ LOCK DAM   9.5 MI

Description:	Lake
Navigable:	Spring, summer, fall
Scenery:	Wild
Maps:	Churchill Lake 15, Umsaskis Lake 15, DL 55 and 56
Portage:	9.5 mi Lock Dam 20 yd
Campsites:	See Allagash Wilderness Waterway map

The boat landing is to the east of the bridge. After you unload, vehicles must be left in the large parking lot across the road and to the southwest. Check at the waterway Ranger Station for updates on weather and parties ahead of you.

Chamberlain is a very large lake with a northwest/southeast orientation, and the prevailing NW wind can make travel difficult and dangerous for small craft. Exercise caution and good judgment when crossing bays in Chamberlain and keep an eye to the sky.

LOCK DAM ➤ CHURCHILL DAM   18.75 MI

Description:	Lakes
Navigable:	Spring, summer, fall
Scenery:	Wild: tramway and trains—southwestern end of Eagle Lake; moose in early morning and evening, especially in Heron Lake
Maps:	Churchill 15, Umsaskis 15, DL 55, 56
Portage:	18.75 mi L Churchill Dam 50 yd
Campsites:	See Allagash Wilderness Waterway map

At the right end of Lock Dam is a short lift-over into the stream below. In 0.5 mile, you reach Martin Cove at the southern end of Eagle Lake. Beaver might have dammed the stream in one or two places, but canoes and kayaks can usually be pushed over the top.

No trip down the Allagash is complete without a visit to the tramway and the locomotives. The trail begins at the end of a narrow inlet on the shore of Eagle Lake located due south of Farm Island (6.0 miles from Lock Dam). Look out for metal spikes in logs underwater as you paddle into the inlet. The trail leads past the locomotives to Chamberlain Lake, parallel to the old tramway, which can be seen in the woods to the right. At the Chamberlain end of the trail are the remains of the engines that powered the tramway.

John's Bridge (12.25 miles) crosses the thoroughfare between Eagle and Churchill Lake, and 6.5 miles beyond is Churchill Dam (18.75 miles), where you take out on the left.

Indian Stream Access

For those wishing to skip Chamberlain Lake and a day of paddling, Indian Stream provides access to Eagle Lake in a cove southwest of Lock Dam and about the same distance from the northerly destinations. The Indian Pond road turns left off the Telos road 9.3 miles north of Chamberlain Bridge. Follow the Indian Pond road to the bridge over Indian Stream. You pass the Indian Pond campsite on the left. When you reach the stream, you see a small parking area to the right and a closed gate just beyond the bridge. Walk your boats for about 0.5 mile down Indian Stream to Eagle Lake.

INDIAN STREAM ➤ CHURCHILL DAM   18.75 MI

Description:	Small stream, lakes
Navigable:	Spring, summer, fall: low water—might have to drag or lift in a few places in stream
Scenery:	Wild
Maps:	Churchill Lake 15, Umsaskis Lake 15, DL 55 and 56
Campsites:	See Allagash Wilderness Waterway map

Indian Stream enters Eagle Lake in a shallow cove at the south end of the lake. In high water the stream can be paddled. You have some rocks to avoid, and low-hanging branches make poling difficult. In most conditions boats have to be walked down the stream.

After you are in Eagle Lake, continue north to Churchill Dam as if paddling from Lock Dam.

Description:	Quickwater, Class I, II, lakes
Navigable:	Spring, summer, fall: chase rapids—controlled release
Scenery:	Wild, moose along river, in delta before Umsaskis
Maps:	Churchill Lake 15, Umsaskis Lake 15, DL 55, 56, and 61
Portage:	0 mi Churchill Dam—50 yd from Churchill Lake take-out
Campsites:	See Allagash Wilderness Waterway map

If paddling from the lakes, the take-out is on the left before the dam. If putting in at the dam, river access is on the left below the dam, and the parking lot is behind the old boarding house building on the west side of the river.

The deteriorating 1968 timber crib Churchill Dam was removed in 1997 and replaced with a concrete dam. During the paddling season, enough Churchill Dam gates are kept open in the morning to provide a medium water level for Chase Rapids. In high water the gates might be kept open longer. Be sure to check with the ranger at the dam to find out what time gates shut down. Waterway rangers provide a portage service for gear around the first 6.0 miles of the river. A minimal fee is charged for the service, and most canoe-trippers use it.

The first 1.5 miles of Chase Rapids are Class II and the most difficult. Just after a big eddy you come upon another drop as the river turns sharply right. About 1.0 mile farther you encounter one more Class II section, and the rest of Chase Rapids is Class I and quick water to the remains of a washed-out bridge. Gear that has been portaged by the ranger can be picked up by landing on the left shore just above or below the old bridge abutment. After the gear pickup, minor rapids and quick water continue for most of the remaining distance to Umsaskis Lake (8.5 miles).

The next 9.75 miles up Umsaskis and Long Lakes and beyond are flat. At the north end of Harvey Pond, you find some riffles at the outlet. About 0.5 mile downriver look for the horizon line formed by the remains of Long Lake Dam (18.75 miles). The portage trail and campsites are on the right. The dam can be run only in high water, and even then must be scouted to find the deepest channel, as metal spikes protrude throughout the underwater woodwork of the dam. **Caution!** Not only have boats been ripped open, but paddlers have also been injured. In medium water some paddlers line their boats along the left shore after checking for spikes underwater. The old logs and cribworks are "slick as a smelt," so watch your step.

LONG LAKE DAM ➤ ST. JOHN RIVER   44.25 MI

Description:	Lake, quickwater, Class I, II
Navigable:	High and medium water: mid-May through July, generally
	Low water: if you can't pole, you might have to wade and drag in places
Scenery:	Wild
Maps:	Umsaskis Lake 15, Round Pond 15, Allagash Falls 15, Allagash 15, DL 61, 62, 66, and 70
Portage:	30.0 mi R Allagash Falls 0.25 mile
Campsites:	See Allagash Wilderness Waterway map

In a dry season, you should not have any illusions that the water level of the Lower Allagash is similar to that in Chase Rapids. The flow from Churchill Dam, where all but the fish ladder might be closed at night, is not sufficient alone to provide good paddling farther downstream, where the riverbed is much wider. The depth of the water below Long Lake depends largely on the contributions of all the small streams along the way. If they are low, you have to pick your channels carefully, and occasionally you might have to pole or walk your boat through shallow sections, particularly below Allagash Falls.

Below Long Lake Dam, intermittent riffles continue for 9.75 miles to Round Pond. After the outlet of Round Pond (11.25 miles) Class I Rapids and quick water alternate for 18.75 miles to Allagash Falls (30.0 miles). The only long stretch of flat water is Musquacook Deadwater, which begins about 2.0 miles before the mouth of Musquacook Stream (15.75 miles) and extends for about 2.0 miles north of it. You come upon a Waterway Ranger Station in the field at Michaud Farm (26.75 miles) beside a wide bend in the river to the right. Paddling parties are expected to stop and check with the ranger at Michaud

Farm. After the farm the river splits into several channels with many islands before coming back together just above Allagash Falls.

Allagash Falls (30.0 miles) is 3.25 miles below Michaud Farm. **Caution!** You should stop at the portage on the right bank above the rapids that precede the falls. Below the falls, the river continues much as it does above for the remaining 14.0 miles to Allagash Village. The only Class II water begins 7.5 miles below the falls at Twin Brook Rapids (37.5 miles). Twin Brook is the end of the state-owned Allagash Wilderness Waterway, but the river continues another 6.75 miles to its confluence with the St. John in the town of Allagash.

You travel one last rapid as the river completes a long oxbow before the ME 161 bridge. You can take out on the left just above the bridge (44.0 miles), or a little way below on the right where the Allagash and St. John waters start to mingle (44.25 miles). Landowners at these sites usually charge a small per-boat fee to take out. Remember to ask for and obtain permission before crossing property lines.

Alternative Routes into the Waterway by Canoe: To Allagash Lake

UPPER ALLAGASH STREAM ➤ ALLAGASH LAKE   3.75 MI

Description:	Small stream, quickwater
Navigable:	Spring and high water
Scenery:	Wild
Maps:	Allagash Lake 15, DL 55

Upper Allagash Stream can be reached by several different roads after passing through the NMW Caucomgomoc Checkpoint. Be aware that although roads might be on the map, they are not necessarily in passable condition.

The stream is flat water with swift current. Be on the lookout for obstructions from blowdowns or beavers. When you see Johnson Stream entering on the right (2.0 miles), it is 1.75 meandering miles farther to Allagash Lake (3.75 miles). The outlet is due east 3.25 miles (7.0 miles).

JOHNSON POND ➤ ALLAGASH LAKE   3.0 MI

Description:	Flatwater
Date checked:	1997
Navigable:	Spring, high water
Scenery:	Wild
Maps:	Allagash Lake 15, DL 55
Campsites:	On island in Johnson Pond

In high water, you can float a canoe most of the way down the stream from Johnson Pond to Allagash Stream. You might come upon obstructions as it is not used frequently anymore. In low water the stream is not passable. If you must portage, a grown-over tote road close to the right bank might or might not be a passable carry trail.

If you fly into Johnson Pond, you land at a small island. It is 1.25 miles from the island in Johnson Pond to Allagash Stream, followed by a 1.75-mile paddle down the latter to Allagash Lake (3.0 miles). To the east 3.25 miles, is the outlet (6.25 miles).

ALLAGASH LAKE OUTLET ➤ LOCK DAM   9.5 MI

Description:	Lakes, quickwater, Class I, II
Navigable:	Spring, early summer: fall or low water, wading
Scenery:	Wild, Little Allagash Falls, remains of trestle of the Eagle Lake and West Branch RR (1927–1933)
Maps:	Allagash Lake 15, Churchill Lake 15, DL 55
Portages:	3.25 mi L Little Allagash Falls 150 yd
	9.5 mi Lock Dam 20 yd
Campsites:	See Allagash Wilderness Waterway map

Below the lake, Allagash Stream flows for 2.75 miles to Little Round Pond. You travel continuous rapids, up to Class I, in the first part, but the last 1.0 mile consists of quick water. The portage around Little Allagash Falls (3.25 miles), at the outlet of Little Round Pond, is on the left through the campsite areas.

The stream below the falls, 2.25 miles long, has Class I rapids, except for three places. The first is a ledge about 0.25 mile below the falls that can be avoided by staying along the right shore and going to the right of a small island. A second ledge farther on must be lifted over on the left. Finally, be on the lookout for a logging bridge, because underneath is a short rapid that you should scout.

The gradient gradually lessens as you approach Chamberlain Lake (5.5 miles). It is a 4.0-mile paddle down the lake, past the railroad trestle (6.5 miles), to Lock Dam (9.5 miles).

If you are en route from Allagash Lake to Churchill Dam, you can avoid 7.5 miles of paddling, an important consideration if a strong headwind exists, by portaging along the abandoned tramway from the northern tip of Chamberlain Lake to Eagle Lake. Included in the bargain is a 0.5-mile carry, as well as a visit to the trains.

By Canoe: The Long Trips to Allagash Lake and Chamberlain Lake

A trip on the Allagash Wilderness Waterway, with Allagash Lake on the itinerary, takes 8 to 10 days if you put in above Allagash Lake. If you wish to plan a longer trip, you can do this by beginning at Chesuncook Lake on the West Branch of the Penobscot. It takes an additional 3 or 4 days from Chesuncook Dam to the Allagash by Mud Pond or Caucomgomoc Lake.

Long before today's network of logging roads into the Allagash region, the earliest trips on the Allagash usually began at Greenville and followed a route that went up Moosehead Lake, across North East Carry to the West Branch of the Penobscot, down the latter to Chesuncook Lake, and then by either Mud Pond to Chamberlain Lake or Caucomgomoc Lake to Allagash Lake. The two routes detailed below use Chesuncook Dam landing at the southern end of Chesuncook Lake as the starting point, but you can drive to the West Branch below Seboomook Lake, paddle downstream to Chesuncook Lake, and head north for either route. You can also drive to Caucomgomoc Lake or Umbazooksus Bridge, or for those with weeks of time, you can still start your trip at Moosehead Lake in Greenville and follow the route paddled and portaged by Thoreau into the Allagash, although that route is not outlined here.

CHESUNCOOK DAM ➤
ALLAGASH LAKE BY CAUCOMGOMOC   35.25 MI

Description:	Class I, II (if traveled in reverse)
Navigable:	Spring, summer, fall
Scenery:	Wild
Maps:	Harrington Lake 15, Ragged Lake 15, Chesuncook Lake 15, Allagash Lake 15, DL 49, 50, and 55
Portages:	26.0 mi L Caucomgomoc Stream 1.5 mi
	32.25 mi Allagash Carry 3.0 mi
Campsites:	10 sites Chesuncook Lake BPL $
	19.75 mi L Black Pond (S end) permit
	26.0 mi L Caucomgomoc Portage NMW $
	32.25 mi (N shore) NMW $ car
	35.25 mi Allagash Portage (N end) AWW $

From the landing at Chesuncook "dam" you have 26.0 miles of paddling up Chesuncook Lake and the length of Black Pond to the 1.5-mile Caucomgomoc Portage. The trail begins a short distance up Caucomgomoc Stream on the left at the campsite and leads to a logging road, which you follow to the right. A second road comes in on the left not far from the Caucomgomoc Dam (27.5 miles).

The rapids in Caucomgomoc Stream are easy enough that you can pull up the stream if you have enough water. The only difficulty, going up- or downstream, is a ledge approximately two-thirds up the stream, about opposite where the trail joins the logging road. When you first see the ledge, take out on the left up a steep bank to the trail leading to the logging road. Go right on the road and follow it to Caucomgomoc Dam.

The next leg of the trip is a 4.75-mile paddle up Ciss Stream (deadwater) and across Round Pond to the campsite (32.25 miles). The 3.0-mile Allagash Carry begins at the campsite and Ts off the logging road that goes around the northern shore of Round Pond. The carry trail is a hardened road. About halfway along the carry, go left where the road forks, onto the less traveled road. You come to a closed gate that can be carried around. Always remember to ask for and obtain permission before crossing property lines. As you near the end of the portage, an old trail at a fork leads left to the ranger camp on Allagash Lake. The right fork, a smaller footpath, leads to a campsite on the lake.

The outlet of Allagash Lake (40.0 miles) lies 4.75 miles northeast of the end of the portage.

CHESUNCOOK DAM ➤ LOCK DAM BY MUD POND   31.25 MI

Description:	Lakes, Class I
Navigable:	Spring, summer, fall
Scenery:	Wild, moose in Umbazooksus Lake
Maps:	Harrington Lake 15, Ragged Lake 15, Chesuncook 15, DL 49, 50, 55, and 56
Portages:	21.5 mi R Umbazooksus Dam 10 yd
	22.25 mi R Mud Pond Carry 1.75 mi
	31.25 mi Lock Dam 20 yd
Campsites:	10 sites on Chesuncook Lake BPL, 2 on Umbazooksus Stream
	22.5 mi Mud Pond Carry (S end) NMW $

It is a 20.25-mile paddle from the landing at Chesuncook "dam" to the head of the lake at Umbazooksus Stream, where in high water you must portage a low bridge. After the bridge, you paddle past dry-ki for 0.75 mile, after which you work your way up Umbazooksus Stream. Carry on the right around the remains of the dam on Umbazooksus Lake (21.5 miles). Be on the lookout for moose while crossing Umbazooksus.

The Mud Pond Carry begins on the northeastern shore of the lake, 0.75 mile from the dam. The trail crosses the old roadbed of the Eagle Lake and West Branch Railroad (1927–1933), passes through the campsite, crosses a logging road flanked on both sides with deep water-filled ditches, and then continues through attractive woods to Mud Pond (24.0 miles). While Mud Pond Carry is named after the pond, the name is an apt one and the carry is notorious for the character-building challenge of its knee-deep muck. Make sure your footwear is securely fastened and have a careful and safe carry.

Across Mud Pond, 1.25 miles, is the outlet (25.25 miles). The brook below can be run in high water, but part of it must be waded, lined, or poled down in medium water. Also, a portage trail to the right of the brook might be brushy. It is 0.25 mile from Mud Pond to

Mud Cove on Chamberlain Lake. Lock Dam (31.25 miles) lies 5.75 miles to the north.

By Canoe: To Eagle and Churchill Lakes

HAYMOCK LAKE ➤ EAGLE LAKE   8.0 MI

Smith Brook is mostly a small, easy stream, with a waterfall to lift over not far above Eagle Lake. This route is rarely used and might need clearing of brush or blowdowns.

CLIFF LAKE ➤ CHURCHILL LAKE   4.0 MI

Cliff Lake lies southeast of Churchill Lake. It is rarely used as an access route to the Allagash. You find a campsite and water access at the southeast end of the lake, although road conditions might or might not be passable. It is 2.0 miles across the lake and through Twin Lake to the outlet at South Twin Brook. If the water is high enough to run, this brook provides 2.0 miles of easy rapids to Churchill Lake. If the water is too low, you might have to wade with the boat. It is then 4.5 miles across Churchill Lake and through Heron Lake to Churchill Dam.

Chemquasabamticook Stream

The stream flows north from the lake of the same name, known also as Ross Lake. The latter has a large surface area, a factor that contributes to a relatively steady flow in Chemquasabamticook Stream, particularly above Clayton Lake. Nonetheless, this river requires the high water of May and early June because above Clayton Lake is a 1.0 mile-plus-long section with a gradient of 40 feet per mile that requires a good flow. The drop in this section is steady, and no large rocks are in the riverbed, so the rapids are Class II.

More than half of the river (17.0 miles) is rapids, all relatively easy, with the most difficult being below Clayton Lake. It is a very scenic, semiwilderness trip that can be done in little more than half a day in high water.

Chemquasabamticook Stream joins the Allagash Wilderness Waterway at Long Lake 4.5 miles north of the American Realty Road, from which Ross Lake can be reached. For paddlers continuing down the Allagash, it is 47.25 miles to the St. John River, in which case the most practical access to Ross Lake might be by floatplane.

ROSS LAKE ➤ LONG LAKE   27.0 MI

Description:	Lake, flatwater, Class I, II
Navigable:	High water: mid-May to early June
Scenery:	Wild
Maps:	Clayton Lake 15, Umsaskis Lake 15, DL 55 and 61
Campsites:	Ross Lake (NE shore) NMW $ car

The first 3.5 miles below Ross Lake are easy rapids, which begin to slacken at a bridge. Then, for 1.5 miles, you have deadwater, with two dry-ki dams; the first must be lifted over, but the second can be paddled around on the left. The flat water ends (0.5 mile), the current picks up, and the river drops steadily for 4.0 miles to an old logging camp (9.0 miles), where the current slackens. After 4.0 miles of meandering, the stream opens into Clayton Lake (13.0 miles). It is about 1.0 mile across the lake to the outlet (14.0 miles).

Below Clayton Lake, the stream drops steadily for 9.5 miles, providing good Class II whitewater. The river gradually becomes shallower and wider until it reaches slack water (23.5 miles). After 3.5 miles of flat water, it ends at Long Lake (27.0 miles). To the north, 3.0 miles, is Long Lake Dam (30.0 miles).

Musquacook Stream

Musquacook Stream flows north from a series of lakes east of the Allagash River, joining the latter 4.5 miles below Round Pond. In the spring when the water is high, the stream offers many miles of enjoyable whitewater up to Class III. The trip from Fifth Musquacook Lake to Allagash Village, a total of 52.5 miles, can be done in 3 days.

The stream begins at Clear Lake, an appropriately named body for water that has no tributaries to bring in the organic matter that colors most of Maine's paddleable waters. Access is difficult because the logging roads to it are not generally open to the public. Thus, a floatplane is the only practical access. The 1.0 mile from Clear Lake to Fifth Musquacook Lake is hard, requiring portaging (including bushwhacking) into and out of a deadwater between the two lakes.

The remainder of the stream from Fifth Musquacook Lake makes an excellent trip of lakes and rapids for 25.25 miles to the Allagash River. Fifth is not accessible by road, but Second Musquacook Lake can be reached at the campground on the American Realty Road.

FIFTH ➤ SECOND MUSQUACOOK LAKE   7.0 MI

Description:	Lakes, quickwater, Class I, II
Navigable:	High water: mid-May to early June
Scenery:	Wild
Maps:	Musquacook Lakes 15, DL 62
Portages:	4.0 mi L Fourth Musquacook Lake outlet
	5.25 mi L Musquacook Dam 0.75 mi

Fifth Musquacook Lake is a horseshoe-shaped lake 2.25 miles long, whose only access is by floatplane. The 0.5-mile long stream from the outlet is wide and deep when the water is high, but narrow and difficult when low. You have a 0.5-mile paddle on Fourth Musquacook Lake to its outlet, which is clogged with dry-ki, requiring a short carry left. The 1.0-mile run to Third Lake (5.0 miles) is a fast run of easy Class II rapids.

It is 0.5 mile across Third Lake to the outlet, where the dam is washed out and easily run in high water. The 1.5 miles of stream to Second Musquacook Lake (7.0 miles) is Class I–II. Just before Second Lake, the American Realty Road crosses the stream.

SECOND MUSQUACOOK LAKE ➤ ALLAGASH RIVER   18.25 MI

Description:	Lakes, flatwater, Class I, II, III
Scenery:	Wild
Maps:	Musquacook Lakes 15, Allagash Falls 15, DL 62
Portage:	1 long portage
Campsites:	0 mi R Squirrel Pocket NMW $ car
	5.25 mi L Musquacook Dam NMW $

The washed-out dam at the end of first Musquacook Lake (5.25 miles) is followed by Horse Race Rapids, which are extremely rough. A portage leads through the campsite left to an old tote road that follows the stream for 0.75 mile to where you can put in.

Below the portage the gradient lessens, and there follows about 2.5 miles of flat water to lower Horse Race Rapids (9.25 miles), which are Class III and can be heard as you approach them. A loaded canoe might have to be lined in a few places. The remaining 8.5 miles to the Allagash River at Musquacook Deadwater are all rapid, Class I–II.

Chapter 6
St. John Watershed

St. John River

The St. John River is 450.0 miles long, which makes it 50.0 miles longer than the Connecticut and, next to the St. Lawrence, the longest river in the Northeast. It starts in the remotest corner of Maine, loops north and east to form part of the border with Canada, and then sweeps south and east through New Brunswick to the Bay of Fundy. It was named by the Frenchman Samuel de Champlain, who was nosing along the coast in 1604 and happened to sail into its mouth on the feast day of St. John the Baptist. For the upper St. John, which Champlain never saw, the original Native American name Woolastook is indeed descriptive: it means "goodly river."

From 4th St. John to Baker Lake, the river starts shallow and narrow with drops and pitches that make it runnable only at spring's high water levels and after heavy downpours. Because no major lakes or dams provide holding waters, the St. John runs off quickly after spring snowmelt. Heavy cutting all

Scale in miles

0   10   20   30   40

QUEBEC

NEW BRUNSWICK

Northwest Branch
Daaquam
Depot Stream
Shields Branch
Big Black River
St. John River
Little Black River
Baker Branch
Baker Lake
Southwest Branch
Fifth St. John Pond
St. Francis River
Estcourt
Beau Lake
Allagash
St. Francis
Fish River Lake
Eagle Lake
St. Froid Lake
Fish River
Fish River
Portage Lake
Eagle Lake
St. John River
Fort Kent
St. Agatha
Mud Lake
Long Lake
Madawaska
Munsungan Lake
Munsungan Stream
Mooseleuk Stream
Mooseleuk Stream
Millinocket Lake
Machias River
Little Machias River
Portage
Beaver Brook
Salmon Brook
Square Lake
Cross Lake
Guerette
Van Buren
Millinocket Stream
Aroostook River
Oxbow
St. Croix Stream
Masardis
Ashland
Squa Pan Lake
Aroostook River
Washburn
Caribou
Little Madawaska River
Presque Isle Stream
Presque Isle
Meduxnekeag River
New Limerick
Cary
South Branch
B Stream
Whitney Brook
Bridgewater
Mars Hill
Prestile Stream
Houlton

along the river contributes to quick runoffs. Because of the vagaries of weather, the amount of snow at snowmelt, and rain (or lack of it), you can pinpoint no guaranteed best time to run the St. John. The surest times are at spring runoff (which can happen in a week or can stretch into a month) and following a downpour, which can happen anytime. The best formula for a successful run on the St. John is as follows: The river rises one vertical foot for each inch of rain; it takes 24 hours to reach that one foot; it will hold 24 hours; it will go back to its pre-rainfall level after another 24 hours. At two points on the river the cubic footage of water is measured 24 hours a day, and this is available online at http://www.maine.gov/mema/weather/weather.htm. At 1,500 cfs at Nine-Mile Bridge and 3,000 cfs at Dickey, the water is spread from the upper to lower St. John. If the weather report includes rainfall pre-trip and during trip, add up the inches, factor in the number of hours, and you can discern ahead of time a scenario of river heights and run-off times. Note that high cfs at Dickey and low cfs at Nine-Mile means good water downriver, not upriver, suggesting a put-in north of Nine-Mile. Conversely, if water is high at Nine-Mile and some rain is forecast, you can expect a sufficient level, especially if you increase your daily mileage and/or put in downriver. A 20,000 cfs at Dickey is a high level for paddling from the put-in at Baker Lake.

Runnable pitches are from 1,000–1,500 cfs and above at Nine Mile and 2,500–3,000 and above at Dickey. This formula obviously works best for those who can pick up at any given time and leave, rather than for those who must stick to an agenda.

The best of plans can be molded by the weatherman and the cfs reports as to where to put in and where to take out and/or whether to start at all. Adding an extra river day in the plan provides flexibility in case of inclement weather or unforeseen circumstances. The weather forecast is available online at http://www.maine.gov/mema/weather/weather.htm. When you are on the river, you might be able to get reception for the NOAA radio broadcast from Frenchville. See the NOAA website at http://www.maine.gov/mema/weather/weather.htm.

Other pre-planning factors include where to put in and take out, how you decide to travel (by road or by air), and how to set up your shuttle vehicles if they are to be used. North Maine Woods, Inc. (207-435-6213), is in charge of the road system, fee schedules, and permits for the St. John area. The North Maine Woods St. John River Planning Guide is essential for planning and running the river. It is downloadable online at northmainewoods.org. That website also has information about fees and payment for road and campsite use.

You have as many methods of accessing and egressing the St. John River as you have drive-in and drive-out sites, each dependent on your itinerary. For the most part, access can be at 4th St. John, 5th St. John, and Baker Lake. Road access to Baker Lake can be made through the province of Quebec, Canada, to Saint Aurelie, and then east on the International Paper Company road to Baker or through Maine to Greenville, NNE to Kokad-jo, left onto the Golden Road, right onto the Ragmuff Stream Road to Caucomgomac NMW gate, and on past Saint Francis Lake to Baker Lake. You can also travel through Maine to Millinocket and then west on the Golden Road to Ragmuff, and then as above. The DeLorme *Maine Atlas and Gazetteer* and the DeLorme map of the Allagash and St. John are very helpful. Contact local resources about road access from Allagash Village, which might change as the roads are maintained by paper companies.

Many paddlers use an outfitter in St. Francis or Allagash Village who drive you to your put-in and/or your vehicles around to your take-out point. If you have the time, inclination, and local road knowledge, you can shuttle your own vehicles to the take-out point.

"Woolastook" (Goodly River), the St. John, is a magnificent river to run. Flowing 154.0 miles, the river begins at 4th St. John with riffles, alder, and fords. It expands from 20 feet of brook at Fourth to 300 to 600 feet of the stream below the Southwest Branch to 800 to 1,500 ft wide at Ft. Kent. The river grows at each inlet, forming major rapids at Big Black and Big Rapids. Four major rivers, each larger than Baker Branch, increase the volume, from Southwest Branch to Northwest Branch to the Big Black to the Allagash. A myriad of brooks and streams from Turner to Brailey to Doucie to Knowles, Burntland to Nine-Mile, Chimenticook, Pockwock, Ouellette, and Fox all add their waters to the expanding St. John.

Because a majority of paddlers put in at Baker Lake, we start the mileage from that point and end the mileage at Allagash Village. We do, however, show mileage from 4th to 5th St. John Ponds, from 5th St. John to Baker Lake, and from Allagash to Fort Kent as separate trips. You can add them if you include them in your trip. As these waters flow geographically from one to the other, we describe them as a continuum— 4th St. John to Ft. Kent.

Description:	Flatwater, Class I, II
Navigable:	High water—after snowmelt and heavy rainfall
	Medium water—following rainfall
Scenery:	Wild
Maps:	Baker Lake 15, Beaver Pond 15, DL 48 and 54
Campsites:	0 mi Baker Outlet
	4.6 mi R Turner Bogan
	8.5 mi R Flaws Bogan
	17.7 mi L Southwest Branch
	18.2 mi L Sunset Island
	21.6 mi L Doucie Brook
	23.2 mi R Knowles Brook
	28.8 mi R Northwest Branch
	31.9 mi L Ledge Rapids
	32.6 mi Moody Bridge

At Baker Lake you find two campsites and an outhouse, near the road. The put-in is just before a bridge, on river left. If you have to duck a bit to go under the bridge, the water is at an excellent level.

You travel numerous easy rapids for 4.69 miles to Turner Brook, which enters on the right. You find a campsite just above at Turner Bogan on the right. For the next 8.0 miles the river is mostly flat. Flaws Bogan campsite (8.57 miles) is located on the high right bank. A second campsite, with a forest service cabin, is about 300 yards farther downstream on river left. The cabin is available on a first-come basis. Approximately 14.0 miles from Baker Lake, the current picks up. In the remaining 4.0 miles, nearing Southwest Branch, the rapids might increase to Class II. The Baker Branch is still small enough so that the forest grows right to the water's edge. As you approach the confluence with the Southwest Branch, you can begin to see the effect of the tremendous force behind the ice as it breaks up in the spring. Where sharp bends and a strong current exist, the ice has scraped and sometimes broken off the trees on the outside of the turns. As you continue downstream, the size of the river increases, and the scouring of the riverbank is such a regular occurrence during ice-out that few trees grow near the water except alders, which are relatively unaffected as the ice rides over them. Often huge blocks of ice wash up on the shore, sometimes over high banks and many yards back in the woods.

At the Southwest Branch are several good campsites. The first is on the left across the confluence with the Southwest Branch, and it must be anticipated in order to reach it without being carried downstream. Eddy left into the Southwest Branch and ferry across stream to the site. The next site, also on the left, is more easily reached. It is a small site at the head of Sunset Island.

Below the confluence with the Southwest Branch (17.74 miles) are 11.14 miles of smooth and quick water all the way to the Northwest Branch. About 4.0 miles below the Southwest Branch is a campsite on the left, across from Doucie Brook; shortly thereafter is a site at Knowles Brook, river-right (23.24 miles). You come upon a few riffles as you approach the Northwest Branch. Just below, on the right, is a nice, small, high-bank campsite. After the confluence with the Northwest Branch (28.88 miles) is a large boulder patch. Just below the boulder patch, which requires careful maneuvering, is a heavy pitch at high water. A good path is to start right, move to center at the first corner, skirt stacks, following right beyond the streamlet, and edge left at the runout. Shortly after this pitch is the Ledge Rapids campsite and a cabin on the left shore. The cabin is available on a first-come basis. Stay right at Ledge Rapids. Moody Bridge soon looms ahead. The take-out is on river left, just below the bridge. You find five campsites here. Note that they are also drive-in sites from Reality Road.

MOODY BRIDGE ➤ ALLAGASH VILLAGE   72.25 MI

Description:	Quickwater, Class I, II, III (at high water)
Navigable:	High water—after snowmelt and heavy rainfall
	Medium water—following rainfall
Scenery:	Wild
Maps:	Beaver Pond 15, Clayton Lake 15, Rocky Mountain 15, Allagash 15, DL 54, 60, 61, 70, and 66

Campsites along this section from Moody Bridge to Allagash are numerous and spaced at convenient intervals. Most sites are on river left; toward the lower sections, the sites are accessible by car.

Campsites:	34.6 mi R Red Pine
	36.4 mi L Burntland Brook
	44.0 mi L Nine-Mile Bridge
	54.0 mi R Connor's Farm
	55.1 mi L Seven Islands
	58.2 mi L Priestly Campsite
	63.9 mi L Simmons Farm
	68.9 mi L Basford Rips
	73.7 mi L Big Black
	75.3 mi L The Birches
	77.2 mi L Ferry Crossing
	79.0 mi L Seminary Brook
	80.4 mi R Boom Chain
	80.6 mi L Long Rapids
	87.7 mi L Castonia Farm
	88.6 mi L Ouellette Farm
	90.5 mi L Fox Brook
	94.9 mi L Poplar Island
	101.9 mi L Dickey
	104.8 mi R Allagash Village

At Moody Bridge, you find a spring on river left, about 50 yards up the dirt road. Some boards are across the ditch on the right to the pipe, which comes out of the bank. Filtering or boiling is recommended.

For the next 25.0 miles, from Moody Bridge to Priestly Campsite, the river has good current with occasional easy rapids. In medium to low water, the river is shallow in many places, requiring that you choose your route carefully. As is so frequently the case of canoe and kayak travel at low water on many Maine rivers, the St. John lends itself to the use of the setting pole. Setting pole notwithstanding, in very low water, occasionally it becomes necessary to handline or walk your boat.

In high water travel is almost effortless. At mid to high water Rocky Rapids are instructive in the art of going slower than the current through high-standing waves; they lead to Red Pine on the right and a real widening and slowing of the river for 2.0 miles to Burntland Brook. Between Burntland and Nine-Mile Bridge are numerous turns hosting fast water that behoove you to start each corner on the inside so as to have the option to go wide or not as the rip develops.

Nine-Mile, as told by Helen Hamlin in her book *Nine-Mile Bridge* (W.W. Norton, 1945), was a settlement through the 1930s and is identifiable by the remains of the bridge abutment. The gauging station can be seen downstream. Some shingles from the Hamlins' cabin are visible behind the picnic table set in their former front yard. To see the remains of a steam shovel and the railroad tracks used to maneuver it around in the woods, go up to the Forest Service Cabin on the road, turn right, go about 20 yards to a path on the right into the woods. Seven Islands, the major logging-resupply and horse-rehab depot of the early 1900s, lies 9.0 miles downriver and stretches, island by island, flat and grassy from Connor's Farm on the right past the Seven Islands campsites on the left. Abandoned farm equipment is scattered in the fields on the left of the Seven Islands campsites. Priestly Campsite, site of the old Priestly Bridge, is a drive-in site off the St. Pamphille Road. Priestly Rapids, below Priestly Deadwater, is a true anomaly of this evasive river—hidden at high water, but a runable rapid at mid to low water. Simmons Farm is a grassy knoll on the west shore across from a large island.

Below Simmons Farm is a shallow section for several miles, and you come upon two small rapids: Basford Rips, located at the two right-hand turns that precede Big Black Rapids. **Caution!** Big Black Rapids are 1.0-mile long and can reach Class III depending on the water level. They begin in a sharp left-hand bend of the river. Because you cannot see them as you approach the corner, it is advisable to stop on the left shore at a small eddy behind a rock where there is a good path on the bank above to look them over. They are the most difficult rapids between Baker Lake and Big Rapids. The rapids consist of two sharp drops with an easier section in between. Here you find boulders, ledges, and standing waves. At high water the safest route to follow is down the right-hand side. At mid to low water start left, go to the middle, go to the eddy on river left, come back out, maneuver around various rocks, and end on river left. After 1.0 mile of mostly smooth water, Big Black River enters on the left. The campsites are at the point. You find a spring on Big Black, on river right about 300 yards from the confluence. You take a steep path down the bank to the spot where a pipe comes out of the bank. Filtering or boiling is recommended.

Swollen by the flow from the Big Black River, the river continues for the next 24.0 miles with a good steady current, broken several times by short drops that are Class I in high water and somewhat more difficult when the river is lower. Basford Rips campsite is a good rest stop before Big Rapids.

After a sweeping left turn in the river with a field and a large orange log house with a red metal roof on the left, look for the eddy behind the rock with a take-out by the road. Some paddlers have vehicles shuttled here to load up their gear. Like Chase Rapids on the Allagash, it is best to run Big Rapids with empty boats. If you choose not to run Big Rapids, you can take out at this spot. **Caution!** Big Rapids is 2.0 miles long, Class III, and difficult in high water. It should be scouted from the left bank. Most of the rapids on the St. John get easier as the water rises because they are flooded out. This one does not because it has many large boulders that produce heavy waves. The best route to run this rapid is to stay left all the way through; the last part is the most difficult. Below Big Rapids, the river flattens, passes under the bridge in Dickey, where you have a take-out on river right, and through Allagash Village, where the Allagash River enters on the right.

ALLAGASH ➤ FORT KENT   27.1 MI

Description:	Quickwater, Class I, II
Navigable:	High: 4,000 cfs or above at Dickey
	Medium: 2,500–4,000 cfs or above at Dickey
Scenery:	Rural
Maps:	Allagash 15, Saint Francis 15, Eagle Lake 15,
	Fort Kent 15, DL 66 and 67
Campsites:	5.0 mi R Cross Rock
	8.5 mile R Rankin Rapids (not easily recognized
	dirt road leads up from river)
	11.0 mi R Pelletier
	Numerous islands below St. Francis

For the first 11.5 miles the northern bank of the St. John is wild, and the southern bank has a few houses and fields along the highway, which follows the river closely some of the way. Below St. Francis it flows between Maine and New Brunswick in a rural setting all the way to Fort Kent. This section can be run easily in less than a day except when the water is low. The current is strong for 11.5 miles to the St. Francis River, which enters on the left. You encounter three short rapids, Cross Rock (4.25 miles), Golden (5.5 miles), and Rankin (8.75 miles). They rate up to Class II in medium water, but they are largely flooded out when the river is high. If you are going to be picked up by floatplane in St. Francis, stop at least 1.0 mile above the town to avoid having to paddle back upstream to the plane. Below the St. Francis River (11.5 miles), the St. John is broader and flatter but with good current for the rest of the way to Fort Kent, where the Fish River enters on the right (28.0 miles).

St. John River (Northwest Branch)

The Northwest Branch rises in Beaver Pond near Lac Frontiere and flows south to Powers Gore, where it is joined by the Daaquam River— a stream running north, parallel to the Southwest Branch, until it turns east and crosses the boundary to join up with the Northwest Branch. The American Realty Road, which comes in from Daaquam, Quebec, follows the Daaquam River and the Northwest Branch and then crosses the main St. John River several miles below. The customs stations on this road are not open nights or Sundays. If the water is high enough, you can paddle down the Daaquam River and the Northwest Branch practically from the border.

DAAQUAM ➤ SOUTHWEST BRANCH   8.5 MI

Description:	Quickwater, Class I
Navigable:	High water
Scenery	Wild
Maps:	Beaver Pond 15, DL 60 and 54

Put in on the Daaquam River at Daaquam Forest Service Headquarters. It is nearly 2.5 miles down the Daaquam River to the junction with the Northwest Branch, where it becomes a broader stream, and then 6.0 miles to the junction with the main stream. In this distance the river is mostly smooth. Below the confluence with the Southwest Branch is a larger boulder patch followed by riffles and good current for the remaining 4.5 miles to the American Realty Road.

St. John River (Southwest Branch)

This is a common approach to the St. John River early in the season, giving the longest continuous run.

4TH ST. JOHN POND OUTLET ➤
5TH ST. JOHN POND OUTLET   6.5 mi

Description:	Ponds, flatwater, Class I, II (depending on cfs)
Navigable:	High water only—following snowmelt and after heavy rainfall
Scenery:	Wild
Maps:	St. John Pond 15, DL 48 and 54
Campsites:	0 mi 4th St. John outlet, E shore, small
	6.0 mi NW shore at canal 5th St. John Pond
	6.5 mi NE shore at outlet 5th St. John Pond

From 4th to 5th St. John Ponds, the Baker Branch is small enough to crowd you with alder and block you with dry-ki dams. The old dam at 4th has long been washed out. Immediately below the outlet, the stream consists mostly of fast, shallow riffles, with no big rocks; then it deepens and slows until, about halfway down, you come to a dry-ki dam in an alder swamp. The lower section speeds up, leading to a short, sharp pitch just above and at a bridge site near the inlet to 5th St. John Pond. At this pitch (as at so many places on the St. John at low- to mid-flow levels) you should stand and pole, slowing the boat to a manageable speed. Shortly below this pitch, the stream enters 5th St. John. Two campsites are at the north end, 3.5 miles down the pond.

5TH ST. JOHN POND OUTLET ➤ BAKER LAKE OUTLET   19.32 MI

Description:	Lakes, flatwater, Class I, II
Navigable:	High water only—following snowmelt and after heavy rainfall
Scenery:	Wild
Maps:	St. John Pond 15, Baker Lake 15, DL 48 and 54
Campsites:	0 mi 5th St. John outlet
	16.5 mi Baker Pond, SE shore
	19.3 mi Baker Pond, N outlet

Below 5th St. John sluiceway, the first 4.0 miles are difficult. The river runs fast with sharp turns and drops that require quick maneuvers to avoid being swept against the outside banks. Stow poles inside and beneath thwarts. (If they trail behind the boat, they can be snapped off.) The rapids are not difficult, but they are continuous and demand constant attention. In this section you come upon two old logging bridges that might block the river (depending on the water level) and two dry-ki dams that require very short portages or drags without unloading gear: first on the left and then on the right. Other than the possibility of a log or fallen tree, you face no more obstacles. For the next 8.0 miles, the current remains strong with rapids most of the way to a long deadwater. After 4.5 miles of flat water, the river empties into Baker Lake. The first campsite is immediately to the right (16.5 miles). The next site is at the outlet on the west shore (19.3 miles). This is a long, arduous 16.5 miles from 5th outlet to Baker inlet—equal to many 30.0-mile days on larger rivers.

Big Black River

In many respects, the Big Black River resembles the St. John. It is a large river with alternating sections of slow- and fast-moving current. The rapids are generally shallow, and they tend to get easier as the water gets higher, although a few might generate large waves at times of heavy runoff. The water level is responsive to rainfall, and the river is likely to show daily fluctuations that can be easily measured.

Below the mouth of Depot Stream and above the bridge near the top of Connors Sluice are a few cabins, but the remainder of the river is wild. Many of the banks are heavily forested, but Ninemile Deadwater, which used to be flooded, is bordered by extensive and open low-lying areas. At the end of Connors Sluice is a large meadow that is similar to the one at Seven Islands on the St. John River.

The Big Black River can be reached by road from Allagash. At Saint Pamphile, a North Maine Woods road crosses the border and soon divides. The road to the left crosses Shields Branch, which provides a flat-water access to Ninemile Deadwater that is used by anglers in motorboats. Straight ahead is the bridge near the top of Connors Sluice. The one to the right crosses the river close to the border. The river from that point to Depot Stream is mostly flat.

An alternative means of access is to fly into Depot Lake.

DEPOT STREAM ➤ ST. JOHN RIVER   22.5 MI

Description:	Flatwater, quickwater, Class I, II
Navigable:	High water: mid-May to early June
	Medium water: scratchy by mid-June
Scenery:	Wild
Maps:	Seven Islands 15, Round Pond 15, DL 61
Campsites:	10.25 mi L Ninemile Deadwater (First right turn
	in T14, R14) NMW $
	13.75 mi L Big Black Dam NMW $
	17.5 mi L Fivemile Brook NMW $
	20.5 mi L Twomile Brook NMW $

Below the mouth of Depot Stream are 2.5 miles of flat water to the beginning of Connors Sluice, a fast and easy 2.5-mile Class II run that ends at the beginning of Ninemile Deadwater (5.0 miles). In 2.75 miles, Shields Branch enters on the left.

Ninemile Deadwater extends all the way to Big Black Dam (13.75 miles). The washed-out dam is runnable. The remaining 8.75 miles to the St. John River are a mixture of intermittent Class I and II rapids and quick water, with the most difficult sections being just above and below Fivemile Brook (17.5 miles).

Depot Stream

Depot Stream is a tributary of the Big Black River. Depot Lake, below which the stream is runnable, is located close to the Quebec border; it is a remote body of water. A trip from the lake to Allagash is 72.5 miles. You have no portages, and the hardest rapids, other than Big Rapids on the St. John, are Class II.

Depot Lake can be reached from Allagash, on the west side. You can drive from Quebec to at least three places along the upper half of the stream.

Description:	Flatwater, quickwater, Class I, II
Navigable:	High water: mid-May to early June
Scenery:	Wild
Maps:	Depot Lake 15, Seven Islands 15, DL 60 and 61
Campsites:	8.0 mi L (grassy area) NMW $

From the outlet at the northern end of Depot Lake are 3.0 miles of flat water to a logging bridge, followed by 0.75 mile of easy Class II rapids that lead to another flatwater section 4.0 miles long. Much of this section is through alder swamps and extensive low-lying areas, where you get occasional views of Depot Mountain ahead.

As it passes around the northern side of the mountain, the stream enters a narrow and densely wooded valley, and Class II rapids begin (7.75 miles). In 0.5 mile, you come upon a bridge where the road to the fire tower crosses. Watch for a ledge drop on a blind corner approximately 1.0 mile after rounding the mountain. (To reach the tower follow the road to the south right. Keep left at the fork. The distance is 1.0 mile.)

Rapids and quick water continue for the next 7.0 miles to the bridge on the logging road from Saint Pamphile to Allagash (15.25 miles). You then travel quick water for most of the remaining distance to the Big Black River (19.0 miles).

Shields Branch

Shields Branch rises in Quebec and flows across the international boundary into Maine. Although the upper part can be paddled, it has no access. The road from Saint Pamphile, mentioned in the description of the Big Black River, crosses Shields Branch about 3.0 miles above the junction of that stream with the Big Black and provides an opportunity to reach the latter below Connors Sluice. The 3.0 miles of meandering river give an easy and pleasant paddle through wild country.

Little Black River

The Little Black River rises in Quebec and flows in a southeasterly direction to the St. John River, which it reaches at Dickey. It is navigable from the international boundary all the way to the St. John. The river is most easily reached by a private road of the Seven Islands Land Company, which runs south from Estcourt in Quebec. This road reaches the river about 2.0 miles from the international boundary. Always remember to ask for and obtain permission before crossing property lines. You find a public campground here, which makes a good starting point. The trip is fast water most of the way, with two rapids, both usually runnable.

T19 R12 BRIDGE ➤ ST. JOHN RIVER   27.0 MI

Description:	Quickwater
Navigable:	High water: spring or after heavy rains
Scenery:	Wild
Maps:	Rocky Brook 15, Rocky Mountain 15, Allagash 15, DL 66

You can put in at the campground on the private road at the bridge over the river in T19 R12. From here, you travel a good current to the fork where the West Branch comes in. You find a very fast rapid here, about 0.6 mile long. Below this rapid the river has a good current for the 9.0 miles to Boat Landing Camp at the end of a spur of the same private road from Estcourt. You come to a public campground here on the northern bank of the river. Below Boat Landing Camp, the river meanders for 10.0 miles through a boggy section, although it does have well-defined banks. About 1.0 mile more below this section, Johnson Brook enters on the right; a public campground is here near the road that comes upstream from the mouth. From Johnson Brook, you travel 5.0 more miles of fast water to the mouth, with a falls about halfway down. This is usually runnable but should be looked over first. In high water, a carry is necessary; the carry trail is on the left. From here to the St. John River, it is all easy but with a good current. Almost directly across the St. John is the town of Dickey, where you can take out on ME 161 if you do not wish to run down that stream.

Saint Francis River

The Saint Francis River rises near Whitworth, Quebec, and flows southeast into Pohenegamook Lake. Upon its exit from this lake, it becomes the international boundary for the rest of its course to its confluence with the St. John River. It flows eastward on a very meandering course to Blue River, Quebec, where it turns almost due south for a number of miles. Finally, just above Glazier Lake, it flows southeast toward the St. John. The water holds up well because of the many lakes, so that from Blue River down, at least, it can be run at any time. The best approach is from the Maine side of the river.

ESTCOURT ➤ BLUE RIVER   24.0 MI

Description:	Quickwater, Class I
Navigable:	Medium or high water: spring and early summer
Scenery:	Wild
Maps:	Beau Lake 15, DL 67

This section is very winding. Although the water holds up well, it can become quite scratchy in a dry summer, so the best time for running is probably spring and early summer. Watch for overhanging trees. No serious rapids and few obstructions are here, but some of the old dams, which have been largely washed out, might require a lift-over or lining down. At Blue River the Riviere Blue enters from the north, adding considerably to the volume.

BLUE RIVER ➤ BEAU LAKE   10.0 MI

Description:	Quickwater
Navigable:	Spring, summer, fall
Scenery:	Wild, rural
Maps:	Allagash 15, Beau Lake 15, DL 66 and 67

This portion of the river carries somewhat more water and can usually be run at any time. It has many meanders but no rapids of any consequence. It provides a pleasant, easy paddle with forested banks on the Maine shore; most of the time, you see fields on the Canadian side.

BEAU LAKE ➤ ST. JOHN RIVER   22.0 MI

Description:	Lakes, quickwater, Class I, II
Navigable:	Spring, summer, fall
Scenery:	Wild
Maps:	Saint Francis, DL 67

This is probably the most interesting stretch of the whole river, as it comprises lake, rapid, and fastwater paddling. Like the Allagash, which it resembles, it can be run at any time. The road running south from Blue River ends at Beau Lake, but it gives you a chance to select this section without necessarily running the 10.0 miles down from Blue River if you wish. You can put in at the upper end of Beau Lake and paddle down the 6.0 miles to the narrows at the southern end, after which you travel 1.0 mile more of wide, lake-like stream. Halfway down you pass the Quebec–New Brunswick boundary on the left, before the river becomes narrow for another 1.0 mile, with a small pond partway down.

The river then enters Cross Lake, which you paddle down less than 0.25 mile to the outlet on the eastern shore or all the way down the lake, 0.5 mile to the southern end. The 0.75 mile of river to the Upper MacPherson Pond includes the 0.33-mile-long Cross Lake Rapid (Class III), which must be scouted. The water is heavy and in high water can be dangerous or impossible for a loaded boat. The 0.5-mile carry from the southern end of Cross Lake to Upper MacPherson Pond would be the wise choice for less experienced paddlers.

Upper MacPherson Pond is 0.75 mile long. At its southeastern corner, the river turns southeastward and in 300 yards flows into Lower MacPherson Pond, down which you paddle 1.0 mile to the short stretch of river leading into Glazier Lake. This lake is 4.0 miles long to the Narrows; then you travel 0.5 mile more to the outlet. From the outlet of Glazier Lake, take 2.0 miles of fast water to Falls Brook. Here, where the brook enters on the right at a sharp left turn, is the 0.33-mile-long Falls Brook Rapid. This can be a difficult spot and should be looked over, especially at high water.

In another 1.0 mile, after the river has made a sharp right turn, you come to the Horseback Rapids. These are composed of two short, but sharp, drops. Scout before running. The next 2.0 miles to the MacDonald Rock Rapid contain a number of twists and turns. This rapid is about

0.33 mile long and has high waves in high water. In low water, you encounter many rocks, and fast boat handling is necessary.

From here it is about 1.0 mile to the St. John River, which you
reach opposite the town of Saint Francis, Maine.

Fish River

The Fish River rises from the confluence of a number of brooks in Township 13 Range 8, 2.0 miles south of Fish River Lake. For all practical
purposes, the lake can be considered as its source. From here it flows
eastward to Portage Lake, on which the town of Portage is located. It
then takes a northerly route to flow into the St. John River at Fort Kent.
The upper headwaters are in wild country and must be paddled early
in the season when the water is fairly high. Except for wet seasons, summer travel might be impractical. From Portage Lake down, the stream is
larger and much of it comprises lakes, so that travel at most seasons is
practical. Many paddlers combine it with the lakes of the East Branch,
which joins it at Eagle Lake, to make a long trip.

FISH RIVER SOURCE ➤ PORTAGE   24.0 MI

Description:	Lakes, flatwater, quickwater
Navigable:	High water
Scenery:	Wild
Maps:	Fish River Lake 15, Winterville 15, Portage 15, DL 63 and 64
Portage:	8.5 mi Fish River Falls

An unmarked private road from Portage crosses the Fish River practically at its source above Fish River Lake. Always ask for and obtain permission before crossing property lines. A branch of this road,
which swings north and down the Red River to Eagle Lake, has a
side road, which reaches Fish River Lake at the outlet. You can also
fly in to the lake, where you find two sporting camps. If you put in
at the road crossing above the lake, you find 2.0 miles of easy travel
with a good current north to the lake. A sporting camp is 0.25 mile
away from the inlet on the western shore and another is halfway
down the lake on the eastern shore. It is 3.0 miles down the lake to
the game warden's camp at the outlet at the northeastern corner.

From the lake, 0.5 mile of river takes you to Round Pond, where you find a public landing and campsite; then it is 0.5 mile across the pond. The Fish River Falls are located just below the pond, and a short portage is necessary. Fish River Falls can be run, but it is a heavy Class III+ section. The next 2.5 miles are quick water, with minor rips. The river then becomes smooth water through marshland fringed by forest, good moose country, for most of the 10.0 miles to Portage Lake. It is then 3.0 miles down the lake to the village of Portage at its southeastern corner.

PORTAGE LAKE ➤ EAGLE LAKE   24.0 MI

Description:	Lakes, flatwater
Navigable:	Spring, summer, fall
Scenery:	Forested
Maps:	Portage 15, Eagle Lake 15, DL 63 and 67

This section is all smooth water or lakes. It is often run in the reverse direction starting at the head of the East Branch chain of lakes. From Portage, it is 4.0 miles down the lake to the outlet at the northern end. For the next 10.0 miles to Saint Froid Lake, the Fish River offers smooth paddling through boggy woodlands. You see an excellent beach as you enter Saint Froid Lake.

Saint Froid Lake is 7.0 miles long and less than 1.0 mile wide. About 4.0 miles down, the Red River enters on the left. In another 3.0 miles, you reach the foot of the lake, and here the 3.0-mile-long Nadeau Thoroughfare leads to Eagle Lake, where this route meets that coming down the East Branch. You can use a good campsite across Eagle Lake from the inlet, at Cozy Point on the northeastern shore just east of Oak Point.

EAGLE LAKE ➤ ST. JOHN RIVER   20.5 MI

Description:	Lakes, flatwater, quickwater, Class I, II
Navigable:	Medium water
Scenery:	Forested, rural
Maps:	Eagle Lake 15, Fort Kent 15, DL 67
Portage:	16.0 mi R Fish River Falls 20 yd

From the inlet of Eagle Lake to Eagle Lake Village is less than 2.0 miles. Eagle Lake is a very beautiful, narrow lake. It is about 5.0 miles from Eagle Lake Village to the outlet near Wallagrass. Below, you travel 4.0 miles of smooth river to Soldier Pond, where you come upon a bridge (10.0 miles). Here the quick water begins.

Below Soldier Pond 1.0 mile is a 4-foot drop, which can be run on the right (Class II) or lifted over on the left. You travel quick water for the next 5.0 miles to the second Fish River Falls, a Class V drop. **Caution!** Stop well above the falls on the right and line the boat down to the carry trail, starting from an eddy at the lip of the falls on the right. If the falls is run, it must be run on the right over the drop, because the easy-looking left chute has many sharp rocks and cross-currents.

Below the falls, it is 2.5 miles to a railroad bridge; then you come to Pelletier Rapids, a Class II drop 200-feet long that must be run on the right. In another 0.5 mile, below the road bridge, the river splits. To the right is easy Class I, but to the left is a Class II+ drop, which can be re-run because of the nice pool at the bottom. The remainder of the way is Class I to the Fort Kent Blockhouse, an excellent take-out just above the confluence with the St. John River.

Fish River (East Branch)

The East Branch of the Fish River is little more than a chain of lakes, which are lined with many cottages and year-round homes. The trip comprises the major part of what is commonly called The Fish River Lake Trip. The northern end of Long Lake, the highest in the chain, is in the towns of Saint Agatha and Madawaska, only a few miles from the St. John River. Most of the lakes run in a northwest-southeast direction, with the short bits of connecting river cutting at right angles to this trend, so that you travel in a zigzag route, which finally brings you to Eagle Lake considerably to the south. Here, you meet the main stream of the Fish River and can either go up that stream to its headwaters or down it to the St. John River at Fort Kent, only a few miles from where you started. This trip is one of the best-known in northern Maine and can be done by careful novice paddlers.

Description:	Lakes
Navigable:	Spring, summer, fall
Scenery:	Forested
Maps:	Frenchville 15, Square Lake 15, Stockholm 15, Eagle Lake 15, DL 68

The usual starting point is Saint Agatha at the northwestern end of Long Lake. Although this lake is 10.0 miles long, the paddler wishing to make a fast trip can turn into the eastern arm in 6.0 miles and follow this 3.0 miles to the town of Sinclair at the western end. You can use three state campsites on the lake: one at Berube Point on the eastern shore opposite the western arm, one on the southeastern shore at the mouth of Mud Brook, and one on the southern shore of the western arm 2.5 miles from Sinclair. At Sinclair you take a short 0.5-mile passage through the thoroughfare to Mud Lake, sometimes called Salmon Lake. You have a 2.0-mile paddle for the length of this lake. A lunch site is located on the southern shore about 1.5 miles down. At the southwestern corner the outlet leaves. It is 1.5 miles down this thoroughfare to Cross Lake, which is reached on the eastern shore about halfway down. The northern end of the lake has a number of cottages on both shores. The only campsite on this lake is 1.0 mile diagonally northwest across the lake from the inlet, at Matrimony Point. From this campground or from the inlet it is 3.0 miles to the outlet at the southwestern corner, where a short thoroughfare 1.0 mile in length leads into Square Lake. This is a large lake some 7.0 miles long and 2.0 miles wide with an extensive shoal in the middle. Because of this shoal and the fact that the wind is funneled between mountains, this lake can be dangerous in the wind, which can come up suddenly; therefore, stay close to the shore.

It is about 3.0 miles northwesterly across the lake to the outlet far up on the northwestern shore. This is a wilder lake than Cross Lake, and you might want to spend some time on it using some of the four campsites available: one at Salmon Point on the southeastern shore, one at Goddard Cove on the southern shore at the mouth of Little Goddard Brook, another on the western shore at the big hill 3.5 miles south of the outlet, and another on the western shore 1.5 miles south of the outlet at Limestone Point. The thoroughfare from Square

Lake to Eagle Lake is 3.0 miles long, with a good campsite halfway down on the northern bank at the mouth of Halfway Brook. Eagle Lake is formed in the shape of an L. The thoroughfare from Square Lake reaches the lake at the halfway point of the east-west leg on the northern shore. From here, it is 4.0 miles west to the inlet of the main stream of the Fish River 1.0 mile east of Eagle Lake village on the southern shore. From this point, you can ascend the main stream or descend to the St. John River. You can use a nice campsite on the northern shore just east of Oak Point, on Cozy Point. You might wish to spend some time on the eastern bay of the lake east of the inlet. You find three campsites here: one on the southern shore in Three Brooks Cove at the mouth of Middle Brook, one on the southeastern shore 3.0 miles east of the thoroughfare, and another one 4.0 miles from the thoroughfare. You can take out at Eagle Lake Village or continue the trip as desired.

Aroostook River

The Aroostook River is formed by the union of Munsungan Stream and Millinocket Stream in the unincorporated townships north of Baxter State Park and follows a winding course northeast to the St. John River in New Brunswick. The first part of the river is forested and wild, the lower portion is through farmland, and the last few miles are difficult whitewater.

Pending settlement of the boundary between the United States and England, the Aroostook valley became the prey of lawless trespassers who removed large amounts of timber. The Maine legislature authorized a company of volunteers to suppress this illegal traffic. On February 8, 1839, 200 men under Captain Rines reached Masardis Stream and fell unexpectedly upon the trespassers, who offered only slight resistance. Flushed with success, the company advanced to the Little Madawaska River, where they met a reverse. Captain Rines was captured and carried off to Fredericton. These events precipitated the Aroostook War, a general call to arms in which there was no loss of life, and which was finally settled by the Webster-Asburton Treaty of 1842.

Around 1900, the Aroostook River was used to gain access to the Upper East Branch of the Penobscot River from Moose Brook, which flows into Millinocket Lake. The Aroostook was also used, as it is still by a few, to gain access to the Seboeis River and Grand Lake Seboeis, with a 0.75-mile carry from the West Branch of Carry Brook. This brook flows into La Pomkeag Stream and then into the Aroostook River about 10.0 miles west of Oxbow.

LIBBY CAMP ➤ OXBOW LANDING   17.0 MI

Description:	Quickwater, Class I
Navigable:	High water: spring
Scenery:	Wild
Maps:	Millinocket Lake 15, Grand Lake Seboeis 15, DL 57

Put in where Pinkham Road crosses Munsungan Stream, or farther down at Oxbow Road. This latter road also crosses Millinocket Stream. Libby Camp is at the confluence of Millinocket Stream and Munsungan Stream and can be reached by either. The first 7.0 miles to Mooseleuk Stream have a fast current with occasional riffles, followed by 1.0 mile of deadwater to La Pomkeag Stream. After 7.5 miles of current to Baste Rips (Class II), it is 1.5 miles to Oxbow Landing, where motorboats can be launched. Watch for poison ivy at the grotty campsites in this stretch.

OXBOW LANDING ➤ WASHBURN   44.0 MI

Description:	Flatwater, quickwater, Class I
Navigable:	Spring, summer, fall: some shallow spots
Scenery:	Forested, towns
Maps:	Grand Lake Seboeis 15, Oxbow 15, Ashland 15, Presque Isle 15, Caribou 15, DL 57, 58, and 64

After 3.0 miles of deadwater, the river swings north, and the barely noticeable entrance to the Oxbow is on the right. You can make a side trip of 1.0 mile to this overgrown marsh. The deadwater continues 3.0 miles to Shepard Rips (Class I), where a camp is on a bluff on the left. The river runs slowly east/north, where you find an excellent campsite at the turn, and then east again for 8.0 miles to the mouth of the Saint Croix Stream (and a good take-out just up Saint Croix Stream at the ME 11 bridge) in Masardis (14.0 miles). Several small ledges are found here. The 5.0 miles of slow water to Squa Pan Brook is largely through farmland, which cannot be seen from the river.

In 5.0 more miles, you pass the site of an old logging bridge, and shortly after that the Machias River (24.0 miles). The next 1.0 mile contains some Class I rapids to the ME 11 bridge in Ashland (access here). It is another 1.0 mile to the Little Machias, and 1.0 mile more to Sheridan, with a railroad bridge and the remains of an old logging dam. This can be run, lined, or carried on the right. Below this 6.0 miles is Pudding Rock, a large rock face on the right with some ledges on the left; you find a good access to the river here.

At the island before Beaver Brook, 3.0 miles farther, the left channel leads to a campsite on a high bank on the left. The river winds through islands for 2.0 miles to Gardner Brook Rapids (easy Class I).

This is the end of the wilderness run; many camps are along the shore for the 6.0 miles of quick water to Washburn. At the railroad trestle are the remains of an old logging dam, and then a landing and a good parking place just above the Washburn Bridge (44.0 miles).

WASHBURN ➤ FORT FAIRFIELD   37.0 MI

Description:	Flatwater, quickwater
Navigable:	Spring, summer, fall
Scenery:	Rural, towns
Maps:	Caribou 15, Presque Isle 15, Mars Hill 15, Fort Fairfield 15, DL 64 and 65
Portage:	14.0 mi e Caribou Dam 0.5 mi

Much of this run is through potato fields, although the banks are often wooded. The river is swift, with many small rips through islands to Crossville, where you see a white church steeple on the left. The river passes under a railroad bridge 1.0 mile below Crossville and enters Rum Rapids, Class II in low water, but tending to wash out in higher water. The next 7.0 miles to the US 1 bridge in Presque Isle (11.0 miles), where Presque Isle Stream enters, have good current and pass many islands. The 14.0 miles to the dam at Caribou are smooth. The carry on the right is shorter but difficult; the left is 0.5 mile on a good road behind the power plant. It is 5.0 miles to the Little Madawaska River at Grimes Mill, and 7.0 miles to the ME 165 bridge at Fort Fairfield (37.0 miles).

FORT FAIRFIELD ➤ ST. JOHN RIVER   11.0 MI

Description:	Flatwater, Class II, III, IV, V
Navigable:	Above 15,000 cfs—dangerous;
	2,800–5,000 cfs—best level for all boats
Scenery:	Wild
Maps:	Fort Fairfield 15, DL 65
Portages:	4.0 mi R Dam
	5.0 mi Dam

If you continue across the international boundary, you must report to customs, located 3.0 miles east of town of ME 167, and also check the dam release for the day.

Flat water continues to the dam, 4.0 miles from Fort Fairfield, and 1.0 mile beyond the Canadian border. Portage right.

The next 1.0 mile is through a canyon, Class IV–V, where the river drops 75 feet. The canyon should be run only after complete scouting because it contains very few eddies and a 180-degree turn in the middle of the gorge. The last drop is the most difficult, where the river makes a right-angle turn against a rock wall.

Below the second dam, you enter immediately into Class II rapids for 1.5 miles, to a Class III ledge with the chute on the left, and then into more Class II rapids to the Limestone River on the left. The last major rapid starts under the Trans-Canada Bridge; the size of this rapid is deceptive because of the height of the bridge, and it can easily swamp an open boat. The last 2.0 miles to the St. John are flat water.

Munsungan Stream

Both the upper end of Chase Lake and the outlet of Munsungan Lake can be reached by good gravel roads.

CHASE LAKE ➤ LIBBY CAMP   16.0 MI

Description:	Lakes, flatwater, Class I, II
Navigable:	High water: spring
Scenery:	Wild
Maps:	Spider Lake 15, Millinocket Lake 15, DL 56
	and 57

Chase Lake is 1.5 miles long. The outlet is a 0.5-mile long, very shallow stream with Class I rapids. It is then 5.0 miles down Munsungan Lake to a broken logging dam, which can be run. You travel 1.5 miles of Class I rapids and ledge drops to Munsungan Falls, a heavy Class III rapid, which should be scouted from the right bank. This is a ledge drop at a difficult angle. Just below are a steel logging bridge, falls, and a possible campsite.

Quick water for 6.0 miles is followed by 3.0 miles of Class I rapids to Libby Camp, where Millinocket Stream joins to form the Aroostook River.

Machias Stream

The Machias Stream flows south and then west from Machias Lake in T12 R8 to the Aroostook River near Ashland. The river is about 39.0 miles long and drops 420 feet, making it an excellent whitewater trip for a weekend. In the early spring, the river can be run in a day with water up to Class IV. The Machias runs through mountainous and heavily forested country, with many signs of the old logging days. Because of heavy logging in the recent years, the river must be run early because of a very fast runoff. It also can be run after heavy rains.

PRATT LAKE ➤ BIG MACHIAS LAKE OUTLET   8.0 MI

Description:	Lake, quickwater
Navigable:	High water: spring
Scenery:	Wild
Maps:	Mooseleuk Lake 15, DL 63
Campsites:	7.0 mi on northern shore at Twentymile Brook
	8.0 mi Big Machias Lake outlet car

The outlet of Pratt Lake is at the northernmost point, where you enter a small but swift stream. This flows through some ponds for about 2.0 miles. After 3.0 miles, you enter Big Machias Lake. The outlet is 3.0 miles down the lake at the eastern end.

Description:	Flatwater, quickwater, Class I, II, III
Navigable:	High water: very fast–Class III)
	Medium water: scratchy
Scenery:	Wild
Maps:	Mooseleuk Lake 15, Greenlaw 15, Ashland 15,
	DL 63, 57, and 64
Campsites:	15.0 mi L Rand Crossing car; many other
	undeveloped campsites

Scout the old dam at the outlet, which can be run but contains many rocks. Below the dam is good current for a mile and then 2.0 miles of Class II rapids to Russell Crossing, where there was once a bridge on the American Realty Road. The heavy rapids continue about 1.0 mile, followed by 3.0 miles of Class II rapids to McKeen's Crossing and Rowe Brook (6.0 miles). After 9.0 miles of good current, you go under the Rand Crossing Bridge from Ashland, where you find a large public campsite on the left side.

Below here, the river has good current 8.0 miles to the deadwater behind a dam. In the middle of the swamp just before the South Branch enters is a set of Class I rapids where a clay deposit was once mined from the river. Below Rand Crossing 6.0 miles is a deadwater 3.0 miles long formed by an old dam now almost gone that can easily be run in the log chute on the right side.

Below are Class II+ rapids for 4.0 miles; then good current follows for 4.0 miles. Suddenly, Ashland is around a bend. Just below the town is a Class III+ set of ledges, which should be run left to right in medium and low water, but on the far right in high water. Then go under a bridge, and in 0.5 mile enter the Aroostook River.

Little Machias River

The Little Machias River rises to the southwest of Portage, flowing southeast to Little Machias Lake. From there, it flows southeasterly through wild but swampy land to the Aroostook River below Ashland.

LITTLE MACHIAS LAKE ➤ AROOSTOOK RIVER   6.0 MI

Description:	Flatwater, quickwater, Class I
Navigable:	High water
Scenery:	Wild
Maps:	Greenlaw 15, Ashland 15, DL 63 and 64

The first 3.0 miles are wild, swampy country; the lower 3.0 miles are swift current with occasional rips. The confluence with the Aroostook is halfway between Ashland and Sheridan.

Beaver Brook

Beaver Brook drains an extensive forest area to the east of Portage Lake. The brook is smooth with good current and about ten good permit campsites along the way. The country is wild and untouched by camps, roads, or signs of logging; it is a good place to see moose and waterfowl. The campsite at the mouth of Beaver Brook is the nicest on the Aroostook River.

WEST BRANCH BEAVER BROOK ➤ EAST BRANCH   5.0 MI

Description:	Quickwater
Navigable:	High water
Scenery:	Wild
Maps:	Ashland 15, Portage 15, DL 64

This section can be run down from the ME 11 bridge in Winterville in high water only and is rapid, with many blowdowns.

CONFLUENCE ➤ AROOSTOOK RIVER   8.0 MI

Description:	Quickwater, Class I
Navigable:	High or medium water
Scenery:	Wild
Maps:	Ashland 15, Portage 15, DL 64

From the bridge on a dirt road just below the confluence, the brook is mostly smooth, with a few rips and chutes for the first 3.0 miles to enliven the trip. It then winds through the alder in a swamp, but in the last 3.0 miles to the Aroostook you again find rips and quick water. When the brook takes a sharp bend to the left, the Aroostook River is beyond the high bank directly ahead.

Salmon Brook

Salmon Brook is a rapid stream, which rises in Salmon Brook Lake and flows southeast to the Aroostook River at Washburn.

NEW DUNN TOWN ROAD ➤ AROOSTOOK RIVER   **4.0 MI**

Description:	Class II
Navigable:	High water: spring only
Scenery:	Wild
Maps:	Caribou 15, DL 64

Put in from the Story Brook Fire Tower road. The stream drops 40 feet to the Aroostook River, all in an even gradient, providing easy Class II rapids for the entire distance. It makes a good stream to warm up on in the spring. Take out at the town landing in Washburn.

Little Madawaska River

The Little Madawaska River rises in Bog Pond about 6.0 miles west of Perham in T14 R5 and flows northeast to Stockholm and then southeast to the Aroostook River at Grimes Mill. The beginning and end of the river are very swift, but the middle section is swampy and slow going. Above Blackstone, access is poor, and you find many blowdowns.

BLACKSTONE SIDING ➤ STOCKHOLM   **13.0 MI**

Description:	Quickwater
Navigable:	High or medium water
Scenery:	Forested, town
Maps:	Portage 15, Caribou 15, Stockholm 15, DL 64 and 68
Portage:	13.0 mi L dam in Stockholm 100 yd

The first 5.0 miles to Madawaska Lake Outlet are quick water and easy rapids through softwood swamps. An alternate starting point is Madawaska Lake, running the 1.0 mile down the outlet, which increases the size of the river considerably. The next 4.0 miles to the ME 161 bridge and the following 2.0 miles are swift, and then 2.0 miles of deadwater and swamp bring you to the dam in Stockholm.

STOCKHOLM ➤ AROOSTOOK RIVER   22.0 MI

Description:	Flatwater, quickwater
Navigable:	High water: dangerous below ME 89
	Medium water: recommended
Scenery:	Forested, rural, towns
Maps:	Stockholm 15, Caribou 15, Fort Fairfield 15,
	DL 68 and 65

You travel 1.0 mile of quick water below the dam and then 7.0 miles of meandering swampland to the US 1 bridge at Acadia. Quick water for 3.0 miles follows; after another 5.0 miles you come upon a dam and then 2.0 miles of meanders through open farmland to another bridge on the Loring Access Highway. There, the river quickens for the next 1.0 mile to the ME 89 bridge, which should be approached on the extreme left.

The last 3.0 miles to the Aroostook are very swift and meandering. Almost every bend has overhanging or fallen trees. Stay near the inside of the bends and be prepared to land should the river be blocked.

Presque Isle Stream

Presque Isle Stream rises in the unorganized townships southeast of Ashland and flows northerly to the Aroostook River at Presque Isle. Starting at Presque Isle Lake, the stream is steep, and blowdowns are frequent; so, the recommended starting point is Grindstone.

GRINDSTONE ➤ AROOSTOOK RIVER   15.0 MI

Description:	Flatwater, quickwater
Navigable:	High water: spring
Scenery:	Wild, town
Maps:	Presque Isle 15, DL 64 and 65

The first 8.0 miles are swift, with the Presque Isle Rapids (Class I) at the foot of Hobart Hill. The next 5.0 miles are the backwater from the rock dam at Presque Isle, located directly below a bridge. This can be run on the right center (Class III+) in high water or lined on the right at low water. The last 2.0 miles to the Aroostook River are quick water with a few rips.

Prestile Stream

Prestile Stream is formed by the junction of a number of brooks in Fort Fairfield. It flows south through Easton, Mars Hill, and Blaine to Bridgewater. There, it turns east, crosses the international boundary, and flows into the St. John River a few miles south of Florenceville, New Brunswick.

WESTFIELD ➤ CANADIAN BORDER   14.5 MI

Description:	Flatwater, quickwater, Class I
Navigable:	High water: upper sections
	Medium or low water: lower section
Scenery:	Wild
Maps:	Mars Hill 15, Bridgewater 15, DL 59
Portage:	6.0 mi R Robinson Dam

From Westfield to Mars Hill, the river runs southeasterly with fine views of the long ridge of Mars Hill. The going is hard, with many low trees and blowdowns, to the backwater of the washed-out Mars Hill Dam (4.5 miles).

Below the old dam are easy rapids for about 1.0 mile, then 3.5 miles of good current to the backwater of the Robinson Dam (10.5 miles), which is carried on the right.

Below Robinson Dam the stream is much larger and passable at most seasons. About 1.0 mile below the dam at Robinsons, the river crosses the town line into Bridgewater and turns east. About 3.5 miles down, Whitney Brook enters on the right, and in less than 0.5 mile you reach the international boundary. The customs station is on the road on the left bank. If you do not wish to continue into Canada, take out here or at the bridge just above the entrance of Whitney Brook.

Whitney Brook

Whitney Brook is formed in Bridgewater by the junction of the northern and southern branches. About 1.0 mile below this junction, the brook is crossed by Rumford Road and US 1. Below here it is navigable, although it is best done with relatively high water. The brook flows on a northeasterly course to meet the Prestile Stream less than 0.5 mile west of the Canadian border.

BRIDGEWATER ➤ PRESTILE STREAM   4.0 MI

Description:	Quickwater, Class I
Navigable:	High water
Scenery:	Forested
Maps:	Bridgewater 15, DL 59

From the pond at Bridgewater, you travel 4.0 miles of easy rapids and fast current to the junction with Prestile Stream, passing a very low bridge 2.0 miles down. Take out in the large field in front of customs.

Meduxnekeag River

The Meduxnekeag River rises in Ludlow, flows southeast to New Limerick, then east to Houlton, where it turns north and slightly east to the Canadian border. Here, it turns east to join the St. John River near Woodstock, New Brunswick.

NEW LIMERICK ➤ HOULTON   11.0 MI

Description:	Flatwater, quickwater
Navigable:	High or medium water: spring, early summer
Scenery:	Forested
Maps:	Myrna Mills 15, Amity 15, DL 53
Portage:	(11.0 mi dam in Houlton)

Below the dam at New Limerick, the river has a good current partly through swamps for the 2.0 miles to Green Pond, where the outlet is only 200 yards away along the southern shore to the east. From here the river is larger, and in 3.0 miles of a somewhat meandering course, you reach the outlet of Nickerson Lake on the right. This lake, a favorite spot for summer cottages, is only 1.0 mile up the outlet. In 3.0 miles more, you reach Carys Mills and the entrance of the South Branch just below on the right. With the added water the stream is now quite large for the 3.0 miles to the dam at Houlton.

HOULTON ➤ CANADIAN BORDER   **9.0 MI**

Description:	Flatwater, quickwater
Navigable:	Spring, summer, fall
Scenery:	Forested, rural
Maps:	Houlton 15, Amity 15, DL 53 and 59

The stream is now large and flows northward for some 8.0 miles with no obstructions; then it turns east and in 1.0 mile more crosses the border between Monuments 27A and 27. The nearest customs station is 1.0 mile south at the road crossing, so you probably want to take out at the road bridge about 2.5 miles upstream from the international boundary.

Meduxnekeag River (South Branch)

The South Branch of the Meduxnekeag River is formed by the junction of a number of brooks in Cary. From there, it flows north through Hodgdon to Houlton, where it joins the main river at Carys Mills.

CARY ➤ MEDUXNEKEAG RIVER   **9.0 MI**

Description:	Flatwater, quickwater, Class I
Navigable:	High and medium water
Scenery:	Forested, rural, towns
Maps:	Houlton 15, DL 53
Portages:	5.0 mi L dam at Hodgdon 10 yd
	(9.0 mi L waterfall at Carys Mills)

Just above the Oliver Road Bridge at Cary, the South Branch is joined by Davis Brook and becomes quite large. You travel 4.0 miles of meandering stream to the big pond at Hodgdon, followed by 1.0 mile down the pond to the town. You come to a dam just above the bridge; portage 10 yards on the left by a small public landing. You find Class I–II rips for 100 yards below the dam, followed by 1.0 mile of good current to a broken log dam. This dam might be runnable but is apt to be blocked by debris. Quick water and riffles for 2.0 more miles bring you to a bridge on the dirt back road from Hodgdon to Carys Mills. Within 0.5 mile you come to an area of meanders and alder that continues for 0.75 mile. After you are out of the bushes, the current quickens again, and occasional Class I rapids appear. These become more frequent and interesting after a nearly right-angle turn to the right. A slight turn to the left signals the beginning of a series of low ledges above the first of two bridges at Carys Mills. A falls drops in several sections just below the bridge. Below the falls you find 100 yards of Class I water to the main river.

B Stream

B Stream rises in Hammond and flows southeast to the Meduxnekeag River in Houlton. It is fed by a number of brooks with swampy areas on their courses, so it should hold water well later in the paddling season. From B School in southeastern Hammond, the river drops 120 feet in 8.0 miles to Houlton.

HAMMOND (SIXTH BRIDGE) ➤ HOULTON 4.25 MI

Description:	Quickwater, Class I, II
Navigable:	Medium water
Scenery:	Forested
Maps:	Houlton, DL 59 and 53

Starting at the sixth bridge above the confluence with the Meduxnekeag, this stream can be paddled in mid-June if it has not been too dry. You travel quick water and Class I riffles, occasionally obstructed by trees, to the high bridge near BM 373 (1.5 miles). Below this bridge, the stream is somewhat larger and deeper, and you are not so hampered by trees. The third bridge marks the beginning of a 1.0 mile-long section where ledges cross the stream at varying angles, creating intermittent Class II rapids, one or two of which might be tricky at high water. This section ends at a bridge on the back road to Ludlow, which is the last convenient take-out; beyond, access from I-95 is impractical, and the area around the US 2 bridge is urbanized, with a low dam just above it.

Chapter 7
Western Coastal Watersheds

Little River

The season is short but exciting on the Little River. Go early in the morning or on an overcast day, because the river heads into the afternoon sun for most of its length.

LEBANON ➤ SALMON FALLS RIVER   11.25 MI

Description: Flatwater, quick-water, Class I, II
Navigable: High water: late March to early May
Scenery: Forested
Maps: Berwick 15, DL 2

The usual put-in is below the broken dam beside an old mill in Lebanon. In high water, the river can be run above the mill, either from Fall Road (1.0 mile upriver) or from ME 11/ US 202 (3.0 miles above the mill). Determined explorers occasionally start even higher up. The river

WESTERN COASTAL
WATERSHEDS

Scale in miles

0   10   20   30

above the mill is quite narrow with Class I–II rapids and numerous obstructions.

From the mill you come upon two rapids, one at a broken dam in the first 1.0 mile. In the next 1.0 mile, from the Lord Road bridge to the bridge on Little River Road, the river is smooth and winding. The next 4.25 miles to Stackpole Bridge pass through an area known as "the Marshes," where the river maintains a good current around numerous tight twists and turns. Occasional breakthroughs create some confusion, but careful observation of the current guides you through easily.

Whitewater enthusiasts frequently begin at Stackpole Bridge (6.25 miles); under the bridge is a small drop over a ledge. The next 2.0 miles are smooth and slow until the river reaches a small Class I rapid, followed soon after by 0.25 mile of Class I rapids up to Messenger Bridge, where Pine Hill Road and Little River Road meet.

Below Messenger Bridge (8.25 miles) is another Class I rapid, an easy Class II rapid, and finally a 0.75-mile-long, hard Class II rapid. The river is narrow enough that you must pick either the left or right side—you can find no room for a middle route—and the only clear passage involves switching occasionally from a course down one side to a course down the other. Stop and scout frequently unless you like piling up onto ledges and into impassable rock gardens. One particularly interesting spot has a car-sized boulder perched on top of a ledge left of center; the usually runnable channels lead you within an arm's length of it.

The long rapid ends with a small ledge in a sharp right turn. The last 0.5 mile of this rapid, down to a back-road bridge (9.5 miles), is very scratchy when the rapids above are marginally runnable; flat water follows. Above the Hubbard Road bridge 0.5 mile (11.25 miles), you come upon a broken dam at the end of a sharp S-turn that can be run with extreme caution or lined from the right bank.

The Little River empties into the Salmon Falls River (11.25 miles) just below the Hubbard Road bridge. Somersworth is 5.0 miles downstream (16.25 miles).

Great Works River

This unassuming little river claims the distinction of having turned the first water-powered mill in the United States, in the section of South

Berwick called Great Works. Mills continued there without a break for more than 300 years, until the 1940s, when the remaining few fell into disuse.

NORTH BERWICK ➤ SOUTH BERWICK   11.5 MI

Description:	Flatwater, quickwater, Class I, II
Navigable:	High water: late March to mid-May, passable at most water levels for last 3.5 mi
Scenery:	Forested
Maps:	Kennebunk 15, York 15, Dover 15, DL 2 and 1
Portage:	11.5 mi Rock Gorge 1.0 mi

The best place to put in is at the bridge on Madison Street. Use the *Maine Atlas and Gazetteer* to find Madison Street, across from where ME 4 and ME 9 merge from the south in the town of North Berwick.

The first 5.0 miles to Emerys Bridge on Hooper Sands Road are narrow and winding, and the river shallows out early in the season. The next 3.0 miles to Junction Bridge, at the western end of Emerys Bridge Road, hold water a little longer. Both sections are prone to blowdowns.

The final 3.5-mile section from Junction Bridge to the village of Great Works is runnable except in very dry summers, and it is entirely flat water. Take out at the Brattle Street bridge (11.5 miles) 0.25 mile below the ME 236 bridge.

Caution! Below the Brattle Street bridge are a dam and falls called Rocky Gorge. Stay well above this area. Continuing to the Salmon Falls River, into which the Great Works River flows, is difficult because this obstruction requires a 1.0-mile-long portage. You encounter another dam 1.0 mile downstream at the confluence with the Salmon Falls River. The deep impoundment above this hydroelectric dam is Leigh's Mill Pond, a local swimming/fishing hole. If you want to explore this section of the river up to Rocky Gorge, the river crossing at Leigh's Mill Pond on Vine Street is the best access.

Mousam River

The Mousam River flows into the sea at Kennebunk. Usually you do not have enough water in the upper section for a good run except in the spring and just after Labor Day, when Mousam Lake is drawn down.

MOUSAM LAKE ➤ ESTES LAKE   14.0 MI

Description:	Lakes, flatwater, quickwater, Class I, II, III
Navigable:	High water: early spring and early September, annual drawdown of Mousam Lake
Scenery:	Forested, rural, towns
Maps:	Berwick 15, Kennebunk 15, DL 2
Portages:	3.5 mi L 1st and 2nd dams in Springvale
	4.0 mi R small dam in Springvale
	4.5 mi e 1st dam in Sanford
	6.0 mi L 2nd dam in Sanford (cross over first bridge)
	(14.0 mi R Estes Lake Dam)

The river below the dam on Mousam Lake can be reached by turning off ME 11/109 at the Emery Mills Market. If you see a boiling flow at the base of the dam, you have sufficient water for this trip.

In the 3.0 miles to the first millpond in Springvale, you need to watch out for three sharp drops. The first is under a power line. The second is a short distance below the ME 11/109 bridge (1.25 miles). This drop could be Class III and should be scouted. If the water is too low for this rapid, it is too low for the trip. Scout this rapid from a bridge about 50 yards downstream from the ME 11/109 bridge. The third drop is about 1.0 mile farther.

At Holdsworth Park on ME 11/109 in Springvale, you have good access to the pond above the first dam. If you are continuing downstream, take out left of the dam (3.5 miles), portage along Water Street about 1,000 feet, and put in below the second dam. A third dam (4.0 miles) is just upstream of an abandoned stone railroad bridge.

The first dam in Sanford (4.5 miles) is followed by quick water to the millpond above the second dam (6.0 miles). Take out on the left, cross the river via Washington Street, follow Pioneer Avenue downstream, and put in by the Emery Street bridge. Then you have quick water with some debris for 3.0 miles to the ME 4 bridge.

Below ME 4 (9.0 miles) is 0.5 mile to the ruins of Jagger Mill Dam, which can be run. Quick water continues for most of the way to Mousam Lake (13.0 miles), which is near the head of Estes Lake. When the lake opens up, turn right to reach the dam (14.0 miles).

ESTES LAKE ➤ KENNEBUNK   12.0 MI

Description:	Quickwater, flatwater, rapids
Scenery:	Rural
Maps:	Kennebunk 15, DL 2, 3

Below the powerhouse is a short rapid, followed in 0.5 mile by a gauging station on the right, the Whichers Mills Road bridge, and a dam. This dam should be carried on the right and the put-in made below a sharp fall and rapid, at the head of Old Falls Pond. Then 1.5 miles of paddling brings you down the pond to the high-power dam at the end. This should be portaged on the left, down a steep hill 150 yards. Below the start about 200 yards, just around the bend, is a sharp rapid, which should be scouted before running if the river is in flood. After you are through the rapid, the river becomes quiet with a fair current and good hemlock woods on the right bank. The valley soon widens out, and in 4.5 miles you come to the bridge at West Kennebunk. The old dam just below the bridge has a short rapid just below it.

In 0.5 mile more, the railroad culvert is reached; in another 200 yards is a dam at a mill, where you face a short, steep carry on the right bank to the rapids. These 0.25-mile-long rapids are easily run to the slack water, which continues for 1.0 mile to the Maine Turnpike bridge. The next 2.0 miles of meandering river to the US 1 bridge in Kennebunk pass through farmlands on both sides. In Kennebunk, it is best to take out above the bridge. The rapids below drop to tidewater.

Tidal Rivers South of Portland

Paddling in tidal marshes does not involve either the risks or the specialized equipment required for paddling along exposed shorelines.

Both open canoes and flatwater kayaks, along with basic quickwater paddling skills are generally sufficient. Birders and amateur naturalists can find salt marsh exploration particularly enjoyable.

SCARBOROUGH, NONESUCH, LIBBY, AND SPURWINK RIVERS

Description:	Tidal
Navigable:	Anytime; check tide chart
Scenery:	Rural, settled, salt marsh
Maps:	Portland 15, DL 3

Scarborough River

The Scarborough River is formed by the joining of Cascade Brook and Dunstan River near West Scarborough, which is also called Dunstan Corner. It is the largest of several streams emptying into the estuary that separates Pine Point from Prouts Neck. For a 4.75-mile trip, put in at the Scarborough Marsh Nature Center (which provides boat rentals and guided trips) near the time of high tide. The Nature Center, a Maine Audubon Society location, is south of US 1 on ME 9 (Pine Point Road).

For the first 0.5 mile or so, you are actually on the Dunstan River. Cascade Brook enters through a culvert on the right. About 3.0 miles farther on, the river passes under a railroad trestle. The current at the strength of the ebb can be quite strong, and it passes through the trestle at a 45-degree angle. Paddlers without whitewater experience, or who are not alert, can get into difficulty here. Another 1.0 mile through the widening estuary brings you to the Pine Point town landing.

Nonesuch River

The Nonesuch River has a long course through the upland parts of Scarborough, but it is so frequently obstructed by alder and fallen trees that it can be recommended only to dedicated bushwhackers.

For the recommended trip, put in at ME 207 just west of Black Point village. The river can be ascended at least 1.5 miles from here or paddled 4.0 miles down with the tide.

Downstream of this point you encounter a railroad trestle. Alternatively, you can put in at the state boat ramp on Clay Pits Road and skip it. Other than that, you face no impediments to the take-outs at either Pine Point or Ferry Beach on Prouts Neck.

Libby River

The Libby River is substantially smaller than either the Scarborough or the Nonesuch. Put in from ME 207 just west of ME 77. Respect the no trespassing signs along the river, and remember to ask for and obtain permission before crossing property lines. The Libby becomes a little scratchy at low tides. This river is excellent for viewing wildlife. You can paddle through the culvert under ME 207. Take out at Ferry Beach, which has a parking fee in the summer.

Spurwink River

The Spurwink River is not connected to the others and is of a somewhat different character. Those wishing to tour the narrow passages of the marsh can put in from Spurwink Avenue for the East Branch or from Fickett Road for the West Branch. From either point, it is 0.5 mile to ME 77, where a side road on the right comes right down to the river. This is a better start for the lower Spurwink.

The side road ends at what appears to have been an old ford, and its remnants form a Class I riffle and eddies on the ebb. You also find a lot of current under the ME 77 bridge. From ME 77 to Higgins Beach is about 1.0 mile past scenery that is more varied than the typical marsh. No good take-out or any free parking is available at Higgins Beach, which is a popular bathing beach. Often, an impressive surf closes out the mouth of the river at half tide or lower. Plan to return to ME 77 (about a 5.0-mile round trip). If you start at high water and set a leisurely pace down and back, you might end up dragging your canoe or kayak over sandbars the last 0.25 mile up to ME 77.

Presumpscot River

The Native Americans named the river the Presumpscot, meaning the "river of many falls." Indeed, it was once an appropriate name: Wescott's Falls, Great Falls, Whitney's Falls, Island Falls, Dundee Falls, Leavitt's Falls, Gambo Falls, Little Falls, Mallison Falls, Saccarappa Falls, Ammonscongin Falls, and Presumpscot Falls all claimed the river as their home in the 1600s.

The river has changed dramatically since Europeans arrived and began developing industries along the Presumpscot's banks. Perhaps the Native Americans would have renamed the river "river of much sludge, pollution and foam" as detritus from saw mills, paper mill effluent, town sewage, and the like poured into the waters that once teemed with salmon and other fish.

At its worst, the Presumpscot became so polluted that no measurable oxygen was found in the river at all. The water in the lower river resembled a "root beer float" and was considered dead. Abandoned by all who lived nearby, its only value was its use as a cheap and convenient place to dump waste. Today the river is much cleaner and is classified as an "A" from the headwaters to the confluence of the Pleasant River. With the removal of Smelt Hill Dam in October of 2002, the lower river is now meeting its water quality classification criteria. Five of the eight dams on the Presumpscot were recently relicensed by the Federal Energy Regulatory Commission. The Friends of the Presumpscot River (FoPR) worked to achieve an order for fish passage on all five dams. Contact FoPR for more information: www.presumpscotriver.org.

The Presumpscot River is the largest freshwater input to Casco Bay. At times the river is a boulder-strewn rapid, at other times a calm ripple in forested ravines, and at others, placid pond water. It discharges 39,000 cubic feet per minute and falls 270 feet during its journey. Eight dams account for most of the elevation drop. The Presumpscot flows 25.0 miles, from Sebago Lake to Casco Bay, passing through Windham, Gorham, Westbrook, Falmouth, and Portland.

SEBAGO LAKE BASIN ➤ SMELT HILL DAM   23.5 MI

Description:	Lakes, flatwater, quickwater
Navigable:	Spring, summer, fall: dam controlled
Scenery:	Forested, rural, settled
Maps:	Portland 15, Gray 15, DL 5
Portages:	1.25 mi R Sebago Lake Basin Dam 80 yd
	2.1 mi R Eel Weir Canal Dam 140 yd
	3.25 mi R Great Falls Dam 140 yd
	5.0 mi R Dundee Dam 340 yd
	8.1 mi R Gambo Dam 150 yd
	9.75 mi L South Windham Dam
	10.33 mi R Mallison Dam 1.0 mi

15.5 mi L Saccarappa Dam 0.33 mi
16.5 mi R Cumberland Mills Dam
2.75 mi around Sappi paper mill
23 mi R above Presumpscot Falls
continue 0.5 mi to put-in

Access at White's Bridge Road is gone. Everything is fenced, and parking is nonexistent. You can paddle down Jordan Bay from the Raymond Beach and Boat Launch on US 302, but that adds about 4.0 miles of big-lake paddling to the trip. Because of the orientation of Sebago, in any wind, trouble waves are guaranteed. From White's Bridge Road it is 1.2 miles across the basin to the Eel Weir Dam, which maintains the lake level.

Portage on the right of all the dam works. It is recommended that Eel Weir canal not be used for boating—use the river itself. Subject to water levels (releases from the Basin dam), the river needs at least April level to be runnable. Put in at the base of the ME 35 bridge. Public parking is on the east side of ME 35. This section of the river is small, mixed Class I and easy Class II, until a small falls at the end of the bypass reach (river). Portage around these falls. A river-wide ledge here is not runnable because of problems at the base of the vertical portion. Line or portage river left (about 200 ft).

The unrunnable ledge is in deadwater where you can see the Eel Weir powerhouse to your right. Portage river right, and put directly into the head of North Gorham Pond. A stand of large pine trees is at the portage site.

It is 1.2 miles to the take-out at the Great Falls Dam. Portage along North Gorham Road to the head of Dundee Pond. You find access at Pettingill Park in 0.33 mile on the left. Then it is a 1.5-mile paddle to Dundee Dam, where you should start a portage at left of center on the right wing dam. Proceed to the dam access road, which is 0.5 mile of private road off Hurricane Road. Go left, then right along the old canal path, and put in at the end of the tailrace. Watch carefully to follow the trail as it leaves the gravel roads—signs are not always in place.

Finally the trip is on the river and not ponds. It is 1.25 miles to Babb's Bridge, a replica of an 1843 covered bridge that burned in 1973 and was rebuilt in 1976. The mouth of the Pleasant River is passed on the left in 0.6 mile. It is 0.5 mile up the river to the River

Road access in Windham. In 1.8 miles, the Gambo Dam is reached by following the trail from Shaw Park off Route 237. Portage to the right of an island before the bridge, and continue along the old gunpowder mill foundations to put in across from the powerhouse.

The riverbanks continue to be mostly forested in the next 1.6 miles to the Little Falls Dam in South Windham. A rather long portage of 0.9 mile is mandatory at this point because of private property, and no easy access or egress exists before the Mallison Falls Dam and its power canal in 0.6 mile. Take out before the US 202/ME 4 bridge on the left and cross the bridge going 0.4 mile south to ME 237. Go left for 0.2 mile to Mallison Street on the left. In 0.1 mile, turn right onto Canal Street and go 0.2 mile to the gate to the powerhouse. Go through the parking lot to the put-in down a steep bank. Again, always be aware that you are on private property, and obtain permission before crossing (postings everywhere).

The next stretch of 5.0 miles is the longest section of continuous paddling on the river. It extends to the Saccarappa Dam in Westbrook passing the Little River on the right in 0.75 mile. On the left approximately 0.13 mile above the dam is a take-out through a brushy area owned by the City of Westbrook. Portage down Lincoln Street to Bridge Street, and put in on river right downstream of the bridge. A short paddle of 1.2 miles through the wooded backyards of Westbrook ends at the Cumberland Street bridge just before the Cumberland Mills Dam. You can take out on the right in the Sappi Fine Paper parking lot. Remember to ask for and get permission before taking out.

From the Cumberland Mills dam the river is steady, deep, and murky down to the US 302 bridge. You find no marked public parking under this bridge. Below this bridge are the remains of Riverton Park on the right, now a patch of woodland. After passing Riverton Park, you come upon a new take-out just before the Blackstrap Road bridge on river right. It is 2.0 miles to the Maine Turnpike bridge, which has some rapids underneath it. The left passage is smoother, whereas the right is more challenging. Continuing with good current and wooded banks, you pass the Piscataqua River, which might offer 1.0 mile or so of flatwater paddling. Smelt Hill Dam was removed, but you face a considerable drop at Presumpscot Falls. Just before the falls on the right is a well marked portage and trail, about 1.0 mile from the Piscataqua. You have the opportunity to follow the trail for a short hike here, which has an overlook for Presumspcot Falls and is maintained by Portland Trails. To continue, put in at tidewater and in 0.25 mile pass under the high bridge. You also find a new take-out on river left just below the high bridge over Allen Avenue Extension at Walton Park. You can see a large dock and stair system, with a trail that leads to a small parking area. Continue 0.5 mile farther to the ME 9 bridge and last take-out before the large estuary. This 0.75-mile section should be timed with a high tide because of mud flats at low tide.

Crooked River

The Crooked River flows from Songo Pond near Bethel south to the Songo River and Sebago Lake. Mostly it is clean and attractive, and for 53.0 miles it has scenery that includes forests typical of northern Maine (alder swamps and stands of red maple). Many sections have a remoteness that road and topographical maps do not suggest. From the river, North Waterford is not very pretty, but the settlements of Bolsters Mills and Scribners Mill farther downstream are slices from New England's past.

In the spring, the river offers a pleasant combination of rapids and smooth water. Below the ME 118 bridge in East Waterford are 10 sets of rapids, which are mostly Class II with a few Class III drops. In high water, you travel several sections with heavy waves. Because of the river's relatively small drainage area, the water level changes from hazardously high to undesirably low in a matter of weeks.

ALBANY ➤ NORTH WATERFORD   9.0 MI

Description:	Flatwater, Class I, II
Navigable:	High water: April
Scenery:	Forested
Maps:	East Stoneham, North Waterford, DL 10

The Crooked River here is small. In a few places, fallen trees block the stream, and in the middle section alder crowds the channel. The current is fastest at the beginning where it flows through forest, portions of which have been selectively cut. Where the gradient lessens, the river meanders through alder thickets.

A convenient starting point within sight of the highway is from a bridge on a logging road that leaves ME 5/35 just more than 5.0 miles north of Lynchville. For 0.75 mile, you go along with a mixture of rapids and flat water. Stop above an old bridge by an abandoned farm (1.5 miles) to scout the rapids below. Below the second highway bridge 0.5 mile, the stream enters an alder swamp through which it meanders for 2.5 miles to the ME 35 bridge in Lynchville (7.5 miles). For the next 1.5 miles to the ME 35 bridge in North Waterford (9.0 miles), the river is flat and wider.

NORTH WATERFORD ➤ EAST WATERFORD   12.0 MI

Description:	Flatwater, quickwater, Class II, III
Navigable:	High water: April
	Medium water: May, shallow rapids
Scenery:	Forested, towns
Maps:	North Waterford, Norway 15, DL 10

The banks of the river in North Waterford are not very attractive. Beginning at the broken dam below town, though, you come upon 2.0 miles of good rapids mixed with quick water. The last 6.0 miles are very crooked, with leaning swamp maple crowding the stream.

Below the ME 35 bridge less than 0.5 mile is a broken dam that you should scout. Then you travel easy rapids as the river flows past a lumberyard. About 100 yards beyond the point where the stream approaches the highway again, stop just above a cabin on the right (1.0 mile) to scout the steep Class III rapids beside the roadside rest area. Near the top, large boulders produce heavy waves in high water with no obvious channel. The lower section is 0.75-mile long, and it contains two easier Class II drops, which can be scouted from ME 118.

Below the last drop (2.0 miles), the river leaves the highway and runs deep and slow. A distance of 2.5 miles below the rapids, the outlet from Papoose Pond enters on the right, and in another 0.25 mile you come to a bridge (4.75 miles). After 1.0 mile, the river passes below the cliffs of Pulpit Rock (5.75 miles). The second bridge below the rock is ME 118 in East Waterford (12.0 miles), and it is reached after 6.25 very crooked miles.

Description:	Flatwater, Class I, II
Navigable:	Spring, summer, fall
Scenery:	Forested, rural
Maps:	Norway 15, Sebago Lake 15, DL 10, 4, and 5
Portage:	(17.0 mi L dam at Scribners Mill 20 yd)
Campsite:	4.75 mi L bottom of first rapids

This stretch makes a pleasant one-day trip with a mixture of rapids and smooth water. Some cabins are along the river below East Waterford and Twin Bridges, and also beside McDaniel's Rips near Sodom Road. Other than that, the river is secluded all the way to Bolsters Mills. The section between Sodom Road (a name that originated in the enmities aroused by a nineteenth-century land feud) and Twin Bridges is especially scenic.

The rapids between East Waterford and Sodom Road provide nice whitewater runs for paddlers with skill and good judgment. Not all who try to run these rapids possess these qualities, and many boats have been wrecked in McDaniel's Rips.

Below the ME 118 bridge are 4.5 miles of winding river that lead to a 0.25-mile-long set of rapids that begin innocently enough. Soon, though, these lead to a very sharp Class III drop followed by easier rapids that have heavy waves in high water. The river should be scouted from the left bank. Below it are two pools separated by some riffles. Then you reach McDaniel's Rips (5.0 miles). Stop on the right bank and scout them, because they begin with a drop over a ledge at the site of an old paper mill.

After the ledges associated with the mill site is a narrow and surprisingly steep pitch ending with a boulder midstream. Because this rock is often covered by water and hard to spot, many paddlers have been too slow to choose a path around it and have broached on it.

Beyond (about 100 yards), the drops continue as Class II or III rapids (depending on the water level), which are 0.5-mile long and taper to smooth water at the Sodom Road bridge.

Below Sodom Road (5.5 miles) you travel slack water for 3.0 miles to a power line (8.5 miles). Shortly after that is a nice, 100-yard Class II rapid with clear channels and large waves in high water, followed almost immediately by another shorter pitch, also with heavy waves in high water. In about 0.5 mile, you come to more Class II rapids at Twin Bridges.

For 0.25 mile below ME 117 at Twin Bridges (9.5 miles), the rapids continue; then, you find smooth water for 4.25 miles to Bolsters Mills (14.0 miles). A human-made rapid replaces the dam; the rapids lead to the 0.5-mile of natural Class II rapids that are below where the dam once was. These rapids are followed by 2.5 miles of slack water broken by one short, easy pitch about halfway to Scribner's Mill (17.0 miles). If you are continuing downstream, portage on the left; or you can run the dam at the right water level.

SCRIBNER'S MILL ➤ US 302   15.0 MI

Description:	Flatwater, Class I, II
Navigable:	Spring, summer, fall
Scenery:	Forested, rural
Maps:	Norway 15, Sebago Lake 15, DL 10, 4, and 5
Portage:	10.0 mi L Edes Falls 10 yd

This section is passable all summer, although a few short rapids might have to be walked down. Between Scribner's Mill and Edes Falls, the river meanders for many miles through a high-banked floodplain where some sandy beaches are exposed in low water.

The portion of the river from US 302 to the Songo River is not recommended. The banks are lined with many small cabins, and you see other encroachments of civilization (such as powerboats) that the sections upstream generally lack.

To reach Scribner's Mill, head south on Maple Ridge Road, about 2.0 miles north of Harrison on ME 117. In about 2.0 miles turn left on an unnamed side road—it's less than 1.0 mile to the river. If you go too far, Maple Ridge Road meets Edes Falls Road in 1.5 miles. Put in below the dam on the left. After 0.5 mile of rapids, the river is flat and winding for 9.25 miles. Near the end of the flat water, you find a few camps on the left, some Class I rapids, and, finally, a portage on the left around the old dam at Edes Falls. Sometimes you can pass the breached dam by running over a sloping ledge on the far right (Class III).

Below Edes Falls (10.0 miles) is 0.25 mile of Class I rapids, ending just below the bridge. The last 5.0 miles are mostly flat water. You find good access on the left bank at the ME 11 bridge (12.75 miles) and fair access at the US 302 bridge (15.0 miles).

The last 4.25 miles to the Songo River (19.25 miles) are flat, crooked, and unattractive. From the mouth of the river, continue straight ahead through the locks to the Bay of Naples (Brandy Pond) (20.0 miles) or turn left to Sebago Lake (21.75 miles).

Pleasant River

This Pleasant River is a tributary of the Presumpscot River, which drains Sebago Lake. The Pleasant River rises east of Little Sebago Lake and flows southwest to its confluence with the Presumpscot.

US 302 ➤ RIVER ROAD   4.0 MI

Description:	Flatwater, quickwater, Class I, II, III
Navigable:	High or medium water: April or May after heavy rains
Scenery:	Forested, rural
Maps:	Yarmouth, DL 5

Put in on the right side of US 302 going north toward North Windham. The Pleasant initially meanders through farm fields and woodlands. The rapids are easy for the first half of the distance to a 6-foot drop in two stages (Class III) with a rescue pool at the bottom. Scout or portage on the right. Quick water continues below for another 0.25 mile to another double-ledge combination (Class II+), a good surfing spot. The remainder of the distance is mostly quick water. Take out on River Road at Lovet Bridge. Watch for trees partially blocking the river. Canoe polers can put-in at Lovet Bridge and pole upstream to the Class II double-ledge drip.

Royal River

The Royal River rises in Sabbathday Pond in New Gloucester and flows east, north, and then south in that town. It continues southward through North Yarmouth to reach the Atlantic at Yarmouth. Except for one or two short bits, it is mostly smooth; the parts that can be most easily paddled are wholly smooth. As a consequence, the river can be run almost any time of year. The upper river can probably be run in high water, but the steep drop at Upper Gloucester must be carried.

MILL ROAD ➤ ME 231   1.75 MI

Description:	Quickwater, Class I
Navigable:	High water: April, early May, passable most summers
Scenery:	Forested, rural
Maps:	Freeport 15, DL 5

Put in where Mill Road spans the Royal River (between ME 115 and ME 231). After a Class I chute below the bridge, it is quick water to the next bridge. This part of the Royal is often interrupted by fallen trees and the thick undergrowth might make portage difficult.

ME 231 ➤ YARMOUTH WATERWORKS   7.5 MI

Description:	Flatwater, quickwater (in spring)
Navigable:	High water: April, early May, passable most summers
Scenery:	Forested, rural
Maps:	Freeport 15, DL 5

You can put in at the ME 231 bridge about 0.75 mile north of BM 167 on the Freeport topographical map, but parking space is limited. You find a Class I rip directly under the bridge. In the spring, this part of the Royal has a strong but smooth current, occasionally interrupted by fallen trees and beaver dams, which might effectively block the small river. Thick undergrowth might make portaging difficult; you can always lift over the dam(s).

In 1.5 miles, the Chandler River enters from the left. At the confluence the Chandler is wider, but the current is slower. You can easily ascend the Chandler 0.25 mile to North Road, where you find a short, rocky rapid (Class II in medium water) under the road bridge. A short carry on either bank gives access to flat water, which continues upstream for about 1.0 mile before the increasing frequency of fallen trees becomes a nuisance.

ME 9 is a little more than 0.25 mile below the confluence of the two streams, at Dunns Crossing, which offers a good off-road put-in. In summer, unless there have been heavy rains, you find no perceptible current below Dunns, and above it the current is not enough to impede upstream travel. The next 5.75 miles are smooth and meandering with no obstructions. You see only a few houses and one lovely farm. The second of two railroad bridges signals the end of this section, with Yarmouth Waterworks on the right. The Waterworks is on East Elm Street, which joins North Road and leads back to Dunns, making for an easy car shuttle.

The Royal River now loses its placid demeanor as it plunges over the dam below East Elm Street and continues to fall until it reaches tidewater at ME 88.

YARMOUTH WATERWORKS ➤ TOWN LANDING   1.0 MI

Description:	Quickwater, Class II, III, IV
Navigable:	High water: April, early May
Scenery:	Settled, urban
Maps:	Yarmouth, DL 5
Portages:	R Below East Elm Street 100 yd
	R First old mill site 150 yd
	L Second old mill site 100 yd

The first half of this section runs through Royal River Park, in Yarmouth. Because of the three portages (total 0.33 mile), it is hard work for the amount of paddling actually done. Water levels are critical for a safe and enjoyable run on those rapids that can be run.

Just below the East Elm Street bridge is a dam built on either side of a sloping outcropping of ledge. At an ideal water level, an expert kayaker might be able to slide down this ledge (Class IV) and run the short rocky Class III rapid just below it. Also, an old 10-foot-wide mill canal exits the pond above this dam very near the Waterworks' parking lot and runs under the street. It looks runnable, but is not, as it contains two 90-degree turns, a 4-foot drop, and a lot of debris. Carry around the dam on either side of the canal.

Less than 50 yards below the confluence of the canal and the main river, the banks become vertical and the river turns into a Class II rapid that is the lead-in to a 12-foot drop over a nearly vertical ledge.

This was once the site of a mill complex, the ruins of which make up the right bank. This fall could be run at some levels in a decked boat, but would be at least Class IV, as the run would require maneuvering both above and below the steep part. Carry by the paved path on the right; by the time you come to a suitable launching spot, the stream has subsided to Class I. In 200 yards, the river passes under US 1 and into the 100-yard-long pond formed by the dam above the Sparhawk Mill.

In high water, you can put in just below the fishway and run a strong Class II–III rapid down past the mill parking lot. Most of this rapid is too rocky to run at medium or lower levels, so you must take out on the right, carry across the bridge down into the mill parking lot, and put in from the left bank. Below the Sparhawk Mill rapid are 200 yards of quick water and easy Class I rips. Now the river swings right and then slides into a series of broken and offset ledges at another old mill site. The lower half of this rapid is under the ME 88 bridge and is flooded out by high tide. With medium water and high tide, you have a choice of highly technical routes through the ledges down to flat water just above the bridge. At low tide and high runoff, you still have several options on the upper part, but all routes lead to two successive heavy drops under the bridge. This rapid can vary from bony Class III to thundering Class IV, depending on the interaction of runoff and the tides.

A gauging station on the right can serve as a take-out, or a little farther downstream you find a take-out on the left at a public parking and picnic area. This spot is marked on the river by a bare ledge. Below the rapid you come to a pool and the high I-95 bridge. The town landing is 200 yards downstream on the left. It is reached by Bayview Street. You then have 2.0 miles of pleasant tidal paddling to the Cousins River and Casco Bay, if you wish an opportunity to relax.

Chandler River

The Chandler River rises in Pownal and flows southwest to the Royal River.

RUNAROUND POND ➤ ROYAL RIVER   **10.0 MI**

Description:	Flatwater, quickwater, Class II
Navigable:	High or medium water: April or May, some sections passable after heavy rains
Scenery:	Forested, rural, settled
Maps:	Freeport 15, DL 5
Portages:	2.75 mi R dam 50 yd
	7.5 mi ledge lift-over

The dam at the foot of Runaround Pond is on Frickett Road halfway between North Pownal and ME 9, which are 3.0 miles apart. A paddle up the pond is possible for a warm-up.

Put in on Runaround Pond Road. To reach the put-in, it is necessary to carry your boat approximately 100 yards down the left side of the millpond below the old mill dam before reaching the stream. Getting into the millpond immediately at the road could be dangerous at high water as you face the possibility of being swept over the dam.

The first 1.0 mile is choked with alder, but the struggle is rewarded by a subsequent 1.0 mile of lovely woodland paddling in fair current to Poland Rang Road. Just below this bridge is 0.25 mile of millpond. Portage on the right along Lawrence Road to where the stream is again large enough for a canoe or kayak. A few yards of riffles bring you to the Lawrence Road bridge. In 0.5 mile you come to a small broken weir that requires a lift-around unless the water is high. In 0.5 mile you pass Sweetser Road, and 0.25 mile below is 0.25 mile of rapids that are Class II when runnable. The one possible channel has lots of turns. Beyond the rapids is 1.0 mile of quick water to Elmwood Road. To Hadsey Road is 0.75 mile of quick water; the hardwood gives way to alder, but you still have room to paddle. The last 1.0 mile is uneventful except for two ledges halfway along. The first is a sloping drop of 1.5 feet, the second is a 1-foot vertical drop. These might be up to Class II in high water and must be lifted around in low water. You can take out at Milliken Road, but the climb up is steep on either side.

Just below Milliken Road is a jagged ledge drop, which probably can never be run clean. The ledge drop is surrounded by barbed-wire fences. The river meanders 3.0 miles with some current to North Road and is occasionally obstructed by fallen trees.

Under the North Road bridge is a short rip. It is 0.25 mile to the Royal River and another 0.25 mile down it to ME 9 at Dunns Corner, where you find good off-road parking.

Paddling upstream from the lower end is also possible for 1.0 mile or more.

Cathance River

The Cathance River rises north of Bradley Pond and flows south to Topsham; there, it turns abruptly and flows northeast to tidewater at Bowdoinham. The river is very small, alternating smooth stretches with short rapids and ledges. These can be run, lined, or carried, depending on water height, type of boat, and skill of party. This is a fun river for paddlers with good skill in whitewater and a realistic estimate of their abilities.

US 201 ➤ BOWDOINHAM		**6.5 MI**

Description:	Flatwater, quickwater, Class I, II, III, IV, V, tidal
Navigable:	Medium water or after heavy rains
Scenery:	Forested, settled
Maps:	Bath 15, DL 6
Portage:	2.5 mi R 15-ft waterfall 50 yd

Put in at the boat launch from US 201 just north of Topsham/Brunswick. From this put-in the river is 20 feet wide, deep, and has almost no current. For 0.5 mile, it follows under and along I-95. As it curves away, the current becomes noticeable. At 1.0 mile from the start the first rapid is reached, runnable but scratchy, a taste of things to come. You encounter many short, steep pitches, each with a quiet pool below, and easy to scout. Several are narrow, sharp curves with a width of 4 to 6 feet. Each drop after the first one should be scouted. The channels often have snags or boulders obstructing them. **Caution!** The 15-foot waterfall (2.5 miles) starts with several small, easy, waves, but do not be fooled; take out on the right as soon as you see the horizon line and before entering the rapid. After you are in the rapid you have only one tiny eddy on the right to save you from being swept over the falls.

Below Cathance Road bridge is a 15-foot waterfall, which can be carried on the right. Access is very poor at the bridge. From this point, the river is a tidal marsh. The scenery is good, with only a few scattered cottages and many birds. The tide is a couple of hours later than Portland. Take out at a boat launching ramp at Bowdoinham.

Sasanoa River

The Sasanoa is an entirely tidal passage that runs northwest-southeast connecting the tidal parts of the Kennebec and Sheepscot Rivers. Midway through its course, at Hockomock Bay, it meets and mixes with the Back River. The Back River also connects the Kennebec to the Sheepscot, but goes northeast-southwest.

You can do the trip in either direction, but timing the tide is critical if you want to go with the current at the two tidal rapids known as Upper and Lower Hell Gate. High water at Bath is 1 hour later than it is at Portland; at Upper Hell Gate, 1 hour and 11 minutes later than it is in Portland; Mill Point, 35 minutes later; and Robinhood, 14 minutes later.

KNUBBLE BAY ➤ BATH   **7.0 MI**

Description:	Tidal, tide race
Navigable:	Anytime: check tide tables
Scenery:	Rural, settled, urban
Maps:	NOS chart 13293 preferred to Bath 15 and
	Boothbay 15, DL 6 and 7

You can reach the AMC Knubble Bay Camp by following Webber Road that turns left off the paved road to Robinhood. From the camp it is about 0.5 mile to Beal Island (camping by previous registration only, www.outdoors.org). Lower Hell Gate is between Beal and Westport islands. The current swirls through the crooked passageway, creating many low waves, irregular eddies, and, occasionally, small whirlpools. It might be considered Class II at maximum strength on the ebb 3 or 4 hours after high water; near slack, it is more like Class I. The correct exit from Hockomock Bay is hard to find without a chart or knowledge of buoy markings. Upper Hell Gate is 1.0 mile west of where the Sasanoa leaves Hockomock Bay; it is nothing more than the constriction of the already-narrow channel and appears trivial to whitewater paddlers. A Class I chute with waves at most times, it can be tricky if powerboats are trying to pass at the same time.

In another 0.5 mile the Sasanoa opens into Hanson Bay, which is shallow and can be choppy in a blow. Follow the current between Preble and Sasanoa points and out into the Kennebec. Give wide clearance to Bath Iron Works and stay out of their safety zone, which is marked by buoys. Take out at the municipal floats just upstream of the US 1 bridge on the west or at the boat ramp near the sewage treatment plant 1.0 mile farther up the Kennebec.

Kennebec River

BATH TO LINES ISLAND AND RETURN   6.0 MI

As a continuation of the Sasanoa River trip, or separately, it is not too difficult to continue up the Kennebec River to round Lines Island and return.

If the tide is ebbing, hug the western bank and use the eddies to get upstream. Then ferry across, go up Burnt Jacket Channel east of Lines Island, and come back down the western channel with the main current.

Sheepscot River

The Sheepscot River rises in Montville and flows southwest through Palermo and Somerville to Whitefield, where it is joined by the West Branch. From there, it flows southward past Wiscasset to the sea between Georgetown and Southport.

SHEEPSCOT POND ➤ COOPERS MILLS   12.5 MI

Description:	Quickwater, Class I, II
Navigable:	Medium and high water
Scenery:	Forested
Maps:	Vassalboro 15, North Whitefield, DL 13

North of ME 3 in Palermo, the Sheepscot is very small. From ME 3, it is 0.75 mile of flat water to Sheepscot Pond. A dam and a state fish hatchery are at the outlet 3.0 miles below the pond. Below the bridge at the hatchery, the river is only a canoe-length wide with steep rapids underneath overhanging branches, runnable only in high water. The river can be reached another 0.75 mile downstream. From this road to just north of ME 105 is flat water with frequent beaver dams.

A short section of quick water begins at an old dam site just north of ME 105 and extends south approximately 1,000 feet to the gravel road south of ME 105, followed by more flat water to Long Pond. Down Long Pond 3.0 miles the pond narrows into a river again. Approximately 1.5 miles more brings you to a 7-foot dam above the old bridge at Coopers Mills.

COOPERS MILLS ➤ WHITEFIELD 9.5 MI

Description:	Flatwater, quickwater, Class II, III
Navigable:	High and medium water
Scenery:	Forested, rural
Map:	DL 13

You travel 1.0 mile of rapids below the dam, the first 0.5 mile of which is Class III in high water and rocky at other levels. It is narrow with one sharp drop and overhanging obstacles, which make it dangerous. The next 1.0 mile to the junction with the West Branch (2.0 miles) is mostly smooth water.

The next 2.0 miles to the ME 126 bridge at North Whitefield (4.0 miles) are smooth going. You find a USGS gauging station at this bridge. Beside the gauging station on river left is a steep put-in. The next 5.5 miles of winding river to Whitefield are smooth, past many fields and some wooded banks to a washed out dam.

Description:	Quickwater, Class II
Navigable:	High water: early to mid-April
	Medium water: late April to early May, or after
	heavy rains
Scenery:	Forested, rural
Maps:	Wiscasset 15, DL 13
Portage:	(6.0 mi dam)

This is a very popular open-canoe run in early to mid-April, as it is not too difficult and it usually ices-out before most other streams. However, it is dry and bony after the spring runoff.

Below the washed-out dam is a 2-foot ledge that makes an interesting souse hole at high water. The put-in is easier from the right, but take care not to block access to the private home just downstream, and always remember to ask for permission before crossing property lines. The pool below the ledge has a fast jet down its middle, which divides around a low island. Most of the river goes left, and beginners often have difficulty crossing the jet to get to a deep channel. In all but the lowest water level you generally have enough water to stay left of the small island.

Fast current with some waves and occasional rocks continues for about 0.5 mile and then winds down to mostly smooth water that continues to a pair of old bridge abutments. There, the Wiscasset, Waterville, and Farmington Narrow Gauge Railway once crossed the river. You find a short Class II pitch here and then 1.0 mile of flat water to the beginning of a 2.0-mile stretch of continuous Class II rapids through wooded banks. These rapids ultimately diminish to Class I riffles; then the river kinks left and right by a large rock outcrop on the left, 100 yards above the muddy take-out on the right bank above the dam at Head Tide. If water is going over the crest of this dam, the rapids above are mostly low waves with few visible rocks. If more than 3 feet of the upstream face of the dam are dry, the rapids are rocky and technical.

Description:	Tidal
Navigable:	Anytime
Scenery:	Forested, rural
Maps:	DL 13 and 7

For the next 1.5 miles to Alna, the river winds, nearly meeting itself, and soon passes under the Dock Road, flowing over a gravel bottom, which causes riffles in high water but is dry going in low water. Although the tidal effect is felt above Alna, the river is still moderate in size and on an outgoing tide provides a pleasant paddle for the next 5.5 miles to the bridge at Sheepscot. Much of this section of river is protected through the work of the Sheepscot Valley Conservation Association. This is the second bridge to replace the original bridge, a toll bridge from 1794 to 1894 that provided the earliest crossing of the river. You might wish to take out here on the left where the Dyer River enters. Below the bridge is the reversing falls. Use caution at mid to low outgoing tide. You might want to go down the widening estuary 5.0 miles to Wiscasset, which is well worth visiting with its charming old houses and interesting museum.

Sheepscot Reversing Falls

The waves and holes are formed by the outgoing tide dropping over a ledge. The flow begins 2½–3 hours after high tide in Portland. (Tide charts are available on the Internet, in the local newspapers, and elsewhere.) The greater the difference in high and low tide heights, the better the wave.

Typically boaters squirt the eddy line while waiting for the wave to form. As the flow changes, the wave gets steeper and more hole-like. A second wave/hole is behind the first one, and you have several other spots along the ledge to play in. If you are a novice, you have plenty of room to play while the wave is busy and also lots of room for swimming and multiple roll attempts/practice.

How to get there: Head north out of Wiscasset on ME 218. Turn right on Sheepscot Cross Road (street sign is on the left). You can cross the river and can see if the falls have "reversed" by looking right. Take the next right.

You pass a church and some houses. Turn down the next right (unpaved) road 0.5 mile and take the next right down a smaller dirt road. Parking is limited. This looks as if you are entering private property, and you are. Remember to ask for and obtain permission before crossing property lines.

Follow the footpath on the right of the parking area down to the put-in on the upstream side of the falls and float around the point. The take-out is on the downstream side of the peninsula.

Sheepscot River (West Branch)

The West Branch rises in Palermo and flows south through China to join the main river in Whitefield. In the first few miles below Branch Pond, the river is small as it wanders through a swamp, is obstructed with debris, and has a few rocky, scarcely runnable rapids. The remainder of the river is a mixture of quick water and rapids, with the blockage by trees becoming less frequent as the river becomes larger.

WEEKS MILLS ➤ SHEEPSCOT RIVER   **11.25 MI**

Description:	Quickwater, Class I, II
Navigable:	Medium or high water
Scenery:	Forested
Maps:	Vassalboro 15, North Whitefield 15, DL 13
Portage:	11.0 mi L ledge 25 ft or 100 yd, depending on water level

This section of river is primarily gentle current flowing between evergreen-lined banks, interspersed by occasional rocky rapids.

The section of river immediately below Weeks Mills might be blocked by fallen trees. Check locally before starting. If the river is blocked, put in at the next bridge.

An abutment 1.5 miles above the ME 105 bridge has a chute through it. Starting shortly above the bridge is a rocky Class II rapid with a small ledge continuing down to the bridge. More smooth water is followed by 0.5 mile of scratchy rapids. You travel more easy rapids and see some interesting rocks by a pool above the ME 11 bridge (9.0 miles). Anyone who has had difficulty with the rapids above should take out here.

Rapids start 0.5 mile above the next bridge, gradually increasing in difficulty and culminating in an unrunnable drop over a ledge. When you see the bridge, you still have enough time and distance to get to shore before the ledge.

Rapids continue below the bridge to the confluence with the Sheepscot River 0.25 mile below. The next take-out is 2.0 miles down the main river.

Damariscotta River

The Damariscotta River is a long freshwater lake separated by a high dam from a tidal inlet. You find a reversing falls above Damariscotta, below Salt Bay.

DAMARISCOTTA ➤ SOUTH BRISTOL   13.0 MI

Description:	Tidal
Navigable:	Anytime
Scenery:	Rural, settled, towns
Maps:	Wiscasset 15, Boothbay 15 or NOS chart 13293, DL 7
Campsite:	10.5 mi Fort Island

Put in from the public boat ramp in Damariscotta at or shortly after high water, which occurs 16 minutes later than it does at Portland. The river is wide, and the well-marked channel is deep enough for sizable yachts. In about 5.0 miles, the channel makes a sharp kink to the right around a hidden ledge off the end of Fitch Point. The ledge, which uncovers at half tide, creates a minor tide rip when covered and large eddies when bare. In another 2.5 miles on the left you see the University of Maine's Darling Center Marine Lab on Wentworth Point. You pass between Miller and Carlisle Islands 1.0 mile farther; they make good lunch stops.

Beyond Carlisle Island 2.0 miles is Fort Island, which boasts a campsite and the remains of a very small redoubt. Between Fort Point, the eastern end of the island, and the left bank is a powerful tidal race. At strength, it sometimes tows the navigational buoy completely under. Give it the same respect as you would a Class II rapid. Even though wide open, the eddy lines are irregular and abrupt.

East Boothbay is 1.5 miles beyond Fort Island on the west. You could take out here, but parking near the water is limited and the shuttle route is circuitous. A better idea would be to cross 1.5 miles to South Bristol on the eastern bank and take out near the town float on the southern side of the gut near a small store.

Pemaquid River

The Pemaquid River starts at Pemaquid Pond and flows through Biscay Pond and then southward past Bristol until it reaches tidewater at Pemaquid.

The dam at Bristol has raised the level of the connecting streams above, but the dams farther downstream are out, leaving shallow rapids.

PEMAQUID POND ➤ BRISTOL DAM   6.5 MI

Description:	Lake, flatwater
Navigable:	Anytime
Scenery:	Forested
Maps:	Waldoboro West, Louds Island, Bristol, DL 7
Portage:	(6.5 mi R Dam at Bristol)

This trip is highly suitable for beginning paddlers as it is all flat water, but pleasant; it is best suited as a lake paddle rather than a through trip.

Start at a launching ramp at the northern end of Pemaquid Pond. Paddle 6.25 miles south to the outlet. You could take a side trip up the outlet stream 1.75 miles to Duckpuddle Pond.

Continuing south, it is 2.5 miles down Biscay Pond to its outlet, a short, marshy paddle to the ponded Pemaquid River and another 2.25 miles to the dam above Bristol.

BRISTOL ➤ PEMAQUID   5.0 MI

Description:	Pond, flatwater, quickwater, Class I, II
Navigable:	Medium to medium-low water
Scenery:	Forested, rural
Maps:	Bristol, DL 7
Portage:	5.0 mi gorge 200 yd

The middle section of this river is a delightful paddle but lacks a good access. It is guarded by awkward rapids at the beginning and end. If runnable, the rapids might be Class III. This section should be enjoyed on a warm day with fairly low water and the boat waded down the rapids. Portaging is not feasible at either end.

Because of the rapids below the dam and the gabions in the river, it is best to put in below the last bridge in Bristol, 0.75 mile below the dam. A short stretch of rapids leads to an open marsh with occasional beaver dams. In another 1.0 mile, you reach the old dam above Bristol Mills Road. The steep drop there should be waded down.

From this bridge (do not trespass on private property) another 0.5 mile of river with some beaver dams leads into Boyd Pond. Going down the pond, keep right into outlet, where it is 1.75 miles of marsh and riffles to the final ledges, 0.1 mile above the ME 30 bridge at Pemaquid. Below the bridge, the river drops steeply for 200 yards through an old mill site and another 200 yards to tidewater.

Medomak River

The Medomak River rises in Liberty and flows south to the ocean at Waldoboro. The river is small and meandering above Medomak Pond. Below the pond, much of the distance is flat and probably passable at most water levels. But this stretch is interspersed with several rapids that are impressive at high water and impassable at low water. All these drops were once dammed, but all traces of the dams are now gone except for the one below Flanders Corner.

CARROLL ROAD ➤ MEDOMAK POND   6.5 MI

Description:	Flatwater, quickwater, Class I, II
Navigable:	Flatwater: most water levels
	Rapids: medium to medium-high water
Scenery:	Forested
Maps:	USGS 1:24,000 Washington, Jefferson, Union,
	Waldoboro West, Waldoboro East, DL 13

The first 1.0 mile below the ME 220 bridge is smooth. Just above the next bridge, the river drops through the rocky site of an old dam.

This section should give a fair representation of water conditions for the rest of the river.

Shortly below the bridge, the Medomak fans out through a boulder field, which necessitates some lifting over for passage at any safe water level. At 0.25 mile below the bridge, a breach in the old dam can probably be run. After dispersing briefly through another boulder pile below the dam, the river flattens out into the beginning of a long, quiet section. Most of the remaining distance to Winslow Mills is flat, with occasional quick water and riffles. Three ledges break this placid run. The first and easiest is around a left turn and ends in a pool. The second is slightly more difficult. The third is at least Class III and might be unrunnable at some water levels. In any case, it should be scouted.

The current picks up as the next bridge (8.0 miles) is reached. Around the corner below, it is a scratchy drop and then easier going to the next bridge (10.5 miles) at Winslow Mills, with a drop through the old dam site. The rapid below soon smoothes out to slow current to the US 1 bridge at Waldoboro. Take out at the picnic area downstream on the right on ME 32.

Rapids start around the corner, leading to a dangerous waterfall at an old dam site behind the Legion hall. In another 0.25 mile (immediately below the next bridge) is a dam. Following a short, rocky section, the river opens up into a wide, flat expanse above town. At the Main Street bridge (another 0.25 mile), the river falls over another rocky drop to tidewater.

Saint George River

Several lakes near Liberty form the headwaters of the Saint George River. West of Searsmont, it becomes large enough to run in high water, and lower down it is passable at all seasons. It is generally an easy river, but nonetheless, you do encounter a few Class III pitches where you must use caution.

The Saint George is an outstanding choice for someone who wants to travel through rural Maine. Although many miles of its banks are forested, the river flows through several small towns and past numerous farms. You come upon three large ponds where the typical view includes hillside fields and barns, although you can see some cottages along the shores. An occasional pair of stone bridge abutments confine the river momentarily, and several washed-out dams suggest that the river is better left unharnessed.

The upper section of the river offers the most interesting paddling. Flat water alternates with rapids and ponds. In high water, you can put in below the dam on Trues Pond in South Montville, but a start above Woodmans Mills is not recommended in medium water. You might also begin on Quantabacook Pond off ME 3 and paddle south to the river at Searsmont.

The lower Saint George River (below Union) can be run at all water levels. It is all lake or flat water except for a total of 0.75 mile of rapids, where you need to wade or drag in low water.

The 5.5 miles from Warren to Thomaston are tidal. The river here, somewhat wider and lined with salt marshes, is attractive.

A road map and the text that follows supply all the information needed to run this river. Of the USGS maps, the Union quadrangle is the most helpful.

WOODMANS MILLS ➤ SEVEN TREE POND   21.5 MI

Description:	Flatwater, quickwater, Class I, II, III
Navigable:	High water: late March, April, and early May
	Medium water: some wading, early June
Scenery:	Forested, rural, towns
Maps:	Washington, Searsmont Union, DL 14
Portages:	5.5 mi L ledge drops in Searsmont
	7.75 mi R dam 100 yd
	17.75 mi e dam 50 yd/0.25 mi
Campsite:	18.0 mi L in pine-hemlock grove

Woodmans Mills is located on ME 173 about 3.0 miles west of Searsmont where West Appleton Road branches south and almost immediately crosses the river. A small ledge drop and some minor rips are just below the bridge. Then, for 0.5 mile, the river is small and occasionally crowded with alder, but the current is strong.

For the next 4.0 miles, the river is mostly smooth. The flat water is occasionally broken by short rips, which in high water are barely noticeable. After the first 1.5 miles, you come upon a 0.25-mile Class II rapid with a ledge near the beginning that must be lined in medium water and should be scouted in high water.

More rapids (4.5 miles) begin as you approach ME 173 west of Searsmont. **Caution!** They begin as Class II, but just above the ME 173 bridge (4.75 miles) is an old washed-out mill dam that must be scouted. Class II rapids continue to a short flatwater section above the bridge in Searsmont.

Caution! In high water, stop **above** the ME 131/173 bridge in Searsmont (5.5 miles). Two difficult ledge drops are directly below this bridge. These should be scouted. In medium water you can lift over the left side of each ledge, but you are likely to get wet doing it. Below, easy rapids taper to flat water by the time you reach the outlet from Quantabacook Lake (5.75 miles). You can use an alternative put-in at Searsmont on ME 173/131 at the Quantabacook outlet. This is the most popular put-in and the starting point for the Saint George canoe race. In approximately 2.0 miles you find a Class III rapid at the former site of a wooden dam.

Below the bridge at Ghent (7.75 miles) is about 1.0 mile of Class II rapids. After 0.5 mile of quick water, you travel a short rapid called Magog Chute. It can be run at any level but should be scouted. Depending on the water level and paddler skills, it can be run left, center, or right. The next 4.0 miles to Appleton are mostly flat. You find a take-out on the right just below the ME 105 bridge. A 0.25-mile Class II rapid begins at the ME 105 bridge (10.25 miles). Another one begins 0.25 mile above Appleton, where the banks of the river become steep (13.0 miles). These last rapids continue past Appleton, but under the bridge is another ledge drop that can be lined or run in medium water and should be scouted in high water.

Below Appleton (13.25 miles), wide, shallow rapids continue for 0.5 mile, followed by 1.75 miles of flat water to Sennebec Pond (15.5 miles). A boat landing is at the southern end where ME 105/131 skirts the pond (17.5 miles). Then comes 0.25 mile of Class II rapids with a sharp Class III ledge drop halfway down in the middle of an S-turn. A steep portage is on the left. You can also portage this drop by following a dirt road between the river and the canal on the left-hand side. Near the end of the canal, continue straight to a stand of conifers where there is a campsite (18.0 miles).

A 1.0-mile section of quick water begins a short distance below the pool by the campsite. The fastwater continues under the ME 17/131 bridge (19.0 miles) to a sharp, Class II rapid (19.25 miles) just above the bridge in Union. After 1.5 miles of quick water and flat water, the Saint George River opens into Round Pond (20.75 miles).

The outlet of Round Pond is directly to the east, with flat water the remaining 0.5 mile to the ME 235 bridge (21.5 miles). This brings you to the edge of Seven Tree Pond where you find a public access ramp.

SEVEN TREE POND ➤ WARREN   8.75 MI

Description:	Lake, flatwater, Class I, II
Navigable:	High water: April
	Medium water: May
	Low water: passable, some lining required
Scenery:	Forested, rural, towns
Maps:	Liberty, Washington, Searsmont, Union, West
	Rockport, Thomaston, DL 14, 8

This section begins with a 3.0-mile paddle to the southern end of Seven Tree Pond, followed by flat water most of the way to Warren. Past an old railroad trestle 0.5 mile is Middle Road bridge (4.25 miles). A further 2.0 miles beyond, the edge of a field on the right marks the beginning of 0.5 mile of Class I rapids. You pass under a power line 0.25 mile before reaching the rapids (8.25 miles) just above Warren.

The rapids at Warren begin with a sharp, turbulent drop between a pair of old bridge abutments. You find a steep portage on the left. Beyond is 0.25 mile of Class II rapids that end at a power line. You have a good take-out point on the right just upstream of the ME 90 bridge (8.75 miles).

Except at high tide, you face a short rip under the bridge in the town of Warren (9.0 miles), with more easy rapids continuing beyond when the tide is out. In the spring, passage down these rapids is blocked by a fish weir.

At low tide, you encounter a Class I rapid 0.75 mile below Warren. The river passes under US 1 (12.25 miles), widens, and then passes through a narrow, wooded valley before reaching the Wadsworth

Street bridge in Thomaston, where you find a boat landing on the right (14.5 miles).

Oyster River

The Oyster River rises in Rockport and crashes its way to tidewater on the Saint George River.

WEST ROCKPORT ➤ WARREN   **11.5 MI**

Description:	Flatwater, quickwater, swamp, Class I, II, III, IV
Navigable:	High water
Scenery:	Wild, forested
Maps:	Thomaston, West Rockport, DL 14
Portages:	Many
	5.0 mi R Falls
	8.0 mi R Falls

From the start at Mill Street in West Rockport, the Oyster River is a tiny stream with more blowdowns than water. Travel 2.0 miles below an old dam site and ford (3.0 miles) to "Dan's Demise," a narrow gorge. Portage on the right. Just past East Warren Road (7.25 miles) is a complicated set of ledges followed by a series of sharp drops ending at Great Falls, where you find good access. Below the falls, the river mellows and is wider to the Saint George.

Although short, it is an intense run, frustrating in low water and hair-raising in high. Unlike most remote streams, it is conveniently located not more than a 30-minute drive from nice, warm eateries in Camden.

Down East Coastal Canoe Trail

Various people have been working to establish a relatively safe tidewater-paddling route with supporting campsites to make a week-long trip from Portland to Pemaquid feasible. This section is a brief excerpt from their material.

The recommended route starts from Spring Point, in South Portland. It goes between Peaks and Diamond Islands and west of Long Island. The first campsite is Little Chebeague Island (6.0 miles).

The route then passes south and east of Great Chebeague Island and west of Hope, Bangs, and Stockman Islands. Turning east, it passes south of Basin and Potts Points to a campsite in Harpswell Sound (12.0 miles).

Continue north up Harpswell Sound; proceed through Erwin Narrows, Long Reach, and the Gurnet Strait, turning southeast into the New Meadows River. The portage to the Kennebec is made from Winnegance Bay to Winnegance Creek (Winnegance is a Native American word meaning "small portage"). Meadowbrook, a commercial campground, is near the portage trail (12.0 miles).

The portage starts at a boat-launching ramp at the eastern end of Brighams Cove. Continue over the ridge and along the trees beyond to the trail down to the water. A short portage must be made at the ME 209 bridge. Go up the Kennebec to Bath and turn east into the Sasanoa River to Beal Island, where advance reservations are required for camping (10.0 miles). You find access at the AMC Knubble Bay Camp 0.75 mile to the southwest.

From Beal Island, continue south down the Sasanoa River, cross the Sheepscot River to Townsend Gut, continue across Boothbay Harbor, and round south of Spruce Point and north to East Boothbay. Portage from the boat ramp across the road into a pool and then through a culvert (when tide conditions permit). Go north up the Damariscotta River to Fort Island (12.0 miles).

Return to South Bristol, and go through the Gut to the finish at the boat ramp just north of Fort William Henry (5.0 miles).

Wind, weather, and fog conditions make it highly likely that the trip will be delayed at some point. Allow for rest days or an alternate take-out when making plans.

The entire route is on National Ocean Survey Chart #13288 (Monhegan Island to Cape Elizabeth). Greater detail is found on #13293 (Damariscotta, Sheepscot, and Kennebec Rivers) and #13290 (Casco Bay).

For further information, contact the Maine Island Trail Association, 58 Fore Street, Portland, ME 04101 (207-761-8225), www.mita.org.

Chapter 8
Eastern Coastal Watersheds

Blue Hill Falls

Blue Hill Falls is a tidal rip that is a good place for practice in handling rough water. You frequently see canoes and kayaks playing in these rapids. Approximately 100 yards of rugged whitewater can be traversed repeatedly using the large eddy on the right. The trip can be run anytime the tide is right. The falls is located by ME 175 where the bridge crosses the entrance to Salt Pond 3.0 miles southeast of Blue Hill. Best runs start 3 hours after low tide. The falls start slowly and within 3 hours build up to Class IV.

Narramissic River

The Narramissic River is the outlet of Alamoosook Lake and is the last freshwater section of a collection of lakes and ponds that flow into the Penobscot River at its mouth. The tidal section below Orland is called the Orland River for the last few miles to the Penobscot.

The largest lake that drains into Alamoosook Pond is Toddy Pond, which is pretty and somewhat wild at the southern end;

EASTERN COASTAL
WATERSHEDS

Scale in miles

0   10   20   30

Castine
Bucksport
Blue Hill Falls
East Orland
Alamoosook Lake
Narramissic River
Union River
Ellsworth
Graham Lake
Tannery Brook
Amherst
West Branch
East Branch
Middle Branch
Great Pond
Brandy Pond
Spectacle Pond
West Branch
Narraguagus River
Millbridge
Cherryfield
Deblois
Pleasant River
Mopang Stream
West Branch
Fourth Machias Lake
Third Machias Lake
Machias River
Columbia Falls
Whitneyville
Machias River
Old Stream
Grand Lake Stream
Grand Lake
Big Lake
Machias
Hadley Lake
East Machias River
Gardner Lake
Rocky Lake
Lake Cathance
Cathance Stream
Meddybemps
Dennys River
Machias River
Marne River
Princeton
Grand Falls Flowage
Woodland
St Croix River
St Croix River
Vanceboro
Chiputneticook Lakes
Whiting
Orange River
Dennysville
Calais

NEW BRUNSWICK

254   AMC River Guide ME

but its outlet is not runnable. The farthest upstream starting point is on Mill Dam Brook near Dedham. This flows into Long Pond, the outlet of which is Moosehorn Stream, which flows through Dead River to Alamoosook Lake.

DEDHAM ➤ ALAMOOSOOK LAKE   10.25 MI

Description:	Lake, flatwater, quickwater, swamp, Class I, II
Navigable:	Medium water, lakes anytime
Scenery:	Forested
Maps:	Orland 15, Bucksport 15, DL 23
Portage:	(10.25 mi dam at outlet)

The put-in is on ME 46 where several brooks join just below Dedham. The going is heavy through a swamp and over deadfalls and beaver dams to Long Pond (2.75 miles).

Continuing on Moosehorn Stream from Long Pond (4.75 miles), the river flows over a short rapid. Take quick water and Class I rapids down to the ME 46 bridge, which is too low to pass under in high water. The stream slows for a while and then drops over the most difficult rapids on the trip. There, the stream is small and full of sharp turns under a small bridge on a dirt track. Soon, it slows down and widens out, passing through a marshy area into the Dead River (7.5 miles), which is really a northern arm of the lake, because of the backwater from the dam. It is 2.0 miles down Dead River to the narrows and another 1.0 mile down the lake and around the corner to the dam.

ALAMOOSOOK LAKE ➤ ORLAND   3.0 MI

Description:	Flatwater, quickwater
Navigable:	Spring, summer, fall
Scenery:	Forested, rural
Maps:	Orland 15, DL 23
Portage:	(3.0 mi dam at Orland)

This is a pleasant run through fields and woods that can be done as a return trip.

Union River

The confluence of the East and West branches of the Union River is now flooded out at the northern end of Graham Lake.

GRAHAM LAKE   14.75 MI

From the last bridge on the West Branch on ME 181, it is 2.75 miles to the confluence with the East Branch, and another 1.0 mile to a boat ramp on the western bank. Beyond a large island the lake opens up, narrowing again toward the southern end and the dam.

GRAHAM LAKE ➤ ELLSWORTH   4.5 MI

Below the dam, the river is mostly smooth for the next 4.0 miles to Ellsworth, except for Ellsworth Falls halfway down. Here the river divides into two islands. River left is at least Class I with a few rocks to be avoided on the left at the bottom. The middle offers a better line for the same rapid, and river right might be too rocky to run. Below the high dam at Ellsworth, the river is tidal.

Union River (West Branch)

The West Branch of the Union River is formed by a collection of brooks south of Passadumkeag Mountain and flows south to meet the sea south of Ellsworth. There, it feeds into the complex of bays around Mount Desert on the eastern side of Penobscot Bay. When the water is high, it offers Class I, Class II, and Class III rapids. It should generally be run before the blackfly season.

GREAT POND (DOW PINES) ➤ AMHERST   11.0 MI

Description:	Quickwater, Class II, III
Navigable:	High water: April and May
Scenery:	Forested, blueberry barrens
Maps:	Saponac 15, Great Pond 15, DL 34 and 24
Portages:	Optional, see text.

Great Pond can be reached by a good road that leaves ME 9 about 1.0 mile past Aurora. You find a landing at Dow Pines; ask for and obtain permission to park there at the main office.

From Dow Pines to the outlet is 1.0 mile of lake paddling. The dam that used to mark the beginning of the Union River is now gone. The river starts with 2.0 miles of flat water that lead to a gentle Class II rapid under a defunct logging bridge. More flat water leads to a Class II, 2-foot ledge drop that is best run on the right center. Next are 200 yards of easy Class II water that lead to a pool above Hell's Gate (3.25 miles). Stop and scout; a portage can be done on either side. Hell's Gate is a three-step, Class III drop that can approach Class IV at high water. To run this drop, start left, go center, and end left.

The next 6.0 miles are mostly smooth, but three significant ledge drops should be scouted. The first of these drops is Class III. You find a clean chute on the left side of the 5-foot drop while the easiest portage is on the right. The next rapid is a 3- to 4-foot drop that is rated Class III, IV. It is best run or portaged right. The Gauging Station is a popular take-out on Tannery Road (10.25 miles). The final drop (Class III) is found in a right turn just past the Gauging Station and just above the Tannery Road bridge. Scout and run on the right. A tricky left turn leaves little margin for error. After the rapid, you find a take-out under the bridge on the right, or you can continue another 0.75 mile to ME 99 and take out there.

AMHERST ➤ GRAHAM LAKE   6.0 MI

Description:	Quickwater, Class II, one unrunnable falls with runout rapid
Navigable:	Spring, summer, fall
Scenery:	Forested
Maps:	Great Pond 15, Ellsworth 15, DL 24
Portage:	3.0 mi R waterfall

The next 3.0 miles are meandering quick water to a 10-foot waterfall, followed by 100 yards of Class II. Following this, you reach the backwaters of Graham Lake. Take out at Goodwin Bridge on ME 181 (6.0 miles).

Union River (East Branch)

The East Branch of the Union River drains a number of ponds east of Beddington, and flows west and then south into the upper end of Graham Lake north of Ellsworth to join the main river.

STEEP LANDING ➤ ME 179   **14.25 MI**

Description:	Lake, flatwater, quickwater, marsh, Class I, II
Navigable:	Spring, after heavy rains
Scenery:	Wild, forested
Maps:	Great Pond, Lead Mountain 15, DL 24
Portages:	7.5 mi R Ledge Falls (optional)
	10.5 mi R Island Rips (optional)
Campsite:	3.0 mi Spectacle Pond

Steep Landing is where the esker crosses the river 2.0 miles below Rocky Pond. Do not try to drive down the hill the last 100 yards to the put-in; it is very steep.

The East Branch is half the size of the West Branch. The crossing of Spectacle Pond and the 2.5-mile flat paddle at the end tend to discourage the whitewater enthusiast, but if you are a paddler with an appreciation for diversity, you will be delighted by the East Branch.

From Steep Landing to Spectacle Pond the river is small and flows through alternating forests and bogs. You come upon a short Class I rip just before the entrance to the pond (2.75 miles). Spectacle Pond has few camps and little boat traffic in spring, as well as good sand beaches and campsites.

A 3.0-mile paddle across the lake through the Narrows brings you to "Poison Ivy Pitch" (5.75 miles), a short, sharp drop, Class II in high water. In 1.0 mile, the Bog River (alternate start) comes in on the left, bringing a substantial volume of water. The bog section ends at Ledge Falls (7.5 miles). Look for granite ledge on left. Portage right if desired. Ledge Falls is the site of an old timber dam; logs from the old dam sometimes tear free and complicate the lower end of this Class II–III drop.

Shortly after, the "Ramp," a delightful 2.0-mile section of narrow, snaky river loaded with blind bends and boulders, begins. **Caution!** Although no drop here is greater than Class II in high water, you can come upon downed trees very suddenly. The ramp ends at the junction with the Middle Branch, where you can take out (9.5 miles).

More rips are just below. Beyond a bridge 0.25 mile you find Island Rip (10.25 miles). A small channel of the river cuts right (not passable) to form a small island and a large island just beyond. The optional portage is on the right at the head of the large island; it is very easy to miss. Island Rip is 100 yards long, Class II–III, with many boulders and holes. The worst part is at the start. Below are two small Class I rips. The "Stanmoddar" (11.75 miles) is a huge, erratic boulder. Local Saxon legend has it that "Stanmoddar" gave birth to a myriad of boulders in this area.

The next 2.5 miles are smooth with little current. Take out at the large sawdust pile on the left or below the ME 179 bridge on the right in the pool.

ME 179 ➤ WEST BRANCH   5.0 MI

Description:	Flatwater, quickwater, Class I, II
Navigable:	High and medium water: until mid-June, after heavy rains
Scenery:	Wild
Maps:	Great Pond, Ellsworth 15, DL 24
Portage:	2.25 mi R waterfall 50–300 yd

This section is seldom paddled. About 0.5 mile below ME 179 is a ledge drop that you should look at. Pleasant paddling takes you in 1.0 mile to a bouldery bend, Class I–II (1.5 miles). Use caution on sharp bends here as they blend together.

Get out before two stone bridge abutments (the jaws of death), and scout the rapids below. Class II–III rips begin and continue right to the brink of Siltstone Falls (2.25 miles), a definite portage. Watch carefully for the portage! As you have no good eddies or rescue spots before the falls, this is one place where "going for it" might result in "getting it." Portage right. Below the falls is another short drop that changes in difficulty as the level of Graham Lake rises and falls.

You have no take-out at the confluence. Paddlers going upstream on the West Branch could drag over a peninsula (4.5 miles) to the right to the West Branch, and paddle 2.0 miles up to ME 181. From the confluence it is 12.0 miles south to Graham Lake dam. Take-out might be possible at a boat ramp on the western shore (6.25 miles).

Union River (Middle Branch)

This smaller branch of the Union River is the least used. The heaviest use is by people fishing; they usually put in at ME 9 and paddle upstream into the large bog paralleling the Whaleback.

ME 9 ➤ EAST BRANCH   6.5 MI

Description:	Flatwater, quickwater, swamp, Class I
Navigable:	High or medium water: spring
Scenery:	Wild
Maps:	Great Pond 15, DL 24

Below ME 9 the Middle Branch flows through a swamp with occasional beaver dams. Swamp gives way to forest, and soon the first of two Class I spots occurs. This is followed in 1.5 miles by the other Class I spot. Access is available at an old bridge crossing just before the East Branch.

Tannery Brook

Tannery Brook begins in Burnt Pond on the border of Dedham and Otis. It flows eastward through Otis and Mariaville to Graham Lake. The river drops 195 feet in 5.0 miles, but much of it is in the first 0.25 mile.

ME 180 ➤ GRAHAM LAKE   4.5 MI

Description:	Class I, II, III
Navigable:	High water
Scenery:	Wild
Maps:	Orland 15, Ellsworth 15, DL 24

Put in at the ME 180 bridge. The river is small, and most of the way is Class I, interspersed with ledge drops, Class II and III. Shortly below the ME 181 bridge, it flows into Graham Lake.

Narraguagus River

The Narraguagus flows from Deer Lake to tidewater at Cherryfield. In the 40.0 miles described here, it drops 391 feet, more than any coastal stream east of the Penobscot, except for the Saint Croix, which is appreciably longer. It also has more access points than the rivers to the east, because a road of some kind parallels it the entire distance. Fortunately, the attractiveness of the river is scarcely affected, and it appears as wild as any in Maine.

DEER LAKE ➤ DEBLOIS   25.0 MI

Description:	Lakes, quickwater, Class I, II, III
Navigable:	High water: May
Scenery:	Forested
Maps:	Tunk Lake 15, Lead Mountain 15, DL 34, 24, and 25
Campsites:	0 mi Deer Lake MFS $ car
	1.25 mi L Twenty-Eight Pond permit
	19.5 mi L Beddington Lake Outlet permit

The drop in this section is 230 feet, virtually all of which is runnable in season. The rapids are Class I and II, except near the end at Rock Dam Rips, a Class III pitch.

The first 4.0 miles are flat and should be avoided if you are pressed for time or unwilling to cope with windfalls and beaver dams. It is worth doing, but it takes 2 to 3 hours to paddle from Deer Lake through the Oxbow to the outlet of Haycock Pond, where the river approaches the road for the first time. Below the Oxbow, where the river flows slowly through a large meadow, is a good current with many interesting rapids.

Lead Mountain, located north of the Airline (ME 9) and just west of the river, is a 1,475-foot landmark that is visible from various points along the Narraguagus as far upstream as the Oxbow.

It is 0.75 mile from the MFS campsite on Deer Lake to the outlet. En route you pass the road from Beddington, and if you can just squeeze a loaded canoe or kayak through the culvert, you will have plenty of water downstream. Below the dam for 1.25 miles the stream is flat, small, and occasionally blocked by deadfalls and choked with alder. After a log bridge (2.0 miles), the widened river meanders for 2.0 miles through the Oxbow, where you find beaver dams and a few trees across the water.

Below the Oxbow, the river approaches the road (4.0 miles), and the current picks up. As it passes Bracey Pond (out of sight to the west), you come to a log bridge (6.0 miles), which is a good access point. In 0.75 mile, you come upon another bridge (6.75 miles); after this is 1.0 mile of easy rapids. The latter might be passable on the left if the water is high enough. You take quick water to Third Pond, and below that more good current to Twenty-Eight Pond (11.0 miles).

After Twenty-Eight Pond, you have good current for 3.0 miles, followed by 1.5 miles of intermittent Class I and II rapids to the Airline Bridge (16.25 miles) and continuing for another 0.5 mile beyond. The paddle down Beddington Lake, beginning 1.0 mile past the Airline, might seem confusing if you follow the topographical map too closely, because the water level has dropped since it was made. About 2.0 miles below Beddington Lake a small stream enters on the left. An easy 100-yard paddle up it brings you to Bog Brook Flowage, a large, wild, pretty lake formed by a dam.

Below the old dam (19.5 miles) is good current for 1.75 miles to Bog Brook, where it picks up. Then, 1.75 miles later, below a huge boulder on the right and out of sight around a bend to the left, is Rock Dam Rips (23.0 miles), a nice Class III rapid less than 100 yards long that should be scouted from the left bank. Beyond the rapids a short distance is an abrupt 3-foot ledge drop, which is easily lined down on the left. Soon the current slackens to quick water. Take a short, easy rapid a little way above Deblois (25.0 miles). Land just above the ME 193 bridge because some very rough water is below called Great Falls. You find a good 0.33-mile-long portage trail on the railroad tracks.

DEBLOIS ➤ CHERRYFIELD   17.25 MI

Description:	Flatwater, quickwater, Class I, II, III
Navigable:	High or medium water: May through June
	Low water: passable
Scenery:	Wild, towns
Maps:	Tunk Lake 15, Cherryfield 15, DL 25
Portages:	0 mi R Ledges at Deblois 200 yd
	0.25 mi R Ledges 150 yd
	15.75 mi L Stillwater Dam 50 yd

The lower part of the Narraguagus is most easily characterized as a flatwater river that winds in a shallow, wooded valley. In a few locations, the blueberry barrens are visible on the hills above. From the power-line crossing to Little Falls, the banks are more open, with a thick growth of bushes and small plants overlooked by numerous dead elm trees.

At the beginning are two sections that must be portaged. Just north of the bridge in Deblois is a path along the river that leads in 0.33 mile past a cabin to the flat water below the second impassable drop. In high or medium water, the part between the drops can be run. Descend to the river when you have reached the lower corner of the field (about 200 yards) and run easy Class II rapids to a pool. Take out a short distance below the pool on the right before a cabin, and portage again about 150 yards around the falls.

In the first 0.75 mile below the second portage, you face a few short Class I–II rips. Then, for approximately 9.0 miles, the river is quick water, with a good current that lessens as you continue downstream. The only landmarks are a power line (4.25 miles) and Schoodic Brook (9.25 miles), which enters on the left as the Narraguagus turns right.

A short distance below Schoodic Brook you reach the first of two easy Class II rapids that precede Little Falls. The falls are, in fact, a Class II rapid, about 100 yards long with heavy waves in high water. The house on the left bank is owned by the Maine Atlantic Salmon Commission (www.state.me.us/asa/), and public access to the river is available here.

Below Little Falls are three Class II rapids, the first of which is almost flooded out in high water. Then flat water continues past the confluence of the West Branch (15.25 miles) to Stillwater Dam.

Below Stillwater Dam (15.75 miles), you travel nearly continuous rapids for 1.5 miles until you reach tidewater. The rapids are Class III, with three difficult pitches: just above and 50 yards below the railroad bridge and just before the first road bridge. The other sections are easier, but here the Narraguagus is a big river. The rapids reach tidewater about 100 yards above the US 1 bridge (17.25 miles).

Narraguagus River (West Branch)

The West Branch of the Narraguagus River rises just west of Beddington in T22 MD and flows southeast more or less parallel to the main river until it joins it a few miles above Cherryfield. The upper part of the river is too small for paddling until it nearly reaches Deblois. You can reach it here and run down to the main steam with easy rapids and good fishing along the way.

DENBOW HEATH ➤ SPRAGUE FALLS   14.0 MI

Description:	Flatwater, quickwater, swamp, Class I, II, III, IV
Navigable:	High and medium water: early June
Scenery:	Wild, forested
Maps:	Lead Mountain, Tunk Lake 15, Tunk Mountain, DL 24 and 25
Portages:	5.0 mi L Rock Dam 10 yd
	10.0 mi R Long Falls 0.5 mi
	14.0 mi R Sprague Falls 150 yd

This is a beautiful, little-used river, much like other eastern Maine streams. The rapids are granite ledges and piles of boulders. Access to the put-in is through Denbow Heath Peat Mine. Ask for and obtain permission at the mine before accessing the river.

Rock Dam is a short ledge drop about 3 feet high that should be looked over closely. Spring River enters right at 7.0 miles. Long Falls, 0.25 to 0.33 mile long and difficult, definitely must be scouted. The first pitch should probably be carried; it is strong, complicated, and narrow. You come upon a nice Class II–III pitch around the corner below. The main portage trail is on the railroad tracks.

You have a good take-out at Sprague Falls. These falls should be portaged on the railroad tracks for 150 yards.

SPRAGUE FALLS ➤ NARRAGUAGUS RIVER   4.0 MI

The last section to the Narraguagus River is mostly smooth.

Pleasant River

The Pleasant River flows from Pleasant River Lake, just south of ME 9 in Beddington, to Columbia Falls. It should be distinguished from the Pleasant River that is a tributary of the Piscataquis in the Penobscot watershed and others. The Pleasant has three distinct personalities: the upper portion is a fine wilderness trip with some whitewater; the middle portion meanders through an extensive heathland ending at Saco Falls; and the lower section is mostly smooth and settled to Columbia Falls, where it becomes tidal.

PLEASANT RIVER LAKE ➤ COLUMBIA FALLS   33.5 MI

Description:	Flatwater, quickwater, Class I, II, III
Navigable:	High water: early May
Scenery:	Wild, towns
Maps:	Tug Mountain 15, Cherryfield 15, Columbia Falls, DL 25
Portages:	27.5 mi L Saco Falls 2.0 mi
	33.5 mi Falls

The Pleasant River starts at an outlet on the southern end of Pleasant River Lake. The river can be reached by taking a dirt road south from ME 9 at about the T30 MD Township line, which is marked. Drive straight on the dirt road for 2.75 miles. Keep to the left as several roads run off to the right to lakeside camps. The trip starts at a small wooden bridge and a dam at the southern end of the lake.

The Pleasant River drops over a series of narrow ledges to a pool 70 yards below. These ledges might be impassable in all but very high water. The best route is to the left. The river then passes through a number of marshes with numerous signs of beaver activity; lodges are scattered through the marshes, and dams block the river at several points.

After 5.5 miles, the river narrows and enters a stretch of Class III rapids west of Beech Hill at a point about 0.5 mile from the "Allison Worcester camp" on Tug Mountain quadrangle. The "hill" is almost indistinguishable in the rolling blueberry barrens. The most prominent landmark is a large boulder, which sits in the middle of the river.

Here, the river narrows to about 20 feet. It cascades some 75 yards through Class II and III rapids. This section should be scouted because it is rocky, and you have little room to maneuver. **Caution!** Fallen trees might cross the river at this point, forming strainers. After these rapids, the river continues narrow and fast moving for 0.25 mile. After another 6.5 miles, you find a road access (12.0 miles) before you enter an extended marsh. If you want to take out here, you should spot a car on the dirt road, which can be reached by turning east off ME 192 almost directly opposite the Deblois airfield.

Pleasant River meanders for 14.0 miles through the heath, following such a convoluted route that it requires almost a full day of paddling. (This great heath is one of the longest peat wetlands of its type in the northeastern United States.)

After the heath, the river passes through a forested area with low, alder-lined banks. The approach of Saco Falls is indicated by several old farm buildings on the left (27.5 miles). The river flows past islands and ledges composed of large rocks and then narrows very sharply before dropping to the falls. Only the first 50 yards of the rapids can be run on the left; scout on the right. You find a take-out on the left in the pool below the rapid. Boats can be carried 150 feet up a gravel path leading to a paved road. **Caution!** An unfinished dam stands below the pool, the footing of which causes a drop of several feet. The falls are 100 yards below; the banks of the river are steep and the current fast.

The river thunders under a bridge several hundred feet over a series of giant rock steps at Saco Falls. Because this would be a 0.25-mile-long and difficult portage, it is better to end the trip here.

Advanced paddlers can choose to continue for the 2.0 miles from Saco Falls to Arty's Bridge. You can scout the Class III boulders and ledge drops from river left. You encounter at least one more portage, river left, in this very beautiful section of the Pleasant.

Putting in at Arty's Bridge, 2.0 miles downstream (29.5 miles), the river is mostly smooth. Several hundred yards below the bridge is a short set of Class II rips, and another set of rips (31.5 miles) where some dragging might be necessary in low water about 2.0 miles above Columbia Falls. The river passes under a railroad bridge to the take-out on the left just above the US 1 bridge. This is also the site of a Maine Atlantic Salmon Commission counting fence and a public boat landing. Below here the river passes over some falls to tidewater.

Machias River

The Machias River rates with the Allagash, the Penobscot, and the St. John as one of Maine's most scenic waterways. It offers semiwilderness travel with lakes, swamps, intermittent rapids up to Class III, ledges, a waterfall, and portages—all in a region that is used much less than the Allagash and that is more accessible than the St. John. When the last of the dams was removed in 1974, the Machias once again became a free-flowing river.

The route from Fifth Machias Lake to the sea offers one of the longest (76.0 miles) and most attractive semiwilderness canoe trips in Maine. The three big lakes have only a few cabins on their shores, and above First Machias Lake you find none along the river.

Extensive clear-cutting of timber has occurred throughout the Machias watershed. This has changed the characteristics of the river, causing a much more rapid runoff in the spring and a definite response to rain.

Many years ago, you had two routes to the Machias River from Nicatous Lake. One went up Gassabias Stream, across Gassabias Lake, and over a long portage to Fourth Machias Lake. The other began with a portage into Upper Sabao Lake (sometimes called "Machias Lake") and continued downstream to Lower Sabao Lake at the head of the West Branch. Although the first segments of each route (to Gassabias Lake and Upper Sabao Lake, respectively) are usable now, the remaining portions are impassable.

Description:	Lakes, flatwater, Class I, II, III
Navigable:	High water: May
Scenery:	Wild
Maps:	Nicatous Lake 15, Wabassus Lake 15, Tug Mountain 15, DL 35 and 25
Campsites:	3.0 mi 5th Lake Outlet permit
	3.75 mi R old dam site permit
	8.25 mi R Knight Dam permit
	13.75 mi L 4th Lake (N of Unknown Stream) MFS
	15.25 mi L 4th Lake Outlet permit car
	20.5 mi 3rd Lake Narrows (island) permit
	21.0 mi Getchel Lakes Outlet (W side) permit
	21.25 mi Prune Island (S side) permit
	23.5 mi 3rd Lake Outlet permit car
	27.75 mi R 2nd Lake Outlet (beach) permit car
	30.25 mi L 1st Lake Outlet permit car

Fifth Machias Lake can be reached from the Stud Mill Road that runs from Princeton to Costigan. A 0.5-mile trail to Greenland Cove leaves that road 4.5 miles west of the crossroads near the northern end of First Machias Lake.

From the end of Greenland Cove it is 2.5 miles across the lake to the beach at the outlet (3.0 miles). This point can be reached by car from the same road by turning north 3.0 miles west of Greenland Cove on Road 42-00-0. This is the usual start for the river trip. From there, Fifth Lake Stream flows through a culvert and then a low, marshy area for 5.25 miles to Knight Dam (8.25 miles). Almost all the way there you travel quick water, but a short, easy rapid is less than 200 yards above the old washed-out dam. Then come 1.5 miles of Class I and II rapids, with five short sections to watch out for. The first three are Class II–III ledge drops that should be scouted. After a little slack water, you reach the fourth sharp drop: a narrow chute. The fifth tricky spot is just around the next corner. Soon thereafter the rapids end, and after 1.25 miles of flat water Fifth Lake Stream empties into Fourth Machias Lake (11.0 miles).

In 1974, the dams on Fourth and Third Machias Lakes were removed, exposing the land that was flooded many years ago. The shores are now vegetated with white birch (particularly at the upper ends of each lake where the land is flatter) and many grass species. Other shrubs and trees will appear with time.

Fourth Machias Lake is 4.25 miles long. At the outlet (15.25 miles), the remains of the old dam can be run in high water. Fourth Lake Stream begins with a short Class II rapid, followed by 1.25 miles of quick water and smooth water. Shoreline Rapids (16.75 miles), exposed when the dam on Third Machias Lake was removed, is a short Class II pitch that carries you below the old lake level. You come upon another Class I rapid before you reach Third Machias Lake (17.75 miles).

It is a 5.75-mile paddle down Third Machias Lake to the outlet (23.5 miles), where the remains of the old dam can be run. A good gravel road runs up the eastern side of the river from First Lake to this point. This is an excellent alternative put-in for those wishing to avoid paddling the three large lakes.

The Machias River begins with 0.5 mile of Class I and II rapids, followed by another 0.5 mile of deadwater. Below the latter is Otter Rips, a 0.25-mile set of Class II rapids that leads to a second deadwater, which is 1.0 mile long.

Long Falls (25.75 miles) begins at the boundary line between T43 MD and T37 MD; it is a 0.25-mile Class III pitch consisting of three ledge drops and a boulder-strewn runoff. A portage on the left-hand side leads to a short stretch of quick water below the rapids. In the remaining 1.25 miles to Second Machias Lake (27.25 miles), you have almost-continuous Class II rapids. These drops below Long Falls, though unnamed, are significant. Paddling for 0.5 mile on Second Machias Lake and 2.0 miles of flat water on the river bring you to First Machias Lake (29.75 miles). Just before reaching the latter, the river flows under the Stud Mill Road, which connects Princeton and Costigan.

From the outlet of First Machias Lake (30.75 miles), the river is mostly smooth for 4.0 miles. Then, in the middle of an S-turn, a few easy rapids lead up to Carrot Rips, also called Karrick Pitch (35.0 miles), a short Class II–III drop that should be scouted or portaged on the right bank (watch for poison ivy). Beyond 0.5 mile, the West Branch enters on the right.

Below the confluence with the West Branch (35.5 miles), 4.5 miles of good current mingle with occasional easy rapids. All of the latter, including the Class II rapids at Boot Rips (38.25 miles), are flooded out when the water is really high. As you approach ME 9, stop well before the bridge (40.0 miles), because the river above it has been channeled and few good stopping places are available in the swift current. Airline Rapids, below the bridge, should be scouted (watch for poison ivy again here).

ME 9 ➤ MACHIAS   36.5 MI

Description:	Flatwater, quickwater, Class II, III
Navigable:	High and medium water: May and June
Scenery:	Wild
Maps:	Tug Mountain 15, Wesley 15, Whitneyville, Machias, DL 25 and 26
Portages:	4.5 mi L Little Falls 0.25 mi
	8.5 mi R First Pitch Wigwam Falls 0.5 mi
	13.5 mi L Upper Holmes Falls 200 yd
	14.0 mi R Lower Holmes Falls 150 yd
	25.0 mi R Great Falls 0.25 mi
Campsites:	0.25 mi L Airline Rapids MFS $ car
	4.75 mi L Little Falls (lower end) permit
	10.0 mi L Wigwam Rapids Third Pitch (poor) permit
	13.75 mi L Upper Holmes Falls (lower end) permit
	23.0 mi L Smith Landing (poor) permit car
	25.5 mi R Great Falls (lower end) permit

The Machias from ME 9 to the sea is a large river with many sections of flat water separated by falls and, in high water, heavy rapids. Depending on the water level and the skill of the paddlers, only Upper Holmes Falls, listed above, might need to be portaged. All should be scouted before a decision is made.

The riverbanks approaching Whitneyville are in the process of recovering from the disturbance of a fire and a dam.

Below Smith Landing, the river passes through an area burned in 1956. It is interesting to note the ease with which the fire jumped the river, while at the same time left isolated pockets of the forest unscathed. A good example of this is at Great Falls, where the island at the beginning was burned, but neither bank of the river at that point was touched. Little evidence of the fire remains. The old lake bed has gone to meadow and is very attractive.

The removal of the dam at Whitneyville, which backed up the water to Great Falls, has allowed the river to return to its original channel. When the old lake bottom was first exposed, it was covered with cords of sunken pulpwood, which has now been salvaged.

Airline Rapids, about 0.33 mile long, begins under the ME 9 bridge and should be scouted. It is Class III, can be run in two stages, and might have some heavy waves in high water. You travel quick water for 2.25 miles to two short Class II rapids followed by fast current to Little Falls (4.5 miles). The upper section is Class IV, but the lower portion is Class II. The portage begins on the left and ends at the campsite below the falls. More flat water continues for 3.75 miles to Wigwam Rapids.

Wigwam Rapids (8.5 miles) extends over a distance of 2.0 miles, with sections of varying difficulty depending on the water level. High water obliterates many riffles; when it does, there remain four more or less distinct pitches. The first, upper Wigwam, begins 0.25 mile below the mouth of Mopang Stream and should be scouted from the good portage, which begins in front of a cabin on the right bank. The upper section contains large boulders that make it Class III when the water is high, Class II when medium. The lower portion of the first pitch is much easier, and you have several places to put in partway down. The first pitch is 0.5 mile long, followed by 0.5 mile of slack water and then the last three pitches, which together make up Lower Wigwam. Within the next 1.0 mile are many small rapids, which are flooded out in high water; the one that is not is the second pitch, Class II. The approach to the third pitch (10.0 miles) is somewhat blind. This rapid should be scouted from the portage on the left bank, as it is a short, tricky drop over a Class III ledge with an almost river-wide hydraulic (a sneak route on the left). The fourth pitch, not far beyond, is a short Class II rapid.

After Wigwam Rapids are 3.0 miles of slack water to Upper Holmes Falls (13.5 miles), a 15-foot waterfall with a portage on the left. A good road runs from ME 9 to Holmes Falls, and you might want to take out here. Below 0.33 mile is Lower Holmes Falls (Class III), which begins at Deadman's Island, on the northern end of which is a memorial to Obadiah Hill, a pioneer who died in 1786. The portage is on the right bank. The dangerous section of the rapids is at the end, and it cannot be seen from the trail. These rapids are separated by a small island that makes scouting difficult. The right side tends to be bony even in moderately high water; the left side is quite pushy and tends to run you up against the ledge on river right.

Flat water continues for 11.0 miles, passing the mouth of Old Stream (20.25 miles) and is interrupted only slightly by Getchell Riffles, which are Class I (21.0 miles), and Bobsled Rips, hardly notable (24.5 miles). At Smith Landing (23.0 miles), a good dirt road leads to ME 192. Great Falls (25.0 miles) is a long, continuous Class III rapid. The easiest route is on the left. Scout first. The portage is on the right bank.

You travel 6.25 miles of quick water to Whitneyville (31.5 miles). The old lake bed forms a wide meadow with views of the surrounding hills, unusual on the lower river. Near Whitneyville are the crumbling remains of cribs and piers from logging days. Almost nothing remains of the old dam. A canal was once built on the left above US 1A, creating an island in Whitneyville. The canal is now closed, and the approach to US 1A is on the right via a Class II+ rapid.

Beyond the highway bridge in Whitneyville, the river is flat for 1.75 miles except for a Class I rapid at the railroad bridge. Then comes Munson Pitch, a river-wide, Class II ledge run on the left.

The river flattens out for another 1.75 miles and then enters 0.75 mile of easy Class I rapids between rocky bluffs. A short, flat stretch leads to a pretty little gorge with a nice Class II rapid. A final Class I rapid ends in a short slackwater behind the partly broken dam just above the bridge in Machias. A fairly large parking lot is on the left just above the bridge, which provides a good take-out.

Just below the take-out is Machias Falls, an unrunnable falls. Do not miss the take-out!

Machias River (West Branch)

The West Branch is small, wild, and seldom traveled. It requires higher water than is needed on the Machias River below ME 9, so it must be run early in the spring. You find a convenient campsite halfway down— at Rolford Dam—if the trip is done in 2 days.

UPPER CRANBERRY LAKE ➤ ME 9
(ABOVE AIRLINE RAPIDS)   19.75 MI

Description:	Lakes, flatwater, quickwater, Class I, II
Navigable:	High and medium water: April, May
Scenery:	Wild, forested
Maps:	Tug Mountain 15, DL 35
Campsites:	0 mi Upper Cranberry Lakes MFS $ car
	9.75 mi R Rolford Dam permit

As you follow the road to the Cranberry Lakes from ME 9 (The Airline), keep right at an intersection about 6.0 miles from the highway.

From the MFS campsite on Upper Cranberry Lake to the beginning of Cranberry Stream, you have 3.5 miles of lake paddling, with a portage around a culvert connecting the two lakes. Cranberry Stream meanders sluggishly for 2.0 miles to its junction with the West Branch (5.5 miles). The West Branch flows for 1.5 miles from Lower Sabao Lake to Cranberry Stream; it is flat and swampy.

You find an alternative put-in at a bridge about 1.5 miles downstream from the confluence of Cranberry Stream and the West Branch. It can be reached by taking the logging road from ME 9 just west of the Airline Rapids on the Machias River for about 6.0 miles and then turning left on Road 59-00-0 and then right on Road 39-00-0. This allows you to avoid the flatwater paddling on the Cranberry Lakes and Stream and a much longer shuttle.

Beyond the mouth of Cranberry Stream, the current begins to pick up after 0.5 mile. Then you have 2.75 miles of intermittent, easy Class I and II rapids, with a low logging bridge near the end, before reaching Rolford Deadwater (8.75 miles). Rolford Dam (9.75 miles) is washed out and is runnable.

Between Rolford Dam and the bridge above the confluence with the Main Branch are 5.25 miles of mixed flat water and Class I and II rapids. You also encounter five ledge drops that should be scouted. All can be run at medium to high water, but in lower water they might have to be lined.

Under the bridge (15.0 miles) is a sixth ledge. If it cannot be run, this is more easily portaged beginning on the left bank. The West Branch soon joins the Main Branch (15.25 miles).

Below the confluence, the Machias River flows with good current and occasional easy rapids for 4.5 miles to ME 9 (19.75 miles). Stop well before the bridge, because the river above it has been channeled, with the result that you find few good stopping places in the swift current. Airline Rapids, below the bridge, should be scouted.

Mopang Stream

The trip from the boat landing on Mopang Lake to the Machias River above Wigwam Rapids is a semiwilderness run of 32.0 miles, with only an occasional cabin or dirt road. Mopang Stream flows through marshes in several locations and past blueberry barrens, so that you get a feeling of space similar to that which travel on lakes provides. The dominant ground cover of sheep laurel and lowbush blueberries, sprinkled with isolated red pine and stands of poplar and gray birch, provides a distinct contrast to most other rivers in Maine.

Below the end of Mopang Stream at Machias Eddy, you come to Wigwam Rapids on the Machias, where a road from Columbia Falls provides access.

The water of Mopang Lake and Mopang Second Lake is clear, but before it flows very far downstream it becomes discolored by organic matter from swamps. The river below Second Lake is small, and its banks are forested as far as the meadow at First Lake. Beyond, it is mostly open.

MOPANG LAKE ➤ ME 9   **8.25 MI**

Description:	Lakes, flatwater, Class I, II
Navigable:	High water: May
Scenery:	Wild
Maps:	Lead Mountain 15, Tug Mountain 15, DL 25
Portage:	3.5 mi L Mopang Lake Dam 15 yd
Campsite:	5.75 mi L First Lake Outlet permit

Mopang Lake is reached by a dirt road that leaves ME 9 (The Airline) at a gravel pit 1.8 miles west of the bridge over Mopang Stream. Keep left at each of two forks. It is 3.5 miles from the landing on Mopang Lake to the dam on Second Lake, which controls the water level on both bodies of water. The rapids below are barely passable at medium water. If the water is high, they should be scouted as far as the culvert 0.75 mile downstream (road close by on left bank); you also come upon a sharp drop over a ledge and sometimes trees across the river.

Beyond the culvert (Road No. 5), the stream is Class I, with one or two blowdowns, becoming flat as it approaches Mopang First Lake. The latter is small. Below the old bridge at the outlet (5.75 miles), the river is wider and for the most part flat for 2.5 miles to the ME 9 bridge (8.25 miles), although you find some Class I rips at and below the remains of an old log-driving dam just above the highway.

ME 9 ➤ MACHIAS EDDY   23.75 MI

Description:	Flatwater, Class I, II
Navigable:	High water: May
Scenery:	Wild
Maps:	Tug Mountain 15, DL 25
Campsites:	10.25 mi R beside Bridge (poor) permit
	15.25 mi R Six Mile Dam permit

Most of the drop in elevation takes place in short pitches and at beaver dams. Only at Penman Rips are the rapids appreciably long and more difficult. The rocks in the riverbed are coarse-grained, so they can scrape a boat with unexpected authority in medium water. Much of the way, the river traverses the blueberry barrens, but in the last 3.0 miles above the Machias River, it passes through conifer forests.

For several miles you travel intermittent, easy rapids, after which the stream meanders through the barrens. Beech Hill Brook enters on the right 8.0 miles below ME 9. After winding for another 2.25 miles, the stream passes under two culverts (10.25 miles) near Duck Pond. For the next 5.0 miles to Six Mile Dam (15.25 miles) the current is slow, with an occasional easy rip.

Six Mile Dam can be run, but you face some nasty spikes on the far left side. Below, the rapids are more difficult and more frequent, and you also find some rather high beaver dams. After 3.5 miles you pass beneath a steel bridge, and reach Penman Rips (18.75 miles), Class II, at least. **Caution!** These rapids begin just above a left turn, and at the top are three ledges. Below the latter, the river is narrow with large boulders for about 50 yards, after which the gradient lessens. The next 4.0 miles to the confluence with the Machias River (23.75 miles) are mostly flat, with occasional rips. You can use a take-out here at Wigwam Rapids; the next take-out, at Holmes Falls, is 5.0 miles down the Machias.

Old Stream

This river flows into the Machias River about 5.0 miles above Great Falls. It flows from a series of lakes in T37 MD. Third and First lakes are wild and Second Lake has only a few cabins along its southern shore. Because Canaan Dam no longer impounds water, a section of the river below First Lake is in the meadowland on the bottom of a once-larger lake.

Much of Old Stream above ME 9 is not far from a logging road. However, below the highway, the river is isolated, and it meanders considerably, occasionally within a narrow valley bordered by steep banks.

As recently as the 1950s, long logs were driven down the river by the Saint Regis Paper Company.

SECOND LAKE ➤ MACHIAS RIVER   **25.0 MI**

Description:	Lakes, flatwater, quickwater, Class II
Navigable:	High and medium water: May
Maps:	Wabassus Lake 15, Tug Mountain 15, Wesley 15, DL 35, 25, and 26
Portages:	4.0 mi L Canaan Dam 20 yd
	11.75 mi L Stinking Jam Rapids 50 yd
	15.5 mi L Longfellow Pitch 30 yd
Campsites:	11.75 mi L Stinking Jam Rapids permit
	14.0 mi R head of rapids opposite wooded island permit

You find a roadside rest area on ME 9 (The Airline) beside Old Stream. Since the Airline has been widened, the rest area has a small road to the east of Old Stream. To the east 0.75 mile a logging road leads north past Canaan Dam and Second Lake.

Put in below the culvert at the outlet of Second Lake, where a portage is necessary if you begin farther along the road. The river here is very small and somewhat choked by alder, but it soon opens into a meadow. Just above First Lake is a washed-out driving dam (now stabilized by boulders and tree saplings), followed by a shallow runout.

Flat water continues from the outlet of First Lake (1.75 miles) to just above Canaan Dam, where you come upon another washed-out driving dam. The remains of the dams above and below First Lake are almost unrecognizable in high water.

Canaan Dam (4.0 miles) can be run, but should be scouted. Travel flat water to Glover Pitch, which can be recognized, in addition to the sound of it, by a large ledge on the right bank. These rapids begin with a low rock dam, which is followed by 50 yards of easy Class II. The flat water and quick water between Glover Pitch and ME 9 are broken by Hayward Dam, a series of ledges, which should be lined on the right.

Below ME 9 (8.0 miles) is quick water for about 0.5 mile, after which the river meanders in a narrow valley between conifer forests. Next come a few rips. Stinking Jam Rapids (11.75 miles) is an unrunnable ledge drop followed by Class II rapids. (Take the ledge at the next left turn to the left of center.)

You come upon a 0.25-mile Class II rapid around an island, and some distance later a runnable ledge before Longfellows Pitch (15.5 miles), a 4-foot ledge, which must be lined or portaged on the left. From that point, you travel flat water nearly all the way past New Stream (24.5 miles), which enters on the left to the Machias River (25.0 miles).

The nearest take-out is 2.75 miles downstream at Smith landing (27.75 miles).

East Machias River

The East Machias River is a pleasing mixture of easy rapids, expansive meadows, and lakes of varying sizes. Because of the rapids close to ME 9, the entire river is runnable only in high water. However, the upper section from Pocomoonshine Lake to Crawford Lake is always navigable when free of ice, and below Round Lake the river can be negotiated at low water with some occasional scraping. You see a few cabins, but most of them are on the lakes below ME 9.

In spring, the 45.0-mile trip takes 3 or 4 days. The island campsite on Crawford Lake and the one on Second Lake are among the nicest in eastern Maine.

POCOMOONSHINE LAKE ➤ CRAWFORD
(VIA MAINE RIVER)   10.0 MI

Description:	Lakes, flatwater
Navigable:	Spring, summer, fall
Scenery:	Wild
Maps:	Big Lake 15, DL 36
Campsite:	8.0 mi L first island close to East shore (S end) permit

From Pokey Lake, a wide, sluggish river winds through wide meadows and small ponds to Crawford Lake. In the summer, it seems as though you are paddling past seas of grass. Seldom do trees grow within 50 yards of the river, so easy access to dry ground is the exception. You also have little protection from a strong wind.

In the town of Alexander, follow the road from ME 9 that leads north 2.5 miles to Pocomoonshine Lake Lodges, where you find a launching area. In 2.0 miles the Maine River flows from the lake. It heads generally south through Upper Mud Lake (3.5 miles) and Lower Mud Lake (4.75 miles) to Crawford Lake (7.25 miles). The Crawford Public Landing (10.0 miles) is a short way below the cove, around which a few houses are located.

CRAWFORD ➤ EAST MACHIAS   35.0 MI

Description:	Lakes, flatwater, quickwater, Class I, II
Navigable:	High water above ME 9: May
	High and medium water below ME 9: May or June
	Low water: passable with some scraping below Round Lake
Scenery:	Wild, settled, towns
Maps:	Big Lake 15, Wesley 15, Gardner Lake 15, Machias, DL 36 and 26

Portages:	2.5 mi L Pokey Dam 20 yd
	35.0 mi Dam at East Machias
Campsites:	2.5 mi L Pokey Dam (poor) permit
	21.0 mi L Second Lake (1st point S of outlet) permit

This portion of the East Machias River makes a nice 2-day trip in the spring when the water is high and the air is faintly scented with the smell of burned or burning blueberry fields. Because the rapids are not too difficult, this river is more suitable for people with limited whitewater skill and experience than is the Machias or Narraguagus.

Put in at the Crawford Public Landing, which is reached by a side road next to the cemetery. The East Machias River, by name, begins 2.5 miles south of the landing at Pokey Dam, the outlet to Crawford Lake. After portaging the dam on the left, you travel easy rapids and quick water for 1.75 miles before reaching a deadwater (4.35 miles). After 0.75 mile are more rapids to the Airline Bridge (5.5 miles).

From the outlet of Second Lake on the west shore, the river is flat for 0.75 mile. Then, within 1.5 miles are five rapids, which get progressively harder, from Class I to Class II. At Wigwam Riffles (22.25 miles) is a low, runnable weir, and within 0.25 mile is another rapid.

Crooked Pitch (23.0 miles) is on both sides of an island, with the clearest channel on the right; and Smith Mill Pitch (23.35 miles) and Lower Riffles (23.75 miles) are straight chutes in high water. After 3.5 miles of flat water, including another large meadow, the river flows into Hadley Lake (27.25 miles). The outlet is 3.75 miles down the eastern shore. In the 1.25 miles between the lake and the ME 191 bridge are two easy rapids at low or washed-out dams.

You travel a short Class II drop under the ME 9 bridge (32.35 miles) and another easier one past the next road bridge. The remaining 1.75 miles to East Machias are flat water.

The dam at East Machias (34.5 miles) no longer impounds water. **Caution!** Keep to the left, the inside of the turn, as you approach the town. Stop above the bridge to scout or portage. In medium and high water, much of the debris and protruding steel is obscured. Caution is strongly advised. In low water, you can let down through the gates. Below the dam are sporty Class II rapids, runnable at all water levels. At low tide, they continue past the last bridge (35.0 miles), but the river fans out, and the water gets noticeably shallower.

Northern Inlet and Rocky Lake Stream

Northern Inlet, the tributary of Rocky Lake described here, is the beginning of an excellent summer trip that continues on the East Machias River below the mouth of Rocky Lake Stream. The lower East Machias is passable at all water levels, although sections of a few rapids, particularly Crooked Pitch, are bony in low water. This trip to the sea at the town of East Machias is 25.75 miles long, and it takes 2 full days when the water level is down.

OFF ME 191 ➤ EAST MACHIAS RIVER 9.25 MI

Description:	Lake, flatwater, quickwater, Class I, II
Navigable:	Passable at all water levels
Scenery:	Wild
Maps:	Gardner Lake 15, Wesley 15
Campsites:	3.5 mi L Mud Landing permit car
	4.5 mi L Rocky Lake (beach at S end) permit car

This trip begins at a bridge on a road that leads off ME 191 in T18 ED, 1.9 miles north of the second railroad crossing from US 1 in East Machias. It is a dirt road; 2.8 miles from the highway it crosses Northern Inlet. It continues on to meet ME 9 at a sharp bend in Crawford, where a side road leads to Love Lake.

Begin on the right bank below the bridge. For most of the distance to Rocky Lake the stream is deep, wide, and flat. However, you do come upon about five very short, narrow sections with Class I–II rapids in high water; they must be lined or dragged in low water. At the last of these, an old log bridge blocks the stream at high water.

Mud Landing (3.5 miles) is on the left just after the last rapid. It is another access point that can be reached via a dirt road, which leads off ME 191 about 1.5 miles north of the aforementioned railroad crossing. Farther on 0.5 mile, Northern Inlet opens into Rocky Lake (4.0 miles).

From the outlet (6.5 miles) near the north end of the lake, Rocky Lake Stream, all flat water, flows for 2.75 miles past the mouth of Northern Stream (8.25 miles) to the East Machias River (9.25 miles).

The first take-out downstream is at the ME 191 bridge below Hadley Lake, 13.75 miles to the left.

Josh Stream, Gardner Lake, and Chase Mills Stream

Lakes and boggy streams combine for a beautiful 10.0-mile trip through surprisingly wild country. It runs from the isolated and remote Josh Pond to the East Machias River.

ACCESS TO JOSH POND VIA SUNKEN LAKE   1.0 MI

From a wooded peninsula on the western shore of a marsh at the end of a shallow, winding, channel off the southwestern end of Sunken Lake, follow a trail first west along the peninsula, then southwest, avoiding bogs to the left. The route is occasionally flagged by red tape. Cross a wet spot and ascend a low ridge. Turn right onto an old tote road 0.3 mile from Sunken Lake. Up the tote road 0.5 mile turn left at a wooden boundary post. The trail descends south through open woods past a rocky outcropping and a mossy green boulder on the left; then it follows a dry ridge south. In sight of the lake it angles left off the ridge, reaching Josh Pond 300 feet east of the prominent point on the northern shore of the pond. The route is dry and the grades gentle—not a hard carry for its length.

Josh Pond can also be reached by paddling upstream from Gardner Lake Road.

JOSH POND ➤ EAST MACHIAS   9.5 MI

Description:	Lake, flatwater, Class I
Navigable:	All seasons
Scenery:	Wild
Maps:	Gardner Lake 15, Machias Bay

From the northwestern corner of Josh Pond, beside a grassy bluff with scattered trees, Josh Stream winds slowly through a broad marsh. The channel is wide and deep; wild geese, ducks, and bald eagles can be seen. Gardner Lake Road is 1.5 miles from the pond; lift over the culvert and push over a log jam below. Just before Second Lake, duck under a low bridge.

Paddle 1.5 miles down Second Lake, and turn left past a point and island into Gardner Lake. A campsite is on the left opposite the island. Gardner Lake is beautiful, with forested bluffs and islands. Chase Mills is 3.5 miles down the lake.

If Chase Mills Stream is high, you have 0.5 mile of Class II rapids to run. If it does not look high enough below the dam, carry 0.5 mile southwest down the road and carry 1,000 feet northwest to the stream.

After a few hundred feet of Class I rapids, the stream flattens out; after 1.0 mile it flows into the East Machias River. Another 1.0 mile downstream is the village of East Machias on the right. In the past, this route, together with the Orange River, was an important route from Cobscook Bay to the Machias. This trip is still possible with 1.75 miles of carrying in three portages. It can be extended for miles by exploring Rocky Lake, Roaring Lake, Harmon or Clifford Streams, and the northern arms of Second Lake.

Whiting Bay and Dennys Bay

Whiting Bay leads from the Orange River out to Dennys Bay and on out to Passamaquoddy Bay. Any paddling on tidewater demands experience and consideration of the weather and wind direction as well as the state of the tide.

WHITING ➤ REVERSING FALLS   7.5 MI

At low tide, the head of Whiting Bay is just deep enough to float a loaded boat. To Leighton Point (2.5 miles) the Bay is narrow, often constricted by rocky points, and very scenic. The tide runs at 3 to 5 knots. Where the bay widens beyond Freds Island you find mild currents down either shore. In the main channel down the center, you might encounter 1- to 2-foot waves.

At Reversing Falls, most of the tidal flow squeezes between Falls Island and Leighton Neck. A large reef exposed at all but high tide forms a big eddy with large wave trains along the eddy lines. The channel between the reef and Falls Island has a long line of 3-foot waves. The west channel has impressive boils and swirls. The mean tide range is 20 feet, and the rapids are probably Class III at mid tide. At high tide, all this mayhem stops briefly for about 10 minutes.

Orange River

Orange River is the outlet for a series of lakes, of which Rocky Lake is the largest, flowing east to Whiting Bay. It is an attractive, semiwild flatwater trip available anytime. Rocky and Sunken Lakes are in remote country.

Rocky and Sunken Lakes

Sunken Lake can be reached from Rocky Lake via a broad, shallow channel dotted with beaver lodges. Since the dam at Halls Mills burned, the lake has shrunk, and the northwestern and southwestern bays shown on the USGS Gardner Lake 15 map have returned to marsh. Wildlife is common.

Rocky Lake extends 3.0 miles north, and Rocky Lake Stream is navigable into the marshes nearly 1.0 mile more. Rocky Lake deserves its name: rugged bluffs and bare rock knobs grace every view.

HALLS MILLS ➤ WHITING   6.25 MI

Description:	Flatwater, Class II
Navigable:	Spring, summer, fall: low water-wading below US 1
Scenery:	Forested, rural
Maps:	Gardner Lake 15, Whiting, DL 26 and 27
Portages:	2.5 mi L
	5.25 mi L LLP Dam and falls at US 1 0.25 mi
	(6.25 mi L Whiting Dam and rapids to tidewater)

In high water, the small connecting stream is runnable. Coming down Rocky Lake, take the left channel and lift over the remains of an old dam. The brook twists through alder to a culvert that is runnable if not blocked by debris. Check first! A few hundred feet beyond is Dumpling Falls, a steep, straight flume dropping 4 feet

(Class II) to the flat water of Orange Lake. In low water this 0.25 mile must be carried.

Orange Lake is 1.0 mile long and pretty, but not as wild or rugged as Rocky Lake. Marshy, gentle river for 1.0 mile with only one riffle under a bridge leads to the next lake, shaped like an X. Down the lake 0.5 mile is a short carry at a house on the left that connects to Roaring Lake, which wanders 1.5 miles back into wild country.

Continuing down "Lake X," take the right channel, then the left in 0.25 mile. After 0.75 mile, turn right again. At the old Lubec Light and Power (LLP) dam, land on the left carefully. Beyond the dam is a Class III–IV chute under the old bridge and a Class IV falls under the new bridge.

To continue to Whiting, turn right and cross the old bridge. Cross US 1 and turn left at a closed-up house. Follow a dirt road 100 feet, and turn left into the woods down a trail to the river below the bridges. The carry is 0.25 mile long.

In the summer, the next 0.25 mile is low and requires some wading. In the spring, you have a Class I–II rapid on the left-hand bend and beyond the next right-hand bend a Class II drop. The remaining 0.75 mile to Whiting is flat water. Land on the left along US 1 to finish an Orange River cruise or to portage to Whiting Bay. Below the dam at Whiting is a long series of Class II rapids that are normally too shallow to run even in the spring. Carry along US 1, and then cut through a grassy area to the head of tide. The length of the carry is about 600 yards at low tide, significantly less at high tide. Beyond is the rapid tidal river known as Whiting Bay.

Dennys River

The Dennys River flows out of Meddybemps Lake in the town of Meddybemps first southward and then southeast to Dennysville, where it flows into an arm of Passamaquoddy Bay. It is mixed smooth and rapid, with a good current and a number of rips, which provide a varied interest to the run.

MEDDYBEMPS ➤ ME 86   18.0 MI

Description:	Flatwater, quickwater, Class I, II
Navigable:	High and medium water
Scenery:	Wild
Maps:	Calais 15, Gardner Lake 15, Pembroke, DL 36 and 26

You find an excellent put-in just east of the river on a private drive-way courteously opened to the public and to the left off ME 191. It is a short, dead-end road that runs to the river. Ask for and obtain permission before crossing property lines.

Below the dam at Meddybemps Lake, the quick water soon slows down for the 7.0 miles of mostly smooth water through a swampy country to the site of Gilman Dam. This can be reached from the west by high-clearance vehicles via a rough logging road from East Ridge Road 2.5 miles south of ME 191.

It is 1.5 miles to Gardner Rips and another 1.5 miles to Ayers Rips. Here, the river becomes much more winding, and after passing around the northern end of the Whaleback reaches Stoddard Rips in 2.0 miles. Little Falls, 2.0 miles below, is somewhat more of a rapid. Just below here, the river turns south for a short bit and in 1.5 miles reaches Camp Rips. You find a good take-out on the right below Camp Rips. It can be reached by taking the dirt road off ME 86 at the Robinson's Cottages sign about 0.5 mile west of the bridge in Dennysville.

Below this take-out, you travel under a railroad bridge and enter a Class III–IV gorge. It can be scouted on the right and is generally run on the right. You also have several possible take-outs in the town of Dennysville.

ME 86 ➤ DENNYSVILLE   2.75 MI

Description:	Class I, II, III
Navigable:	Medium water
Scenery:	Forested
Maps:	Pembroke, DL 26 and 27

Scout the Class III, IV gorge that is 200 feet beyond the bridge. It can be run by keeping as close as possible to the ledge along the right bank. Intermittent Class I–II rapids continue for the next 0.5 mile. Soon Cathance Stream enters on the right (0.75 miles). Tidewater begins just below the Dennys River Sportsmans Club (1.5 miles). At mid tide, a Class II run can be made through Dennysville to take out on the left bank at the US 1 bridge where the river widens into Dennys Bay. A Maine Atlantic Salmon Commission counting fence (weir) crosses the river in Dennysville.

Cathance Stream

Cathance Stream rises in Lake Cathance, which is located in Cooper and Township 14, and flows south and east to the Dennys River shortly above Dennysville.

LAKE CATHANCE ➤ ME 86   9.0 MI

Description:	Quickwater, Class I, II
Navigable:	High water
Scenery:	Wild
Maps:	Gardner Lake, Pembroke, DL 36, 26, and 27

You can find two places to put in on the western side of Cathance Lake, from ME 191. The outlet leaves from a long bay on the southeastern side of the lake. To put in at the outlet take the 90-00-0 road from ME 191. After 1.0 mile, go left on the 90-05-0 road to the river.

Because the grade is unusually consistent, you find no rapids of special note; instead, you find pleasant, mild, talking water. The rapids are steepest at the start, gradually moderating, with the last 2.0 miles quick water.

A series of unrunnable drops begins just above the ME 86 bridge. Portage and put in below the bridge. In 4.0 miles you come to the Great Works Flowage, an excellent wildlife area. Portage the Great Works dam. Where Dodge Road crosses, 1.0 mile below, is a small flume you can run. The granite walled feature is 6 feet wide and about 60 feet long. From the flume down to the take-out on the Dennys River in Dennysville, the Cathance is a riffle run.

Saint Croix River

The Saint Croix River flows from North Lake on the Maine–New Brunswick border and runs generally south, forming the southern portion of the international boundary. The upper part is largely a succession of lakes; the middle section has a number of Class I and II rapids, which are runnable much of the year; and the lower portion also has some rapids, although it is more developed.

A good map is available from St. Croix International Waterway Commission, P.O. Box 610, Calais, ME 04619, or staff@stcroix.org.

Report to customs in advance when planning to cross the border on your trip. Bring valid picture identification.

ORIENT ➤ VANCEBORO   36.0 MI

Description:	Lakes, flatwater, quickwater
Navigable:	Spring, summer, fall
Scenery:	Forested, cottages
Maps:	Amity 15, Danforth 15, Forest 15, Vanceboro 15, DL 53, 45, and 46
Portages:	16.0 mi L (Canadian side)
	36.0 mi R Vanceboro

The highest point on the river that is easily accessible is at the northern end of Grand Lake, where you can put in just below the U.S. Customs office on Boundary Road east of Orient. From here, you can go eastward through the thoroughfare to North Lake if desired. But the more usual route is to proceed directly down Grand Lake, the first of the Chiputneticook Lakes.

At the northern end, Grand Lake is narrow (less than 1.0 mile wide), but after about 5.0 miles it opens out into a very large body of water. Although you find a few settled spots here and there, most of the lake is wild. After about 7.0 miles in the larger part of the lake, you approach the southern end, where you should be careful to keep on the eastern side, where in 1.0 mile more you arrive at the outlet. On the southwestern side is a long arm, some 4.0 miles, which runs down to a dead end. This makes a pleasant paddle between high hills, if you wish to make a side trip.

At the outlet is 1.0 mile of fast current past Forest City to the long deadwater below. This deadwater is followed 2.0 miles north to a steep drop, necessitating a long carry on the Canadian side (left). After 1.0 mile more of river, Spednik Lake is reached. This is a long, narrow, and winding lake, which is followed 19.0 miles to Vanceboro. There the dam should be carried on the right, that is, on the American side.

You have alternate portages from Mud Lake to Spednik Lake (see USGS Forest 15). The first runs from west to east and reaches Spednik Lake 0.5 mile north of Forest City Landing. The second begins just before entering the narrows at the northern end of Mud Lake and runs northeast to Booming Ground Cove on Spednik Lake.

VANCEBORO ➤ KELLYLAND   33.0 MI

Description:	Lakes, flatwater, Class I, II
Navigable:	Spring, summer, fall, controlled release
Scenery:	Wild
Maps:	Vanceboro 15, Kellyland 15, Waite 15, DL 46 and 36
Portage:	33.0 mi R Kellyland Dam 100 yd
Campsites:	6.5 mi R Tunnel Rips
	9.5 mi R Little Falls MFS
	13.0 mi L Grassy Island
	19.5 mi R Loon Bay MFS car
	25.0 mi L High Banks
	29.5 mi R Spednic Falls permit

The Saint Croix has runnable rapids when most other streams in New England are too low. This is because the dam on Spednik Lake regulates part of the flow of water to the generator at Grand Falls Dam. The other regulated drainage area that supplies water to the power plant is that of the Grand Lake chain, but it enters the Saint Croix at Grand Falls flowage. Therefore, it does not affect the river between Vanceboro and Kellyland.

The rapids below Vanceboro are all relatively easy, Class I and II, with Little Falls being the most difficult. Topographical maps name a dozen rapids in the first 20.0 miles to Loon Bay. However, most of them are easy, and some are apt to be flooded out in high water. If one gate at Vanceboro is open 5 feet, the river below it will be "high."

You find two campsites at about 4.0 miles below Vanceboro: Picnic Grounds Campsite and Gravel Rip Campsite.

The best part of the river is the 30.0 miles between Vanceboro and Grand Falls flowage, and it can easily be run in 2 days. The middle portion of the river is accessible by car at Loon Bay, and another road reaches Grand Falls flowage near Spednic Falls. Information on these roads is most easily obtained from the district ranger in Topsfield (just east on ME 6).

As you begin the trip, you pass under a railroad bridge, which was the scene of an early act of sabotage prior to the United States' involvement in World War II. The bridge was blown up to prevent the Canadian Pacific from hauling supplies destined for England.

"Kill-Me-Quick" rapids, which is directly below the dam at Vanceboro and the highway bridge, ends under the railroad bridge.

It is followed by 1.5 miles of flat water, then an easy Class I–II rapid, and then Wing Dam Island. An optional, slightly technical route is available to the right of Wing Dam Island—caution at end of pool; it is a sharp II–III chute.

At the end of Wing Dam Island (1.0 miles), you reach Elbow Rips (easy Class I). It is 1.5 miles to Mile Rips (easy Class II) and another 2.5 miles to Tunnel Rips (easy Class II). The trip to George's Rips (easy Class II) is 0.5 mile. It is 1.0 mile to Hall's Rips (easy Class II) and another 1.5 miles to Little Falls (Class III). Little Falls can be run on either side; it is easier on the right, more technical on the left. You can find a good portage trail on the right.

Then it is 1.0 mile to Fork Rips. (Old-timers maintain that the original name was Pork Rips, not Fork Rips, as listed now.) It was here that a barrel of salted pork was lost when a freight canoe was upset in the logging days 100 years ago. Another 1.0 mile brings you to Cedar Island Rips (easy Class II). After Cedar Island, watch for a clearing on the right with a large, white birch tree. Here is the grave of a baby found in the river by loggers, and it has been maintained by them since the late 1800s.

It is then 1.0 mile to Tyler Rips (easy Class II), and 2.0 miles to Albee Rips (easy Class II). You find a large picnic and camping ground on the left (Canadian) side. It is 1.0 mile to Rocky Rips (easy Class II), with another Canadian campground on the left. Then it is 1.5 miles to Split Rock Rips (Class II), 1.0 mile to Meetinghouse Rips (Class II), and 2.5 miles to Haycock Rips (Class II), which empties into Loon Bay (2.0 miles long). Paddle 1.5 miles below Loon Bay to reach Canoose Rips. **Caution!** Scout here; water level is the key to passage. If it is low, line on left; if medium, paddle chute on left. On the right is a rocky Class III; in the center, a Class IV. Watch for obstructions at Canoose—logs and debris.

Below what is now called Canoose Rips follows about 1.0 mile of easy Class I rapids called Canoose Rapids.

Canoose Rapids can be run in three spots:

1. The ledge can be run at virtually any level on far left—a steep, but short, easy chute.

2. On the far right is a rocky winding Class II+ run.

3. The most interesting run is approximately one-third out from the left shore, directly over the ledge. It should be scouted first, however; it could be considered Class III at certain water levels. The rapid below Canoose is actually Class II, approximately 0.5 mile long.

At Dog Falls, you find a runnable ledge on either side of the island, easier on the left. Below Dog Falls is 1.5 miles of moving water/riffles and then 6.0 miles of flat water to Kendricks Rips. Kendricks Rips are the first rips in several miles and are pretty easy to identify. A cabin is on river right just before the rips. The Kendricks Rips campsite is at the northern end of the island, which is hard to see. You come upon one more campsite before you reach the flowage. From here on is open flat water to Kellyland Dam. You pass the flowage, an open body of water with many peninsulas. You should have a topographical map with you; otherwise, you could spend the day looking for Kellyland Dam.

The first dam (actually the Kellyland Dam; used for many years) is no longer available as a take-out; you must proceed beyond the next point and then head left into the canal to the power generation plant.

KELLYLAND ➤ CALAIS   21.0 MI

Description:	Quickwater, flatwater, Class II
Navigable:	Spring, summer, fall
Scenery:	Forested, towns, settled
Maps:	Kellyland 15, Calais 15, DL 36
Portages:	9.5 mi L Woodland Dam and rapids 1,000 ft to 0.33 mi
	19.5 mi L Saint Croix Rapids and Milltown Dam 0.66 mi
	21.0 mi R Calais Falls 0 to 500 ft per tide level
Campsites:	3.5 mi R informal sites on islands

The lower portion of the Saint Croix River is a mixture of complete isolation and heavy industry, flat water and very difficult rapids, and rural countryside and large towns. The former of each pair predominates. It is a very large river because it has picked up substantial drainage from the west. The flow is good all summer, but occasionally it is low if Georgia Pacific's generators are not running.

From the power plant in Kellyland, the river races downstream. After an exuberant but easy Class I mile, it settles down to a slow, deep coast through the forest. It is an attractive, almost wild northern woods setting. If you look underwater in the shallows, you see sunken logs from the old river drives. Keep to the right of the island at Ash Brook for the deep channel. The deadwater of Woodland Lake begins here. The narrow channel to the left of Mosquito Island is blocked by stranded logs. On the right shore is a boat landing, 6.5 miles from Kellyland.

Beyond here, the wild character of the river is traded for a more-settled, but still attractive setting, at least after Woodland is passed. Where the lake narrows at Woodland Junction, slip over a log boom, near the left shore. Approaching the dam and pulp mill at Woodland, stay left to pass another boom; land at the left end of the dam to portage.

If the river channel is dry below the dam, carry 1,000 feet down across the first dry channel, up to the power-line pylons, and down and along the major dry channel to where the flow is restored from the mill. The footing is loose and rocky on this carry.

If the river is not dry below the dam, carry 0.33 mile down the railroad tracks and then to the right down to the river at the head of a small rapid.

In the first 0.5 mile are two Class I rapids, then the river is flat but shallow to Bailey Rips, a slightly harder Class I–II rapids. Below the deadwater of Loon Bay is another riffle at Butler Island and another Class I where the river turns left. When the river narrows just below Haywood Island, you come upon a little Class I–II rapid.

At Upper Mills the river runs through a curving Class II rapid 0.66 mile long, ending in a broad, shallow bay. The next 3.5 miles to Milltown are flat water curving through marshes and hardwood forest. Take out on the left (Canadian) shore to carry Saint Croix Rapids and the Milltown dam. Carry 0.66 mile either along the railroad or the road paralleling it on the left to a landing below the dam on the left shore.

Saint Croix Rapids are really a falls, Class IV–V. The pool behind the dam is short and complicated by a boom, so the carry is not worth breaking into two carries (around the falls and dam separately).

Below Milltown is 0.5 mile of Class II rapids ending at Union Mills. At high tide, this is the end of the flowing river. At low tide, a pool extends 0.5 mile to Calais (pronounced "Cowlus") Falls, which drops to tide. The low-tide carry is on the right, 500 feet long. At mid tide, the rapids are a heavy Class II–III. At high tide, the falls are drowned, not even a ripple left. Take out on the right just beyond the bridge in Calais.

Grand Lake Stream

Grand Lake Stream flows from West Grand Lake to Big Lake, the first in a series of lakes that connects with Grand Falls flowage on the Saint Croix River. The flow is dam-controlled, with the drainage area being the entire Grand Lake chain. If one and a half gates are open at the dam, that provides a good Class II, III run through everything except Big Falls, which has several large holes and would be very difficult to run. The dam is reached over a public road from US 1 north of Princeton.

A USGS gauging station is on left bank at Big Falls, 0.5 mile southeast of village of Grand Lake Stream and 0.8 mile downstream from outlet dam of Grand Lake.

Description:	Class II, III
Navigable:	High and medium water, controlled release
Scenery:	Rural, towns
Maps:	Wabassus Lake 15, Big Lake 15, DL 35
Portage:	0.75 mi L Big Falls 75 yd

If the water is high enough to run the rapids below the bridge in town and low enough to run Little Falls (reached by a road down the left bank 2.0 miles to a picnic area), the rapids are Class II except for Big Falls, which should be carried.

Put in below the dam from either bank. Class II rapids extend 0.75 mile to Big Falls, around a sharp S-curve starting to the right with a house on the left bank; line or carry on the left. Rapids continue another 1.0 mile to the picnic area at Little Falls. (Camping not permitted.) This is a Class III–IV drop. You come upon a river-wide hole at the bottom, and it is best punched on the far right.

After another 1.0 mile, the rapids end at a group of cottages. You must obtain permission from one of the landowners in advance to take out here. If you continue to Big Lake, you can enjoy a beautiful paddle through the marsh. A public boat launch is along the northern shore of Big Lake.

Appendix A
Safety Code of American Whitewater
(formerly the American Whitewater Affiliation)

The following code, adopted in 1959 and revised in 2005, is reprinted with the permission of American Whitewater, P.O. Box 1540, Cullowhee, NC 28723, 1-866-BOAT-4-AW, info@amwhitewater.org.

This code has been prepared using the best available information and has been reviewed by a broad cross-section of whitewater experts. The code, however, is only a collection of guidelines; attempts to minimize risks should be flexible, not constrained by a rigid set of rules. Varying conditions and group goals may combine with unpredictable circumstances to require alternate procedures. This code is not intended to serve as a standard of care for commercial outfitters or guides.

Safety Code of American Whitewater

I. PERSONAL PREPAREDNESS AND RESPONSIBILITY

1. *Be a competent swimmer*, with the ability to handle yourself underwater.
2. *Wear a life jacket.* A snugly-fitting vest-type life preserver offers back and shoulder protection as well as the flotation needed to swim safely in whitewater.
3. *Wear a solid, correctly-fitted helmet* when upsets are likely. This is essential in kayaks or covered canoes and recommended for open canoeists using thigh straps and rafters running steep drops.
4. *Do not boat out of control.* Your skills should be sufficient to stop or reach shore before reaching danger. Do not enter a rapid unless you are reasonably sure that you can run it safely or swim it without injury.

5. *Whitewater rivers contain many hazards which are not always easily rec-ognized. The following are the most frequent killers:*

   A. *High Water.* The river's speed and power increase tremendously as the flow increases, raising the difficulty of most rapids. Rescue becomes progressively harder as the water rises, adding to the danger. Floating debris and strainers make even an easy rapid quite hazardous. It is often misleading to judge the river level at the put in, since a small rise in a wide, shallow place will be multi-plied many times where the river narrows. Use reliable gauge information whenever possible, and be aware that sun on snow-pack, hard rain, and upstream dam releases may greatly increase the flow.

   B. *Cold.* Cold drains your strength and robs you of the ability to make sound decisions on matters affecting your survival. Cold-water immersion, because of the initial shock and the rapid heat loss which follows, is especially dangerous. Dress appropriately for bad weather or sudden immersion in the water. When the water temperature is less than 50 degrees Fahrenheit, a wetsuit or dry suit is essential for protection if you swim. Next best is wool or pile clothing under a waterproof shell. In this case, you should also carry waterproof matches and a change of clothing in a waterproof bag. If, after prolonged exposure, a person expe-riences uncontrollable shaking, loss of coordination, or difficulty speaking, he or she is hypothermic, and needs your assistance.

   C. *Strainers.* Brush, fallen trees, bridge pilings, undercut rocks or anything else which allows river current to sweep through can pin boats and boaters against the obstacle. Water pressure on anything trapped this way can be overwhelming. Rescue is often extremely difficult. Pinning may occur in fast current, with little or no whitewater to warn of the danger.

   D. *Dams, weirs, ledges, reversals, holes, and hydraulics.* When water drops over an obstacle, it curls back on itself, forming a strong up-stream current which may be capable of holding a boat or swim-mer. Some holes make for excellent sport. Others are proven kill-ers. Paddlers who cannot recognize the difference should avoid all but the smallest holes. Hydraulics around man-made dams must be treated with utmost respect regardless of their height or the level of the river. Despite their seemingly benign appearance, they can create an almost escape-proof trap. The swimmer's only exit from the "drowning machine" is to dive below the surface when the downstream current is flowing beneath the reversal.

    E. *Broaching.* When a boat is pushed sideways against a rock by strong current, it may collapse and wrap. This is especially dangerous to kayak and decked canoe paddlers; these boats will collapse and the combination of indestructible hulls and tight outfitting may create a deadly trap. Even without entrapment, releasing pinned boats can be extremely time-consuming and dangerous. To avoid pinning, throw your weight downstream towards the rock. This allows the current to slide harmlessly underneath the hull.

6. *Boating alone is discouraged.* The minimum party is three people or two craft.

7. *Have a frank knowledge of your boating ability,* and don't attempt rivers or rapids which lie beyond that ability.

8. *Be in good physical and mental condition, consistent with the difficulties which may be expected.* Make adjustments for loss of skills due to age, health, fitness. Any health limitations must be explained to your fellow paddlers prior to starting the trip.

9. *Be practiced in self-rescue,* including escape from an overturned craft. The Eskimo roll is strongly recommended for decked boaters who run rapids Class IV or greater, or who paddle in cold environmental conditions.

10. *Be trained in rescue skills, CPR, and first aid* with special emphasis on recognizing and treating hypothermia. It may save your friend's life.

11. *Carry equipment needed for unexpected emergencies,* including footwear which will protect your feet when walking out, a throw rope, knife, whistle, and waterproof matches. If you wear eyeglasses, tie them on and carry a spare pair on long trips. Bring cloth repair tape on short runs, and a full repair kit on isolated rivers. Do not wear bulky jackets, ponchos, heavy boots, or anything else which could reduce your ability to survive a swim.

12. Despite the mutually supportive group structure described in this code, *individual paddlers are ultimately responsible for their own safety and must assume sole responsibility for the following decisions:*

    A. The decision to participate on any trip. This includes an evaluation of the expected difficulty of the rapids under the conditions existing at the time of the put-in.

B. The selection of appropriate equipment, including a boat design suited to their skills and the appropriate rescue and survival gear.

C. The decision to scout any rapid, and to run or portage according to their best judgment. Other members of the group may offer advice, but paddlers should resist pressure from anyone to paddle beyond their skills. It is also their responsibility to decide whether to pass up any walk-out or take-out opportunity.

D. All trip participants should consistently evaluate their own and their group's safety, voicing their concerns when appropriate and following what they believe to be the best course of action. Paddlers are encouraged to speak with anyone whose actions on the water are dangerous, whether they are a part of your group or not.

II. BOAT AND EQUIPMENT PREPAREDNESS

1. *Test new and different equipment* under familiar conditions before relying on it for difficult runs. This is especially true when adopting a new boat design or outfitting system. Low-volume craft may present additional hazards to inexperienced or poorly conditioned paddlers.

2. *Be sure your boat and gear are in good repair* before starting a trip. The more isolated and difficult the run, the more rigorous this inspection should be.

3. *Install flotation bags* in noninflatable craft, securely fixed in each end, designed to displace as much water as possible. Inflatable boats should have multiple air chambers and be test-inflated before launching.

4. *Have strong, properly sized paddles or oars* for controlling your craft. Carry sufficient spares for the length and difficulty of the trip.

5. *Outfit your boat safely.* The ability to exit your boat quickly is an essential component of safety in rapids. It is your responsibility to see that there is absolutely nothing to cause entrapment when coming free of an upset craft. This includes:

   A. Spray covers which won't release reliably or which release prematurely.

   B. Boat outfitting too tight to allow a fast exit, especially in low-volume kayaks or decked canoes. This includes low-hung thwarts in canoes lacking adequate clearance for your feet and kayak foot braces which fail or allow your feet to become wedged under them.

C. Inadequately supported decks which collapse on a paddler's legs when a decked boat is pinned by water pressure. Inadequate clearance with the deck because of your size or build.

D. Loose ropes which cause entanglement. Beware of any length of loose line attached to a whitewater boat. All items must be tied tightly and excess line eliminated; painters, throw lines, and safety rope systems must be completely and effectively stored. Do not knot the end of a rope, as it can get caught in cracks between rocks.

6. *Provide ropes* which permit you to hold on to your craft so that it may be rescued. The following methods are recommended:

A. Kayaks and covered canoes should have grab loops of ¼" + rope or equivalent webbing sized to admit a normal-sized hand. Stern painters are permissible if properly secured.

B. Open canoes should have securely anchored bow and stern painters consisting of 8–10 feet of ¼" + line. These must be secured in such a way that they are readily accessible, but cannot come loose accidentally. Grab loops are acceptable but are more difficult to reach after an upset.

C. Rafts and dories may have taut perimeter lines threaded through the loops provided. Footholds should be designed so that a paddler's feet cannot be forced through them, causing entrapment. Flip lines should be carefully and reliably stowed.

7. *Know your craft's carrying capacity,* and how added loads affect boat handling in whitewater. Most rafts have a minimum crew size which can be added to on day trips or in easy rapids. Carrying more than two paddlers in an open canoe when running rapids is not recommended.

8. *Car-top racks* must be strong and attach positively to the vehicle. Lash your boat to each crossbar and then tie the ends of the boats directly to the bumpers for added security. This arrangement should survive all but the most violent vehicle accident.

III. GROUP PREPAREDNESS AND RESPONSIBILITY

1. *Organization.* A river trip should be regarded as a common adventure by all participants, except on instructional or commercially

guided trips as defined below. Participants share the responsibility for the conduct of the trip, and each participant is individually responsible for judging his or her own capabilities and for his or her own safety as the trip progresses. Participants are encouraged (but are not obligated) to offer advice and guidance for the independent consideration and judgment of others.

2. *River conditions.* The group should have a reasonable knowledge of the difficulty of the run. Participants should evaluate this information and adjust their plans accordingly. If the run is exploratory or no one is familiar with the river, maps and guidebooks, if available, should be examined. The group should secure accurate flow information; the more difficult the run, the more important this will be. Be aware of possible changes in river level and how this will affect the difficulty of the run. If the trip involves tidal stretches, secure appropriate information on tides.

3. *Group equipment should be suited to the difficulty of the river.* The group should always have a throw-line available, and one line per boat is recommended on difficult runs. The list may include carabiners, prussic loops, first aid kit, flashlight, folding saw, fire starter, guidebooks, maps, food, extra clothing, and any other rescue or survival items suggested by conditions. Each item is not required on every run, and this list is not meant to be a substitute for good judgment.

4. *Keep the group compact,* but maintain sufficient spacing to avoid collisions. If the group is large, consider dividing into smaller groups or using the "buddy system" as an additional safeguard. Space yourselves closely enough to permit good communication, but not so close as to interfere with one another in rapids.

   A. *A point paddler* sets the pace. When in front, do not get in over your head. Never run drops when you cannot see a clear route to the bottom or, for advanced paddlers, a sure route to the next eddy. When in doubt, stop and scout.

   B. *Keep track of all group members.* Each boat keeps the one behind it in sight, stopping if necessary. Know how many people are in your group and take head-counts regularly. No one should paddle ahead or walk out without first informing the group. Paddlers requiring additional support should stay at the center of a group and not allow themselves to lag behind in the more difficult rapids. If the group is large and contains a wide range of abilities, a "sweep boat" may be designated to bring up the rear.

C. *Courtesy.* On heavily used rivers, do not cut in front of a boater running a drop. Always look upstream before leaving eddies to run or play. Never enter a crowded drop or eddy when no room for you exists. Passing other groups in a rapid may be hazardous; it's often safer to wait upstream until the group ahead has passed.

5. *Float Plan.* If the trip is into a wilderness area or for an extended period, plans should be filed with a responsible person who will contact the authorities if you are overdue. It may be wise to establish checkpoints along the way where civilization could be contacted if necessary. Knowing the location of possible help and planning escape routes can speed rescue.

6. *Drugs.* The use of alcohol or mind-altering drugs before or during river trips is not recommended. It dulls reflexes, reduces decision-making ability, and may interfere with important survival reflexes.

7. *Instructional or commercially guided trips.* In contrast to the common adventure trip format, in these trip formats, a boating instructor or commercial guide assumes some of the responsibilities normally exercised by the group as a whole, as appropriate under the circumstances. These formats recognize that instructional or commercially guided trips may involve participants who lack significant experience in whitewater. However, as a participant acquires experience in whitewater, he or she takes on increasing responsibility for his or her own safety, in accordance with what he or she knows or should know as a result of that increased experience. Also, as in all trip formats, every participant must realize and assume the risks associated with the serious hazards of whitewater rivers.

8. It is advisable for instructors and commercial guides or their employers to acquire trip or personal liability insurance:
   A. An "instructional trip" is characterized by a clear teacher/pupil relationship, where the primary purpose of the trip is to teach boating skills, and which is conducted for a fee.
   B. A "commercially guided trip" is characterized by a licensed, professional guide conducting trips for a fee.

IV. GUIDELINES FOR RIVER RESCUE

1. *Recover from an upset with an Eskimo roll* whenever possible. Evacuate your boat immediately if there is imminent danger of being trapped against rocks, brush, or any other kind of strainer.

2. *If you swim, hold on to your boat.* It has much flotation and is easy for rescuers to spot. Get to the upstream end so that you cannot be crushed between a rock and your boat by the force of the current. Persons with good balance may be able to climb on top of a swamped kayak or flipped raft and paddle to shore.

3. *Release your craft if this will improve your chances,* especially if the water is cold or dangerous rapids lie ahead. Actively attempt self-rescue whenever possible by swimming for safety. Be prepared to assist others who may come to your aid.

   A. *When swimming in shallow or obstructed rapids,* lie on your back with feet held high and pointed downstream. Do not attempt to stand in fast-moving water; if your foot wedges on the bottom, fast water will push you under and keep you there. Get to slow or very shallow water before attempting to stand or walk. Look ahead! Avoid possible pinning situations including undercut rocks, strainers, downed trees, holes, and other dangers by swimming away from them.

   B. *If the rapids are deep and powerful,* roll over onto your stomach and swim aggressively for shore. Watch for eddies and slack water and use them to get out of the current. Strong swimmers can effect a powerful upstream ferry and get to shore fast. If the shores are obstructed with strainers or under cut rocks, however, it is safer to "ride the rapid out" until a safer escape can be found.

   C. *If others spill and swim, go after the boaters first.* Rescue boats and equipment only if this can be done safely. While participants are encouraged (but not obligated) to assist one another to the best of their ability, they should do so only if they can, in their judgment, do so safely. The first duty of a rescuer is not to compound the problem by becoming another victim.

4. *The use of rescue lines requires training;* uninformed use may cause injury. Never tie yourself into either end of a line without a reliable quick-release system. Have a knife handy to deal with unexpected entanglement. Learn to place set lines effectively, to throw accurately, to belay effectively, and to properly handle a rope thrown to you.

5. *When reviving a drowning victim,* be aware that cold water may greatly extend survival time underwater. Victims of hypothermia may have depressed vital signs so they look and feel dead. Don't give up; continue CPR for as long as possible without compromising safety.

V. UNIVERSAL RIVER SIGNALS

These signals may be substituted with an alternate set of signals agreed upon by the group.

Stop: Potential Hazard Ahead: Wait for the "all clear" signal before proceeding, or scout ahead. Form a horizontal bar with your outstretched arms. Those seeing the signal should pass it back to others in the party.

Help/Emergency: Assist the signaler as quickly as possible. Give three long blasts on a police whistle while waving a paddle, helmet, or life vest over your head. If a whistle is not available, use the visual signal alone. A whistle is best carried on a lanyard attached to your life vest.

All Clear: Come ahead (in the absence of other directions proceed down the center). Form a vertical bar with your paddle or one arm held high above your head. Paddle blade should be turned flat for maximum visibility. To signal direction or a preferred course through a rapid around obstruction, lower the previously vertical "all clear" by 45 degrees toward the side of the river with the preferred route. Never point toward the obstacle you wish to avoid.

I'm Okay: I'm okay and not hurt. While holding the elbow outward toward the side, repeatedly pat the top of your head.

VI. INTERNATIONAL SCALE OF RIVER DIFFICULTY

This is the American version of a rating system used to compare river difficulty throughout the world. This system is not exact; rivers do not always fit easily into one category, and regional or individual interpretations may cause misunderstandings. It is no substitute for a guidebook or accurate first-hand descriptions of a run.

Paddlers attempting difficult runs in an unfamiliar area should act cautiously until they get a feel for the way the scale is interpreted locally. River difficulty may change each year due to fluctuations in water level, downed trees, recent floods, geological disturbances, or bad weather. *Stay alert for unexpected problems!*

As river difficulty increases, the danger to swimming paddlers becomes more severe. As rapids become longer and more continuous, the challenge increases. There is a difference between running an occasional Class IV rapid and dealing with an entire river of this category.

Allow an extra margin of safety between skills and river ratings when the water is cold or if the river itself is remote and inaccessible.

VII. THE SIX DIFFICULTY CLASSES

Class I Rapids
Fast-moving water with riffles and small waves. Few obstructions, all obvious and easily missed with little training. Risk to swimmers is slight; self-rescue is easy.

Class II Rapids: Novice
Straightforward rapids with wide, clear channels that are evident without scouting. Occasional maneuvering may be required, but rocks and medium-sized waves are easily missed by trained paddlers. Swimmers are seldom injured and group assistance, while helpful, is seldom needed. Rapids that are at the upper end of this difficulty range are designated Class II+.

Class III: Intermediate
Rapids with moderate, irregular waves that may be difficult to avoid and that can swamp an open canoe. Complex maneuvers in fast current and good boat control in tight passages or around ledges are often required; large waves or strainers may be present but are easily avoided. Strong eddies and powerful current effects can be found, particularly on large-volume rivers. Scouting is advisable for inexperienced parties. Injuries while swimming are rare; self-rescue is usually easy but group assistance may be required to avoid long swims. Rapids that are at the lower or upper end of this difficulty range are designated Class III- or Class III+, respectively.

Class IV: Advanced
Intense, powerful but predictable rapids requiring precise boat handling in turbulent water. Depending on the character of the river, it may feature large, unavoidable waves and holes or constricted passages demanding fast maneuvers under pressure. A fast, reliable eddy turn may be needed to initiate maneuvers, scout rapids, or rest. Rapids may require "must" moves above dangerous hazards. Scouting may be necessary the first time down. Risk of injury to swimmers is moderate to high, and water conditions may make self-rescue difficult. Group assistance for rescue is often essential but requires practiced skills. A strong

Eskimo roll is highly recommended. Rapids that are at the upper end of this difficulty range are designated Class IV- or Class IV+, respectively.

Class 5: Expert
Extremely long, obstructed, or very violent rapids that expose a paddler to added risk. Drops may contain large, unavoidable waves and holes or steep, congested chutes with complex, demanding routes. Rapids may continue for long distances between pools, demanding a high level of fitness. What eddies exist may be small, turbulent, or difficult to reach. At the high end of the scale, several of these factors may be combined. Scouting is recommended but may be difficult. Swims are dangerous, and rescue is often difficult even for experts. A very reliable Eskimo roll, proper equipment, extensive experience, and practiced rescue skills are essential. Because of the large range of difficulty that exists beyond Class IV, Class 5 is an open-ended, multiple-level scale designated by class 5.0, 5.1, 5.2, etc. Each of these levels is an order of magnitude more difficult than the last. Example: increasing difficulty from Class 5.0 to Class 5.1 is a similar order of magnitude as increasing from Class IV to Class 5.0.

Class VI: Extreme and Exploratory Rapids
These runs have almost never been attempted and often exemplify the extremes of difficulty, unpredictability, and danger. The consequences of errors are very severe and rescue may be impossible. For teams of experts only, at favorable water levels, after close personal inspection and taking all precautions. After a Class VI rapids has been run many times, its rating may be changed to an appropriate Class 5.x rating.

Appendix B
Northern Forest Canoe Trail

The Northern Forest Canoe Trail is a 740-mile waterway from Old Forge, New York, to Fort Kent, Maine. The trail follows Native American travel routes and now serves to encourage canoe/kayak travel in the Northern Forest regions of New York, Vermont, New Hampshire, and Maine.

Below is an outline of the route, from west to east. This is not sufficient information to make the trek (just enough to get you interested), but you can get detailed information from Northern Forest Canoe Trail, P.O. Box 572, Waitsfield, VT 05673 (802-496-2285), www.northernforestcanoetrail.org.

New York: Begin at Old Forge, ascend the Moose River via the Fulton Lake Chain, and portage to the Raquette River. Descend the Raquette and portage to the Saranec River. Descend the Saranec to Lake Champlain.

Vermont: Cross Lake Champlain and ascend the Missisquoi River to the North Branch of the Missisquoi River. Ascend the North Branch of the Missisquoi River to above Mansonville, Quebec. Portage to Lake Memphremagog. Paddle down Lake Memphremagog to Newport, Vermont. Portage to the Clyde River. Ascend the Clyde River and portage to the Nulhegan River. Descend the Nulhegan River to the Connecticut River.

New Hampshire: Descend the Connecticut River to the Upper Ammonoosuc River. Ascend the Upper Ammonoosuc River and portage to the Androscoggin River. Ascend the Androscoggin River to Lake Umbagog.

Maine: Portage the Rapid River to the Richardson, Mooselook-meguntic, and Rangeley Lakes. Portage to the South Branch of the Dead River. Descend the Dead River to Spencer Stream. Ascend Spencer Stream to Little Spencer Stream. Ascend Little Spencer Stream to Whipple Pond and portage to the Moose River. Descend the Moose River to the Penobscot River. Descend the Penobscot River to Chesuncook Lake. Cross Chesuncook Lake to Umbazooksus Lake and portage to the Allagash River. Descend the Allagash (Wilderness Waterway) to the St. John River. Descend the St. John River to the mouth of the Fish River at Fort Kent.

List of Waterways

Tidal rivers south of Portland,
    222–224
Time estimates, xxiii
Trip suggestions, xxx–xxxiv
Twenty-Five Mile Stream, 95–96

U

Umbagog Lake, 26
Union River, 256
Union River (East Branch),
    258–260
Union River (Middle Branch), 260
Union River (West Branch),
    256–257
U.S. Geological Survey (USGS),
    xxvii
USGS gauges, xxvii–xxix

W

Wassataquoik Stream, 132–133
Water levels, xviii, xxiii–xxiv
Water releases, xxiv
Webb River, 37–38
Webster Stream, 127–128
Western coastal watersheds,
    217–252
Whiting Bay, 282–283
Whitney Brook, 214
Wild River, 32–33
Wilson Stream, 88–89
Wytopitlock Stream, 137

The Appalachian Mountain Club

Founded in 1876, the AMC is the nation's oldest outdoor recreation and conservation organization. The AMC promotes the protection, enjoyment, and wise use of the mountains, rivers, and trails of the Northeast outdoors.

People

We are nearly 90,000 members in 12 chapters, 20,000 volunteers, and over 450 full time and seasonal staff. Our chapters reach from Maine to Washington, D.C.

Outdoor Adventure and Fun

We offer more than 8,000 trips each year, from local chapter activities to major excursions worldwide, for every ability level and outdoor interest— from hiking and climbing to paddling, snowshoeing, and skiing.

Great Places to Stay

We host more than 135,000 guest nights each year at our AMC Lodges, Huts, Camps, Shelters, and Campgrounds. Each AMC Destination is a model for environmental education and stewardship.

Opportunities for Learning

We teach people the skills to be safe outdoors and to care for the natural world around us through programs for children, teens, and adults, as well as outdoor leadership training.

Caring for Trails

We maintain more than 1,400 miles of trails throughout the Northeast, including nearly 350 miles of the Appalachian Trail in five states.

Protecting Wild Places

We advocate for land and riverway conservation, monitor air quality, and work to protect alpine and forest ecosystems throughout the Northern Forest and Highlands regions.

Engaging the Public

We seek to educate and inform our own members and an additional 1.5 million people annually through AMC Books, our website, our White Mountain visitor centers, and AMC Destinations.

Join Us!

Members support our mission while enjoying great AMC programs, our award-winning AMC Outdoors magazine, and special discounts. Visit www.outdoors.org or call 617-523-0636 for more information.

THE APPALACHIAN MOUNTAIN CLUB
Recreation • Education • Conservation
www.outdoors.org

Leave No Trace

The Appalachian Mountain Club is a national educational partner of Leave No Trace, Inc., a nonprofit organization dedicated to promoting and inspiring responsible outdoor recreation through education, research, and partnerships. The Leave No Trace Program seeks to develop wildland ethics—ways in which people think and act in the outdoors to minimize their impacts on the areas they visit and to protect our natural resources for future enjoyment. Leave No Trace unites four federal land management agencies—the U.S. Forest Service, National Park Service, Bureau of Land Management, and U.S. Fish and Wildlife Service—with manufacturers, outdoor retailers, user groups, educators, organizations like the AMC and the National Outdoor Leadership School (NOLS), and individuals.

The Leave No Trace ethic is guided by these seven principles:

• Plan ahead and prepare.
• Travel and camp on durable surfaces.
• Dispose of waste properly.
• Leave what you find.
• Minimize campfire impacts.
• Respect wildlife.
• Be considerate of other visitors.

The AMC has joined NOLS—a recognized leader in wilderness education and a founding partner of Leave No Trace—as the providers of the Leave No Trace Master Educator course. The AMC offers this five-day course, designed especially for outdoor professionals and land managers, as well as the shorter two-day Leave No Trace Trainer course, at locations throughout the northeastern United States.

For Leave No Trace information and materials, contact:

LEAVE NO TRACE, INC.
P.O. Box 997
Boulder, CO 80306
800-332-4100
www.LNT.org

AMC Book Updates

AMC Books strives to keep our guidebooks as up-to-date as possible to help you plan safe and enjoyable adventures. If after publishing a book we learn that trails are relocated or route or contact information has changed, we will post the updated information online. Before you hit the trail, check for updates at www.outdoors.org/publications/books/updates.

While hiking or paddling, if you notice discrepancies with the trail description or map, or if you find any other errors in the book, please let us know by submitting them to amcbookupdates@outdoors.org or in writing to Books Editor, c/o AMC, 5 Joy Street, Boston, MA 02108. We will verify all submissions and post key updates each month.

AMC Books is dedicated to being a recognized leader in outdoor publishing. Thank you for your participation.

AMC BOOKS & MAPS

EXPLORE THE POSSIBILITIES

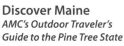